NEW YEATS PAPERS XIX

GENERAL EDITOR: LIAM MILLER

SHIRLEY NEUMAN

SOME ONE MYTH
YEATS'S AUTOBIOGRAPHICAL PROSE

NEW YEATS PAPERS XIX

THE DOLMEN PRESS
in association with HUMANITIES PRESS INC.

General Editor: Liam Miller

Copyright © Shirley C. Neuman 1982

Yeats quotations copyright Anne Yeats and Michael Butler Yeats

Set in Baskerville type and printed in the Republic of Ireland
by Irish Elzevier Printers, for the publishers,

THE DOLMEN PRESS
The Lodge, Mountrath, Portlaoise

North America:
Humanities Press Inc., Atlantic Highlands, New Jersey 97716, U.S.A.

First published 1982

BRITISH LIBRARY CATALOGUING IN PUBLICATION DATA

Neuman, S C
    Some one myth. - (New Yeats papers).
    1. Yeats, William Butler - Prose
    I. Title   II. Series
    828'.8'08   PR5906. A3

ISBN 0 85105 369 6   The Dolmen Press
ISBN 0 391 02150 8   Humanities Press

FOR MY LATE FATHER

You most of all, silent and fierce old man

CONTENTS

ILLUSTRATIONS

ACKNOWLEDGEMENTS

I wish to make grateful acknowledgement to all holders of copyright for material quoted in this book.

Acknowledgement is made:

To Miss Anne Yeats, Senator Michael Yeats, A. P. Watt Ltd., and MacMillan Company of London Limited for permission to quote from the published work and letters of W. B. Yeats; ·

To Miss Anne Yeats, Senator Michael Yeats and Wayne State University Press for permission to quote from William Butler Yeats, *John Sherman & Dhoya;*

To MacMillan of Canada for permission to quote from *Yeats and the Theatre,* eds. O'Driscoll and Reynolds;

To Routledge & Kegan Paul Limited for permission to quote from *W. B. Yeats and T. Sturge Moore: Their Correspondence 1901–1937,* ed. Ursula Bridge;

To Miss Anne Yeats, Senator Michael Yeats and McClelland and Stewart Limited for permission to quote from W. B. Yeats, *The Speckled Bird;*

To Miss Anne Yeats and Senator Michael Yeats for permission to quote from unpublished Yeats manuscripts;

To the staffs of Dublin National Library and The Centre for Contemporary Arts and Letters, SUNY, for knowledgeable and gracious help;

To the secretarial staff of the Department of English, University of Alberta, for accurate and prompt typing, always done cheerfully, of several drafts of the manuscript;

To Liam Miller, for encouragement and suggestions about the manuscript.

ABBREVIATIONS

A: W. B. Yeats, *Autobiographies* (London: MacMillan, 1966).

AM: W. B. Yeats, *The Adoration of the Magi* in *The Tables of the Law* and *The Adoration of the Magi* (London: Elkin Mathews, 1904).

CT: W. B. Yeats, *The Celtic Twilight: Men and Women, Dhouls and Fairies* (London: Lawrence and Bullen, 1893).

EI: W. B. Yeats, *Essays and Introductions* (London: MacMillan, 1961).

Ex: W. B. Yeats, *Explorations* (London: MacMillan, 1962).

FMY: Joseph Ronsley, "Yeats's Lecture Notes for 'Friends of My Youth,' " in Robert O'Driscoll and Lorna Reynolds, eds., *Yeats and the Theatre*, for Yeats Studies Series (Canada: MacMillan Company of Canada Limited; U.S.A.: MacLean-Hunter Press, 1975).

IR: E. H. Mikhail, ed., *W. B. Yeats: Interviews and Recollections* (London: MacMillan, 1977), 2 volumes.

JS&D: William Butler Yeats, *John Sherman & Dhoya*, ed., Richard J. Finneran (Detroit: Wayne State University Press, 1969).

L: Allan Wade, ed., *The Letters of W. B. Yeats* (London: Rupert Hart-Davis, 1954).

L-SM: Ursula Bridge, ed., *W. B. Yeats and T. Sturge Moore: Their Correspondence 1901–1937* (London: Routledge & Kegan Paul Ltd., 1953).

L-WBY: Richard J. Finneran, George Mills Harper and William M. Murphy, eds., *Letters to W. B. Yeats* (London: MacMillan, 1977).

M: W. B. Yeats, *Mythologies* (London: MacMillan, 1959).

Mem: W. B. Yeats, *Memoirs: Autobiography – First Draft*, ed., Denis Donoghue (London: MacMillan, 1972).

NI: W. B. Yeats, *Letters to the New Island*, ed., Horace Reynolds (1934; rpt., London: Oxford University Press, 1970).

OB: W. B. Yeats, *On the Boiler* (Dublin: The Cuala Press, [1939]).

RH: Michael J. Sidnell, ed., "Versions of the Stories of Red Hanrahan," in *Yeats Studies: Yeats and the 1890s*, 1 (Ireland: Irish University Press, 1971). N.B.: The text of *Stories of Red Hanrahan* found in *Mythologies* is followed except where the argument demands reference to earlier versions of the stories.

S: W. B. Yeats, ed., *Samhain: October 1901 – November 1908* (London: Frank Cass and Company Limited, 1970).

SB: William Butler Yeats, *The Speckled Bird*, ed., William H. O'Donnell, for Yeats Studies Series (Canada: McClelland and Stewart, 1976).

SR: W. B. Yeats, *The Secret Rose* (London: Lawrence & Bullen, Ltd., [1897]).

TL: Robert O'Driscoll, "*The Tables of the Law*: A Critical Text," in *Yeats Studies*, 1.

UP: W. B. Yeats, *Uncollected Prose*, ed., vol. 1, John P. Frayne; vol. 2, John P. Frayne and Colton Johnson (London: MacMillan, 1970, 1975).

VI: William Butler Yeats, *A Vision: An Explanation of Life Founded upon the Writings of Giraldus and upon Certain Doctrines Attributed to Kusta Ben Luka* (London: T. Werner Laurie, Ltd., 1925).

VII: W. B. Yeats, *A Vision* (London: MacMillan, 1937).

VP1:   Russell K. Alspach, ed., *The Variorum Edition of the Plays of W. B. Yeats* (London: MacMillan, 1966).

VPo: Peter Allt and Russell K. Alspach, eds., *The Variorum Edition of the Poems of W. B. Yeats* (New York: MacMillan, 1973).

YP: Robert O'Driscoll, "Yeats on Personality: The Unpublished Lectures," in *Yeats and the Theatre*.

ONE: PERSONAL UTTERANCE and THE LUNAR PARABLE: EARLY PROSE and *A VISION*

I

At sixty-nine, Yeats feared he "had grown too old for poetry" (VPl, 1309). Forcing himself to turn again to verse after two years of writing little but prose, praying that he might seem "A foolish, passionate man" (VP1, 1310; VPo, 553), he wrote the first version of *The King of the Great Clock Tower,*[1] a version in which the action is in prose, the words of the attendants singing the song of the severed head in lyrics. In a "Commentary" on the play, he draws attention to the queen's dance with the swineherd's head (VP1, 1311) which, he suggests, both recalls Wilde's *Salomé* and evokes the myth of Cybele. The "mother goddess and the slain god" (VP1, 1311) he would allude to again in his reworking of the Salomé theme in *A Full Moon in March.* That Yeats, in both these plays and in "The Tragic Generation," should evoke the theatrical image of Salomé "dancing seemingly alone in her narrow moving luminous circle" (A, 321), that he should in each case link the image with the 1890s, with the literature of Wilde, of Mallarmé and of Symons, suggests the extent to which he identified with that generation and saw himself as its sole survivor; that he should go on to cite his use of the myth in the story "The Binding of the Hair," published in *The Secret Rose* in 1896,[2] and that the head should sing of "The King that could make his people stare,/Because he had feathers instead of hair" (VP1, 1007) from that same book, suggest an attempt to trace a unity between his early and his late work; that he should both give the image a Greek prototype and employ it in *A Vision* suggests that it had become for him a symbol mediating between civilizations, between the natural and the supernatural, between life and myth.

Outlining a cyclic theory of history in *A Vision,* Yeats had used Salomé's self-absorbed and self-expressive dance as symbolic omen of the turning point at which one civilization begins to fall and its opposite to rise:

When I think of the moment before revelation I think of Salome...dancing before Herod and receiving the Prophet's head in her indifferent hands, and wonder if what seems to us decadence was not in reality the exaltation[3] of the muscular flesh and of civilisation perfectly achieved. Seeking images, I see her anoint her bare limbs...that she may gain the favour of a king, and remember that the same impulse will create the Galilean revelation and deify Roman Emperors whose sculptured heads will be surrounded by the solar disk. Upon the throne and upon the cross alike the myth becomes a biography. (VII, 273)

Yeats's symbolic use of Salomé, who is paradoxically "indifferent" while dancing to "gain the favour of a king," is analagous to his description of the thirteenth cone of the system of *A Vision* as "sufficient to itself" and "conscious of itself," "like some great dancer, the perfect flower of modern culture, dancing some primitive dance and conscious of his or her own life and of the dance" (VII, 240). In Yeats's formulation, modern dancer and primitive dance, Christian revelation and Roman worship become "equivalent expression" (A, 482), similarly significant events occurring in different places. So too, he suggests, should life and art, myth and biography expand each into the other: Christ incarnates the redemptive myth; representational statues of Roman emperors are mythologized by the addition of the solar disk; the dancer watches herself, conscious of her art — the dance — and of her life — herself dancing.

Yeats saw "world history, personal history" (L, 887) as each other's doubles; so he wrote the day after he finished correcting the proof sheets to the second edition of *A Vision*. That work, with its use of biographical data as evidence for a system compounded of psychology, history, astrology and myth, attests to the poet's active belief in all manner of doublings[4] and particularly in the equivalence of the personal and the historic, the biographical and the mythic. Much of *Autobiographies* clearly alludes to it for its principle of organization[5]; it has been suggested that Yeats's decision to publish the 1938 edition of that work as *The Autobiography* is an indication of the unity he had discovered between the separately published volumes, of his success in shaping his life to a symbolic pattern.[6] But the change of title may have been motivated more by a desire to emphasize his intentions than by a personal conviction that he had realized himself apocalyptically for Yeats seems finally to have found life recalcitrant to his ideal of Unity of Being. Only four months before MacMillan published *The Autobiography* in 1938, Yeats, recalling those ancestors who figured so centrally in *Reveries over Childhood and Youth,* summed up his life: "I am not content" (VPo, 604–05). At the same time he returned to autobiography, adopting the persona of "a mad ship's carpenter" who was "very good at his trade if he would stick to it" (OB, 9) but who seldom did stick to it. The persona of *On the Boiler* is opinionated, ferocious, angry. The inclusion of *Purgatory* in this volume of autobiography in which Yeats poses as absolutely frank suggests that he felt that he and his country were condemned to much "dreaming back," to many reincarnations. Both persona and play raise the questions of Yeats's attitude towards *Autobiographies,* of the extent to which the doubling of biography and myth in it had been merely dramatic device, or the extent to which it had transformed biography and myth each into the other and transcended both in what Yeats termed Unity of Being.

Even Yeats's earliest work had been informed by a nascent vision of myth and biography, art and life, as antithetical and doubled. He himself traced the vision to a moment of revelation which probably occurred in 1886 or shortly before [7] and which followed upon his reading of a patriotic poem written by a returned emigrant. Recognizing the verses as "badly written," Yeats was nonetheless moved "because they contained the actual thoughts of a man at a passionate moment of life" (A, 102). He felt that "every thought" came to the poet "for life's sake and that the writing was an afterthought" (FMY, 71). The recognition is recollected as seminal to all his work: "Probably at that moment a vision presented itself to me that I have never since lost. Lyric poetry also could be made personal, it would... recover its old poignance again if we could speak once more simply and naturally..., expressing the emotions that came to us in life, thinking nothing for the sake of literature, everything for the sake of life..." (FMY, 71). He decided to dedicate himself to "the most *powerful* thing in all literature — personal utterance" and opposed that utterance to "poetry of abstract personality" (YP, 30).[8] Life and literature are antithetical here as they are forty years later in *A Vision* but so too, as in *A Vision,* are life and literature intimately related in a mode that transcends the limitations of both.

In his journalism throughout the 1890s, Yeats suggests that the poet must establish what he later termed "equivalent expression" between his life and his poetry, that out of the transcendence of these antithetical modes through "personal utterance" comes the unity of expression that is the greatest art. In 1891, we find him dwelling on self, the world and their unity, all within the context of Irish nationalism. Reviewing the collected edition of William Allingham's poems, he concludes that Allingham "was no national poet," that he "had no sense of the great unities — the relation of man to man, and all to the serious life of the world" and that it "was this that kept him from feeling Ireland as a whole" (UP, I, 212). Within the year, Yeats returns to Allingham, who, he decides, "saw neither the great unities of God or of man, of his own spiritual life or of the life of the nation about him." Failing to so see, he failed to create a lasting verse: in "greater poets everything has relation to the national life or to profound feeling; nothing is an isolated artistic moment; there is a unity everywhere, everything fulfils a purpose that is not its own..." (UP, I, 260). Implicit in the assessment are the two unities which shape the "Lunar parable" (A, 344) of *A Vision:* unity with the self; unity with that outside oneself, with the world or God.[9]

Yeats's emphasis on these antinomies which foreshadow the system of *A Vision,* if by no means logically enunciated or rhetorically precise, is insistent throughout 1892. Describing literary London to the politicized Dublin of that time, he recalls an earlier speech at The Rhymers' Club. There he had attempted "to explain a philosophy of poetry... and to show the dependence... of all great art and literature upon conviction and upon heroic life." Romantic in both its conception and formulation, Yeats's statement was received by his fellow poets with "irritated silence" (UP, I, 248). Had they been more prescient, they would have recognized in it and in his later recollection of it in an article written for *United Ireland* ("Hopes and Fears for Irish Literature") Yeats's enduring preoccupations with a philosophy of poetry based on "conviction," with Irish literary nationalism, and with the necessary coherence and doubling of life and art.

By 1895, the credo was becoming more specific in its antitheses. In a series of four articles on "Irish National Literature," Yeats distinguished literature from expository writing by drawing an analogy with the traditional dichotomy of body and soul. Literature is "wrought about a mood... as the body is wrought about an invisible soul" and such "moods are the labourers and messengers of the Ruler of All," he writes, setting forth the formal pattern which would assume the nomenclature of self, anti-self, and true self in *A Vision*. The artist is one who possesses the vision to transform base metal into spiritual gold; he discovers "immortal moods in mortal desires, an undecaying hope in our trivial ambitions, a divine love in sexual passion" (UP, I, 367). [10] The conviction that such antithetical emotions might yet be each other's double persists in Yeats's journalism. Writing of A.E.'s poetry in 1898, he stresses the body-soul analogy in a paraphrase of his subject: "All emotions are double, for either we choose 'the shadowy beauty,' and our soul weeps, or the invisible beauty that is 'our high ancestral self,' and the body weeps" (UP, II, 123). The idea appears yet again in Yeats's last piece of journalism of the decade: still explaining "The Literary Movement in Ireland," this time to the December, 1899 audience of the *North American Review,* he makes the Apocrypha the source of his image: "a change of thought is making us half ready to believe with Ecclesiasticus, that 'all things are made double one above another,' and that the forms of nature may be temporal shadows of realities" (UP, II, 195). [11]

The tenor of Yeats's early philosophical statements, then, is towards contraries which are necessarily related; opposing emotions, life and art, are but each other's doubles pointing to a unity beyond both. But his statements of this conviction are often vague, always symbolic, doubtless because the source of much of his belief lay in theosophy and the rituals of The Order of the Golden Dawn. His concealment of those sources hardly made for the simplicity or the directness of "personal utterance."

Precisely because he was unwilling to acknowledge many of the sources from which he shaped his "conviction," Yeats seems to have found fiction more congenial to its initial expression. If John Butler Yeats disapproved of his son's vision of the possibilities inherent in "personal utterance,"[12] he did direct him towards fiction that would draw on the young poet's experience by suggesting that "he should write a story, partly of London, partly of Sligo."[13] Instead of a story set in London and Sligo, Yeats wrote one which conveyed through legend all his romantic identification with the landscape of Western Ireland and all his feelings of alienation from England.[14] Dhoya is literally an outcast; physically grotesque and frequently possessed by uncontrolled rage, he is abandoned by the Fomorians in the Bay of Ballah. His identification with his natural surroundings is both complete and an index of his alienation from all human life. For friends he has only bats, owls and frogs, "the outcasts from they knew not what" (JS&D, 116); to receive his prayers he has only huge pines, "each one alone," a "dark outlaw" (JS&D, 119). Prefiguring the contemplative man's union with his self which characterizes the ideal Phase Fifteen of *A Vision*, Dhoya directs his fury against his own shadow and, having pledged himself a knight ready to "avenge" (JS&D, 117) the feminine lunar principle, if she be wronged, he offers sacrifice to the moon. Dhoya is monstrous, however, because he has failed to discover harmony within himself through union with his opposite, that same feminine principle; because he lacks such moral beauty, the moon refuses the sacrifice of Yeats's uncouth Endymion.

Nearly thirty-five years after writing *Dhoya*, Yeats would cite the example of Dante and Villon to argue that the poet must "become conjoint" to his buried self through the encounter with "the greatest obstacle he may confront without despair" (A, 272-73), the choice of "whatever task's most difficult/Among tasks not impossible" (VPo, 376). The pattern is implicit in *Dhoya*. His sacrifice having been refused, the first human voice Dhoya has heard since his exile calls his name and he returns to his cave to find a woman in white awaiting him. Clearly an embodiment of the moon-goddess, she is of the spirit world, he of this; as a result of their sexual union, Dhoya finds a harmony of spirit which, in its seeming immutability, suggests a divine world.

In his introduction to *John Sherman & Dhoya*, Richard J. Finneran notes that Yeats has altered the typical Irish legends of liaisons between mortals and immortals by having all the action remain in the physical world and suggests that, having structured the story about the "tension" between mutability and immutability, Yeats firmly declares himself for this world of passion and change (JS&D, 18, 20). A "pale and mutable light" (JS&D, 124) does indeed illuminate all the natural cycles which lend substance to the threnody of Section II that "All things change save only the fear of change" (JS&D, 120, 122). Dhoya's love for his fairy-mistress ends in tragedy because both deny the change on which their love is founded, for "Only the changing, and moody, and angry, and weary can love" (JS&D, 120). Dhoya has been granted the opposing principle with which he can complete his self, but his refusal to recognize the nature of the gift leads to self-destruction rather than self-discovery.

While *Dhoya* may be unconsciously autobiographical about Yeats's feelings of inadequacy at the time it was written, [15] it formally tends towards myth rather than biography. The diction and rhythms of the prose are clearly meant to poeticize the events of the story and both the concluding paragraph and the earlier digression about the naming of Pooldhoya, which is reminiscent of the etymologies of early Irish compilations like *The Tain*, serve to generalize and to mythologize the narration. John Butler Yeats was dissatisfied with the direction his son had taken in his first attempt at fiction and demanded that the young man populate a story with "real people."[16] Where Yeats had attempted to raise the biographical details of Dhoya's life to mythic significance, in *John Sherman* he embedded the dualities of his mythic approach to the world in biographical detail about his characters.

That *John Sherman* is intensely autobiographical and that Yeats parcelled out aspects of himself and his loves and hates among the novella's characters and settings has been frequently noticed.[17] What is of interest is this morcellement is Yeats's irony. Sherman may well be the first of Yeats's characters to find union with the self,[18] but he pursues spiritual wholeness in worldly and unheroic ways. If he does not perform particularly well or willingly as a clerk in his uncle's office, the indulgence granted his nepotic position nonetheless keeps him from failure. If he is determined to remain a meditative lounger (JS&D, 47), he is frank about his need to marry well in order to finance that life and Margaret's money is at least as significant as Margaret herself in their courtship. Similarly, Howard's role as man of action or Sherman's anti-self,[19] is ironically undercut by his spiritual profession. Accusing Sherman of being content to "live with mere facts" (JS&D, 47), Howard doubts he can find a woman with sufficient sincerity and spirituality to be a fitting mate to him on his ministerial way. For a brief moment during Margaret's transference of her feelings from Sherman to himself, Howard sees her features as "quite commonplace." The recognition is tellingly placed to mark the moment of Howard's betrayal of what he imagines to be his true self; it follows immediately on Sherman's suggestion that Margaret's money could buy a bishopric and is immediately followed by Howard's fancy that the light which radiates from her belladonna-brightened eyes touches the tawdry objects around her with the chameleon's mystic light, the light "which all men are seeking" (JS&D, 97).

While Sherman does opt for the contemplative life, Howard for the active, the delineation of the woman through whom Sherman achieves his spiritual knowledge shares some of the irony Yeats has already displayed in his choice of his protagonists' professions and in his description of Howard's courtship. Mary Carton's spirituality is neither aesthetically nor morally unblemished. Beautiful and distinctive she may be, but Sherman also notes the distastefully crumby remains of her philanthropic tea and the unwholesome appearance of the children she teaches. That Yeats names her after the Mother of God[20] suggests an ideal spirituality but, despite his emphasis on her maternal qualities, Mary's spirituality does not really parallel the Virgin's, for her self-sacrifice ironically rests on ambition. That the ambition is for Sherman and only indirectly for herself does not lessen the irony of his attaining spirituality through such a limited medium. Nor does the calculated ruse by which Sherman frees himself of Margaret and London so as to reunite himself with Mary and Ballah sort well with his supposed spiritual redemption. Writing a novel in which the setting and characters initially seem to be schematized to the point of allegory, Yeats remained unable to make a moral choice untinged by an ambiguous irony. The pattern by which both Sherman and Howard come to terms with their real personalities through the initial pursuit of activities most opposite to them and by which Sherman finds his way to spirituality through union with a woman who is neither a pure nor vibrant embodiment of that spirituality lacks schematic clarity and leaves the reader unconvinced and unsatisfied. However, it does reveal Yeats groping towards the system he would enunciate in *A Vision* in which each person attains to what Sherman calls "his centre of unity" (JS&D, 104) through pursuit of an activity antithetical to it. Writing about "real people" in unadorned prose, Yeats has this time attempted to make the myth a biography.

IV

With *The Celtic Twilight,* Yeats attempted another uneasy doubling of myth and biography. The work in many ways anticipates his pre-occupations in *The Secret Rose* where he described the "Celtic twilight" as that region "in which heaven and earth so mingle that each seems to have taken upon itself some shadow of the other's beauty" (SR, 143).[21] His "one subject," Yeats announced in his dedication of *The Secret Rose,* would be "the war of spiritual with natural order" (SR, vii); so too did each incident of *The Celtic Twilight* confront the natural with the supernatural or spiritual. The spiritual world, "perfect and kindly," represents what we in this "fallen world" have lost; consequently "the more innocent of the spirits" (CT, 184-85) and

Yeats himself mourn our incompleteness, our imperfection, throughout *The Celtic Twilight.* Yeats insists on the confrontation, from the epigraph, which contrasts "Time" and "the fire-born moods," to the closing piece, "The Four Winds of Desire," which suggests the value he gave to both Hyde's and his own collection of folk beliefs: "such stories are not a criticism of life but rather an extension...resembling Homer.... They are as [an] existence and not a thought, and make our world of tea-tables seem but a shabby penumbra" (CT, 200; UP, I, 187). The passage formulates a literary aim Yeats never abandoned: literature must infuse the natural with the spiritual and so enlarge and exalt life beyond quotidian concerns. At the end of his life, in "A General Introduction for my Work," he replaces Homer by Dante and Milton and by Shakespeare and Shelley, "existence" by an "idea" which the poet is "reborn" as in order to breathe life into it, the despised tea-table by an even more prosaic breakfast table, but literature remains the extension and completion of the natural by the spiritual: a poet "is never the bundle of accident and incoherence that sits down to breakfast: he has been reborn as an idea, something intended, complete.... He is part of his own phantasmagoria and we adore him because nature has grown intelligible..." (EI, 509). His *"Phantasmagoria"* completes not only the "physical and moral life" "but imagination" (VII, 230).

This description of Hyde's and, by implication, his own stories also recalls Yeats's earlier discovery of "personal utterance." His revisions of *The Celtic Twilight* for the 1925 edition suggest that he was dissatisfied with the style in which he had attempted to body forth that "personal utterance" and his excision of local detail and of assertions of actual belief suggests that by 1925 he preferred to treat the stories as a patterning of experience rather than as evidence for literal belief in the world of faery.[22] Yet initially the stories represented an advance in his narrative aims. Their real distinction is in Yeats's refusal to efface his presence. In this they serve him as a form of "personal utterance" where two earlier collections of folk tales had not.[23] He described his method in the introductory remarks he titled "This Book": "I have... written down accurately and candidly much that I have heard and seen, and, except by way of commentary, nothing that I have merely imagined. I have, however, been at no pains to separate my own beliefs from those of the peasantry, but have rather let my men and women, dhouls and faeries, go their way unoffended or defended by any argument of mine" (CT, ix). Yeats's refusal to separate his own beliefs from those he reports makes his own presence in the stories dramatic rather than evaluative. Sometimes he casts himself as the necessary listener or eyewitness, reporting as accurately as he can the speech and experiences of his subject. At other times he assumes the role of participant, turning himself into a dramatic vehicle for spiritual incidents which are themselves " 'dramatizations of our moods' "

(CT, 87), of our psychological or mental, as opposed to our physical, states.[24]

That Yeats intended his presence in *The Celtic Twilight* to be dramatic and personal rather than dogmatic or scholarly is attested to by his revisions of the text in the early editions. Between the 1893 and 1902 editions, he added seventeen stories,[25] all of which dramatize the confrontation of the natural with the spiritual. He also withdrew the review of Hyde's *Beside the Fire* which had concluded the first edition. That he should delete a review which contains a statement of literary principle parallel in both its conviction and its form to the statement of "A General Introduction for my Work" and which is obviously central to a lifetime of writing points to the narrative strategy of *The Celtic Twilight*. Yeats's decision to omit "The Four Winds of Desire" in spite of its statement of principle must have been dictated by its generic and stylistic incompatibilities with the rest of the collection: it is a review where the remainder of *The Celtic Twilight* is folk narrative and its method is expository where the tales rely on the dramatic methods of either direct or indirect discourse. Its excision allows the tales to speak for themselves as "personal utterance." Yeats's desire to let incidents speak for themselves without superimposed exposition is also attested to by his manuscript revisions of the stories. Curtis Bradford's examination of the manuscript versions of "The Religion of a Sailor," for example, reveals several excised passages, among which is the following: "Alas that he who does may not dream, and that he who dreams cannot do, and that the world sees no one man who unites them into a double mystery."[26] Clearly central to Yeats's thought, the passage points forward to his opposition of "the writer" and the "man of action" (A, 516) in *The Death of Synge* and of antithetical and primary man in *A Vision*. Clearly too, Yeats has cancelled the passage because it obscures the action of the sailor's tale by appealing to our intellect to universalize it rather than letting it speak "simply and quietly"[27] to our emotions.

The progeny of this union of opposite principles, the "double mystery" Yeats sought to set before his readers in *The Celtic Twilight*, was to be Art. Rounding off an over-extended metaphor in the prefatory "This Book," he had invoked the muse: "Hope and Memory have one daughter and her name is Art, and she has built her dwelling far from the desperate field where men hang out their garments upon forked boughs to be banners of battle. O beloved daughter of Hope and Memory, be with me for a little" (CT, x). Yeats himself evidently felt that the collection failed Art in its uneasy hovering between the poeticized and inverted constructions meant to suggest the speech of the Irish peasant and the dramatic and quasi-journalistic narrative meant to make the experiences immediate. Late in life, he indicated that the mythic subjects of *The Celtic Twilight* had begun a movement towards

19

the literature he most valued in Ireland but that its style — "a bit of ornamental trivial needlework sewn on a prophetic fury" (Ex, 333) — substituted a patchwork for the garments worn by Art. Well before the 1902 edition, he had begun stripping the text's diction of many of its poeticized and convoluted phrases. Still more convincing testimony to his doubt that he had succeeded in giving birth to Art in the attempt of *The Celtic Twilight* to present myth in terms of literal experience is Yeats's return to the shapeliness of fiction in *The Secret Rose*.

V

Yeats directly acknowledges his Rosicrucian iconography in the poem which opens that volume; the "great wind of love and hate" of the Secret Rose is to create unity out of contraries. At the same time, he stresses in the epigraphs biography and myth as an embodiment of contraries. One recalls Villiers de l'Isle-Adam's now legendary phrase to characterize the spiritually exalted: "As for living, our servants will do that for us." The other undercuts the myth with biographical irony: "Helen, when she looked in her mirror, seeing the withered wrinkles made in her face by old age, wept, and wondered why she had twice been carried away." The stories, which Yeats had published in magazines since finishing *The Celtic Twilight* and many of which he revised only in page proof when he collected them,[28] nearly all focus on a moment when biography confronts and crosses the barrier separating it from myth, when the natural meets the supernatural. Often the occasion is death, literal moment when biographical constraints yield, we hope, to a final and perfect shape in an immortal world. In some of these stories, the spiritual self transcends physical death: Aodh's severed head sings out his song praising a queen[29]; the Rosicrucian knight dies " ' filled with a great joy' " (SR, 66) at being released from an imperfect world into the spiritual world promised him in his youth[30]; the old wizard of "The Heart of Spring" enters in death an immortal world of eternal youth the promise of which is made pervasive in the story by seasonal and floral symbols of rebirth and by the culminating song of the thrush[31]; Proud Costello, thwarted in life by her kin and by his own pride of the embrace of Una MacDermot, is spiritually united with her as the trees above their grave symbolically intergrow like those surrounding the mystic rose of the book's cover design.[32]

However, not all the characters of *The Secret Rose* are able to cross the barrier between natural and supernatural. The boys present at the deaths of the old knight of "Out of the Rose" and the wizard of "The Heart of Spring" are so constrained by mortal desires that they can see only the impracticality of the spiritual quest; their very limitations before the epiphanies they are privileged to witness insist upon those epiphanies' contrary, upon the mortal clay which mires their spirits.

The cock crows for the death of the Rosicrucian knight as it crowed "Three hundred years before the Fall" (VPo, 388) and as it crowed to mark the beginning of Christ's passion; such lads think of it as but a participant in a cock-fight, parodic and debased acting out of Yeatsian contraries. Others, such as the Puritan soldiers in "The Curse of the Fires and Shadows" have not only repudiated the spiritual world but violated it; the supernatural becomes for them a world of deceitful phantoms luring them on to a violent and punitive death reminiscent of Dhoya's. In "The Rose of Shadow," the spirit calling the young woman across the grave's barrier brings death with him and her love for one so violent surely carries her to destruction rather than immortality and perfection of the self.

While such stories serve Yeats by fictionalizing aspects of a good deal of his own experience during the 1890s — his passage through the grades of The Order of the Golden Dawn, his attempt to organize an order of Celtic Mysteries with a literary "procession of the Gods" that would forge "a symbolical, a mythological coherence" (A, 193) for an Ireland riven by factionalism —, they are no unequivocal apologia for the extension of the natural by the supernatural. They dramatize Yeats's fears as well as his hopes in his confrontation of the natural with the spiritual, the biographical with the mythic. As a result, the transcendence of biographical limitations is often approached as uncertainly as it was in *John Sherman*. "The Old Men of the Twilight," for example, have been imprisoned in birds' flesh because they have denied knowledge in their absorption with mere learning. Because their transgression is that of unaware self-absorption, they are appropriately enough incarnated as grey herons narcissistically contemplating themselves in grey pools. Their punishment, doomed as they are to live far too long and never to know the moment of their death, is rigorous enough in a personal context. When we recall, however, that Yeats would later make a "moon-crazed heron" that will "not dare/Dip or do anything but stare/Upon the glittering image of a heron,/That now is lost and now is there" (VP1, 780-81), an image of the completely unified phase of personal life and of civilization, the phase closest to that of the ideal poet, the killing of the heron seems to be significant in a context larger than and contradictory to the mere end of the personal purgatorial experience suggested by the story's plot. The Hawk-King may know enough "to make all darkness light" (SR, 18), but his subjects are only diminished by his knowledge, the woman he loves still prefers yellow hair and physical strength to supernatural wisdom, and the story-teller cannot tell us in what the King's wisdom consists except that it is inaccessible to us and "deadly to mortal things" (SR, 23).[33] Aengus, the Lover of God, becomes revered as spiritual leader of the monks but the narrator does not tell us what Aengus sees when he looks "at the sun going down into the unknown darkness" (SR, 35).

Similarly, the crucified gleeman, in his parallel with the myth of Christ, seems to promise us salvation through spirituality, yet we hear from the story-teller only of the biographical details of his death, not of the nature of the knowledge he finds.

Yeats seems to mediate between the physical and the spiritual, between biography and myth without specifying either the path to the spiritual or the nature of the mythic. But one formulation of the possible ways to unity does recur; the opposition between the man of action and the man of reverie, nascent in the excisions from "The Religion of a Sailor" and central to the lunar types of *A Vision* and to Yeats's personal myth in *Autobiographies,* appears also in *The Secret Rose.* Those, like the Rosicrucian knight, who attain to spiritual unity are "the dreamers who must do what they dream, the doers who must dream what they do" (SR, 53). And in *The Tables of the Law,* which Yeats had originally meant to publish in *The Secret Rose,*[34] he describes Owen Aherne, bearer of mystic knowledge, as possessed of a "nature, which is half monk, half soldier of fortune, and must needs turn action into dreaming, and dreaming into action" (TL, 103). The distinction is another version of the active and contemplative men of Yeats's later work. Where *The Secret Rose* both becomes specifically autobiographical and attempts to transform Yeatsian biography into myth is in its emphasis on contemplative men, on dreamers. In this collection, these reverie-burdened men fall into two broad types: mystics and gleeman, men who might write *A Vision,* men transformed by poetic knowledge. For each type, Yeats created personae.

VI

The monks who do obeisance before Aengus or defend their altar against soldiers, the wizard who surrounds himself with hazel, lilies and roses to die, or the Rosicrucian knight: these are bodies wrought about a mood of mystery. But in the volume's concluding story, "Rosa Alchemica," and in two stories initially meant for *The Secret Rose* and then published separately, "The Tables of the Law" and "The Adoration of the Magi," Yeats created personae who both embody the Rosicrucian mysticism which had become a large part of his own life[35] and present its conflict with his worldy concerns.

The narrative technique of these last three stories is considerably more complex than that of the others collected in *The Secret Rose.* Like the other stories, these concentrate on a moment in the protagonist's life when he confronts the supernatural; unlike many of the other stories, these embody the supernatural in personae of Yeats himself, in what he would later term Masks. These stories too are written in the first person, traditionally the "person" of confession as opposed to the historical and/or omniscient fictional third person. The first person narrator looks back to moments at which he confronted the supernatural and reports the conversations of Aherne or Robartes and his own near loss of self to the supernatural in the context of his present life. In "Rosa Alchemica" this comparative narrative sophistication both lets Yeats present Robartes' case for overthrowing the "God of humility and sorrow" (SR, 257) and, at the same time, seem, since his narrator rejects the esoteric for "refuge in the only definite faith" (SR, 240), not to offend orthodoxy.[36] It also lets him split a personal conflict among characters much as he had done in *John Sherman*. Aherne and Robartes, with their esoteric convictions, and the narrator of these stories, with his pious retreat to the rosary, dramatize Yeats's commitment to the occult and the conflict of that commitment with the views of certain of his family, his readers, and his nationalist friends.

Robert O'Driscoll has pointed out that in these stories our sympathies lie not with the narrator but with the personae who speak for the occult.[37] In this the stories are a paradigm of cabbalistic documents; they present a secret doctrine to those willing to heed it but present it in such a way that the text can be satisfactorily misconstrued by the unsympathetic. But in terms of Yeats's own interest and of the receptive reader's narrative sympathies, the texts are also cautionary tales. Particularly in "Rosa Alchemica," the narrator is not one who defends himself against "the spirits whose name is legion" (TL, 118) so much as he is a failed mystic.

The narrator has sought to follow the alchemical way by writing "a fanciful reverie over the transmutation of life into art, and a cry of measureless desire for a world made wholly of essences" (SR, 222). He fails, as alchemist and artist, because he refuses to recognize the contraries and the experience on which such transmutation is based. Instead of transmuting life into art, he withdraws from life and surrounds himself with the artifacts of others' creativity.[38] His isolation in a world of medieval paintings, of books bound in colours appropriate to their authors' temperaments, of silent servants, identifies Huysmans' des Esseintes as the narrator's prototype[39] and reveals how disenchanted Yeats had become with the decadence of the 1890s by the time he wrote "Rosa Alchemica." This withdrawal marks a part of the narrator's failure, for by it he denies his mortality; he cannot, in Robartes' dialectic, " 'forget he is miserable in the bustle and noise of the multitude in this world and in time' " (SR, 232). Conversely, his "pride of . . . connoisseurship" (SR, 225) marks his failure to transcend life through art for the very self-consciousness of his good taste asserts his separateness from his plaster or bronze gods and goddesses and prevents his feeling the "limitless energy" (SR, 225) which brought them into being in the first place. Holding himself "apart, individual, indissoluble, a mirror of polished steel" (SR, 224),[40] he cannot, again in Robartes' dialectic, " 'seek a mystical union with the multitude who govern this world and time' " (SR, 232).

With Robartes' appearance and his dialectical statement of the choices open to the dreamer, the narrator is given a second chance. That it is a chance to penetrate the world of essences, to seek union with the gods who "govern this world and time," is made clear not only by Robartes' words but by the symbolism of "the trembling of the veil" which pervades the story. The narrator lives in a room in which a "tapestry, full of the blue and bronze of peacocks," alchemical symbols of unity, completion,[41] "fell over the doors" (SR, 222). At the climax of Section I of the story, the narrator, contemplating his own discontent and fancying the stars "divine alchemists" able to turn "lead into gold, weariness into ecstasy, bodies into souls, the darkness into God," has drawn "aside the curtains" (SR, 226). Leading Robartes up the old stairs, he is moved to recall "simpler days" before "men's minds... began to tremble on the verge of some unimagined revelation" (SR, 228-29) and, closing the door, letting "the peacock curtain" fall between the two of them "and the world," he feels himself on the verge of "some singular and unexpected thing" (SR, 229). That the imagery of "the trembling of the veil" intimates the moment of revelation of mystical and divine truth is evident from the other two stories. An allusion in "The Tables of the Law" to "souls trembling between the excitement of the flesh and the excitement of the spirit" (TL, 105)[42] is made plain in "The Adoration of the Magi." There the timidly orthodox narrator characterizes himself as "always in dread of the illusions which come of that inquietude of the veil of the Temple, which M. Mallarmé considers a characteristic of our times" (AM, 45).[43] Yeats's attitude to his narrator's anxiety, as in all these stories, is almost certainly ironic. By the time he writes the "Epilogue" to *Per Amica Silentia Lunae,* he is no longer coy or ironic but openly associates the phrase with the tradition of the poet as mage. The "trembling of the veil," he tells us in the later work, presages revelation, revelation of Unity of Being, of a "tradition... more universal and more ancient" (M, 369), of another order of reality.

Yeats's symbolic use of a literal curtain in "Rosa Alchemica" and his allusion to Mallarmé in "The Adoration of the Magi" in fact serve to introduce his symbol without indicating its ultimate source to readers uninitiated into and presumably unsympathetic to occult rituals. His real familiarity with the image certainly antedates Mallarmé's essay. Behind Mallarmé's veil, for Yeats, lay the "UNVEILED TRUTH" which Mme. Blavatsky promised "true souls" who lifted "aside the curtain."[44] The curtain itself is the "Veil of Matter" between "Physical and Ethereal *Divine* Man," a veil "too dense for even the Inner Man to penetrate."[45] Blavatsky's reference is obviously to the Veil of the Tabernacle and to Masonic and Rosicrucian rituals in general.

Eighteenth-century French Rosicrucian documents record the phrase as central to the depiction of the moment of chaos and terror before divine revelation. In the ceremony of the opening of the Temple, one of the participants demands, "Quelle heure est-il?" and receives the response, "L'instante où le voile du Temple se déchira, que les ténèbres et la consternation se répandirent sur la Terre, que la lumière s'obscurcit, que les voiles de la Maçonnerie se brisèrent, que l'Etoile flamboyante disparut, que la Pierre Cubique sua sang et eau et que la Parole fut perdue."[46] The Postulant in this rite pledges to recover the Word. Golden Dawn notebooks among Yeats's papers demonstrate the recurrence of the image in the ceremonies for the opening and closing of the Order's Temple. One moved, in Golden Dawn symbology, from material to spiritual perception by going behind the "Veil of Isis," identified with "the Veil of the Tabernacle."[47] In the "4°=7° Philosophus" Ritual, the Hierophant recounts the Creation: "From the Father of Waters went forth the Spirit, rending assunder the Veils of Darkness."[48] At the culmination of the 7°=4° Ritual, the Magus appears from behind the Veil, admits the Postulant to the new rank, and retires behind the Veil again.[49] Adepti entered the Portal of the Vault of the Adepti by "the sign of the rending asunder of the veil" and closed the Portal by "the sign of the closing of the veil."[50] The action seems always to have been represented by a sign, and sometimes to have been indicated by a password:

3rd Ad [ept] : What is this sign?
As: [sociate] **Ad:** The sign of the rending asunder of the Veil.
3rd Ad: What is the Word?...
As: Ad: The whole Word is PARÒKETH, meaning the Veil of the Tabernacle.
3rd Ad: In and by that Word I declare the Portal of this Vault of the Adepts duly opened.[51]

In a meditation which Yeats wrote in 1909, he makes the symbolic value of this rending of the veil explicit in terms of spiritual quest. The initiate, whom Yeats directs the reader to imagine himself as, is able to "go no further," and is lost on the Path of the Chameleon "among confused cries of birds of the night & in the gathering darkness." He makes "the sign of the rending of the veil," says "Pawketh," and is rewarded with vision; there "is a light suddenly."[52]

In "Rosa Alchemica," as Robartes begins to make his case for the occult, the veil trembles repeatedly: the peacocks on the curtain in the narrator's room "glow with a more intense colour" (SR, 232), then "glimmer and glow as though each separate colour were a living spirit" (SR, 233), and finally "grow immense" (SR, 236); Robartes himself becomes "a shuttle weaving an immense purple web whose folds had begun to fill the room" (SR, 234). The climax of this vision in which the boundaries between physical and spiritual matter dissolve comes with a prophetic voice announcing that " 'The mirror is broken in two pieces' " (SR, 237). The narrator, who had imaged his withdrawn self as "a mirror of polished steel," has momentarily achieved the visionary ecstasy the absence of which had so discontented him. But he proves unequal to that ecstasy and so fails his own desire. He implies his inability to become pure spirit in the suffocating quality of his descriptions first of "the purple web," then of the peacock feathers as they begin to expand and fill the room; he makes his failure explicit in the assertion that "I had never again known mortality or tears, had I not suddenly fallen from the certainty of vision into the uncertainty of dream" (SR, 238). When he fails a second time to call up the divine powers, "trembling out of existence, folding up into a timeless ecstasy, drifting with half-shut eyes, into a sleepy stillness" (SR, 252),[53] he renounces the spiritual world.

The initiation rites of Robartes' Rosicrucian Order generally promise a spiritual revolution and particularly intimate an overthrow of Christianity — the members dance " 'To trouble His unity with their multitudinous feet' " (SR, 257) — so that many gods may again govern man.[54] Just as in "The Adoration of the Magi" this Second Coming is presented by an inversion of Christian symbolism — the Virgin becomes a harlot and, in later versions, the God born man becomes man transformed into symbol of pure spirit, the unicorn[55] —, so in "Rosa Alchemica" the plea for a new order of the spiritual is presented in an inversion of the Annunciation. The narrator dances with no humble and mortal Virgin but with "an immortal august woman" (SR, 260) who wears black lilies to symbolize the overthrow of Christianity and whose gestures, "laden...with a love like the love that breathed upon the waters" (SR, 260), announce a second Creation. Stricken by fear of her, the narrator renounces vision forever; the shining temple can never again be more for him than an ill-painted, prosaically proportioned, coldly-lit room. His failure of vision is ironic because, breaking his trance and so permitting his escape from the angry villagers, it also prevents his achieving the death he sought at the story's opening.

Demon est deus inversus. The strong tincture of diabolism in the dance with the alluring woman wearing black lilies probably owes a good deal to some of the Parisian occult groups of the 1890s.[56] However, while Yeats's occult beliefs increasingly demanded the recognition of some "rough beast" replete with the necessary evil, he also sought spiritual gold from his involvement with the occult and not the mere perversity of diabolism; witness his later distaste for Aleister Crowley's meddling with the rites of The Order of the Golden Dawn. While Robartes obviously speaks for Yeats's interests and while Yeats's irony makes the narrator's pious return to the rosary seem an inadequate response, the narrator does embody some aspects of the occult experience which certainly must have troubled Yeats during the 1890s. Robartes' speech and the vellum book given the narrator to read before initiation are rich in symbols and allusive promise but never specific as to the nature of the knowledge to be obtained. Undoubtedly germane to this is Yeats's pledge to keep secret the rituals and knowledge of The Order. Probably even more germane is the fact that The Order of the Golden Dawn posited a gradual growth towards a knowledge that had to be taken on faith as the Postulant moved through its grades. This is, of course, consonant with mystic arguments generally which insist that the demand for particularity of knowledge belongs to the rationalist mode and is inimical to the knowledge sought by the postulant. While Yeats undoubtedly felt that he sometimes fleetingly glimpsed the spiritual world,[57] in the 1890s, he remained unable to specify the knowledge Robartes promised. Professing his belief in magic in a 1901 essay, he nonetheless confessed that he did not know what the spirits whom he sought were (EI, 28). Many years later, "the wisdom one had once hoped for" remained "still far off" (Mem, 27), his symbolic tower "a place set out for wisdom/That he... [would] never find" (VPo, 377). Involved as he was in the 1890s in politics, in journalism and publishing, in various concrete activities to bring about a new literary nationalism in Ireland, he must have sometimes felt the undefined mystical knowledge hidden behind the veil of elaborate ritual to be perilous; his treatment of Owen Aherne, cast away from the possibility of redemption by virtue of his knowledge, hypothesizes the possible peril in terms of Christian allegory. Most importantly, the idea of following rigidly outlined ceremonies and "paths" with no specific knowledge of their end, of committing oneself to an act of faith, even if non-Christian faith, could lead the inquisitive neophyte astray. The narrator of "Rosa Alchemica" feels "plucked out of the definite world and cast naked upon a shoreless sea" (SR, 239); in *Autobiographies* Yeats would characterize himself as being "astray upon the Path of the Chameleon" (A, 270) during these years. Robartes and Aherne have their prototypes among Yeats's acquaintances[58] but, more importantly, they dramatize certain of his personal and intellectual conflicts during the 1890s[59] : Robartes, his philosophy and his aspirations; Aherne, his fears about the psychological dangers of immersion in the occult; the narrator — who, like the revived Robartes of the later poems, finds himself "caught between the pull/Of the dark moon and the full" (VPo, 384) —, his fascination with it, his sense of indirection, his possible loss of identity and failure of courage before it.

VII

When, working on *A Vision* more than twenty years later, Yeats resurrected Robartes and Aherne in several dialogue poems and short stories that he might dramatize his self and his thought in poetry, fiction and philosophy, the tone of mockery for the timid seeker after knowledge endures as does the intensity of Robartes' vision. Perhaps the fact that he received the form of his philosophy through first Mrs. Yeats's automatic script and then through the words of "communicators" who spoke through her in her sleep and whom he queried prompted Yeats's return to the dialogue poem. His initial decision to cast *A Vision* in the form of a dialogue between Robartes and Aherne [60] and his later revision of this plan to introduce the text by a biographical account of the circumstances by which the book came into Robartes', then his, hands clearly do point to *A Vision* as the impetus to the dialogue poems of the period. However, the dialogue originally written for *A Vision* was even more unsuccessful than that of the abandoned *The Speckled Bird;* manuscript fragments[61] of it reveal Robartes as a wooden character, mouthing obscure doctrine in obscurer English and altogether taking himself too seriously. Poetry provided the discipline that Yeats's prose in these early versions of *A Vision* lacked while the idea of the dialogue enabled him to dramatize the "doubling" central to his thought without seeming either fanatic or pedantic about its origins in the occult.

The dialogue form brings irony, and occasionally downright mockery, to the poems. With *A Vision* in hand, critics have identified Yeats beneath the persona of *Ille* in "Ego Dominus Tuus" or *He* in "Michael Robartes and the Dancer."[62] What gives wit and shape to the poems, however, are the pointed comments of *Hic* and *She* which undercut Robartes' rhetoric, comments with the dry mordancy of *She's* "You mean they argued" (VPo, 385). Yeats mocks the style of his own formulations here and approaches himself, whether as *Ille,* Robartes, or Yeats, with the mixture of sympathy and irony which distinguished the tone adopted towards the narrator of "Rosa Alchemica." That the mockery is self-directed becomes plain in "The Phases of the Moon" where Aherne, diminished from his earlier tragic role, acts as foil to both Robartes and the tower-dwelling poet, drawing out Robartes' explication, laughing at the poet's ineffectual study:

> I'd stand and mutter there until he caught
> 'Hunchback and Saint and Fool,' and that they came
> Under the three last crescents of the moon,
> And then I'd stagger out. He'd crack his wits
> Day after day, yet never find the meaning. (VPo, 377)

This farcical vein persists in *Stories of Michael Robartes* with which Yeats prefaced the second edition of *A Vision.* Duddon, the narrator, is impotent out of shyness, Denise de l'Isle Adam is a coquette, and she and her two lovers further trivialize their auto-biographical accounts by their ludicrous quarrels. Huddon, Duddon and Denise become students as the result of a travesty of the already travestied heroism of *The Playboy of the Western World;* mistaking Aherne for Huddon, Duddon has knocked him down by hitting him over the head with a stick: "I thought, 'I have knocked down my only patron, and that is a magnificent thing to have done', and I felt like dancing" (VII, 36). O'Leary's entry into the group by virtue of having thrown his boots at — and missed — two ill-spoken actors is no more dignified. Aherne is stereotyped as a devout Catholic who serves Robartes out of an inner compulsion and picks petty arguments over details the while. But however inadequate these characters are for the adventure before them, Mary Bell's and John Bond's dedication to Robartes' cause is founded on a much deeper irony. Mr. Bell's missionary zeal finds an absurd outlet in his decision to help those who lack the familial stability he thinks he rests in; cuckold himself, he is more capable than he knows of teaching cuckoos nestbuilding. Through a second deception by his wife and her lover, he dies convinced of his success. The interplay of appearance and reality through the traditionally comic theme of cuckoldry simultaneously reveals not only the primacy of vision but its false bottom.[63] All in all, these characters and their activities seem but poor instruments with which to realize Robartes' directive to " 'Love war...that belief may be changed, civilisation renewed' " (VII, 52-53).

Set beside the figure of Robartes, however, Yeats's tolerant mockery of his characters and his theme becomes autobiographical gesture. Duddon may not understand Robartes' discourse any more than Aherne anticipates the poet in "The Phases of the Moon" would, but Robartes is presented in total seriousness and, in the context of the initial fictional framework of *A Vision,* the notes to the first edition (1920) of *Michael Robartes and the Dancer,* and those to the first publication of "The Gift of Harun Al-Rashid" (VPo, 460-70), he becomes responsible for both philosophy and poems. Duddon knows no more of where he is really going than did the narrator of "Rosa Alchemica," but Robartes does know much more than did his earlier incarnation and, through the rewriting of *A Vision,* can be increasingly specific about it. He conveys his achievement of Unity directly with his summation of his life: " 'I have completed my life, balanced every pleasure with a danger' " (VII, 41). Yeats conveys it indirectly with the recurrence of the image of the dance. In "Ego Dominus Tuus," Robartes has left his book for one of the journeys which, in the past, have taken him to the Judwalis whose "children are taught dances which leave upon the sand traces full of symbolical meaning" (VII, 41). *Ille* too traces "characters upon the sands" (VPo, 370). In "The Double

Vision of Michael Robartes," Robartes comes to knowledge at the full of the moon by looking into himself. There he sees antithetical man ("A Sphinx with woman breast and lion paw"), primary man (Buddha), and a solitary dancer whose symbolic value in the poem is multivalent. She is self-absorbed, self-expressive antithetical man, whose "Body perfection brought": "O little did they care who danced between,/And little she by whom her dance was seen/So she had outdanced thought." Dancing "between" the two figures and making Robartes realize that he is "caught between the pull/Of the dark moon and the full," she is symbol of the moment of reversal from primary to antithetical civilization. She is the whole process of change, a gyre, "a spinning-top." She is revelation itself: "I, ignorant for so long,/Had been rewarded thus/In Cormac's ruined house" (VPo, 382-84).[64]

"Ignorant for so long": looking back on the 1890s and particularly on his adeptship under Mathers, Yeats concluded that he had "known none mount" into Hodos Chameliontos "and come to good that lacked philosophy" (A, 337). The increased clarity and specificity of Robartes' doctrine and the intensification of irony and self-mockery in the poems and stories contemporary with *A Vision* he owes to the systematization of his thought; the antinomies on which he based the philosophy were central even to his moments of adolescent rebellion. "I have been preoccupied," he wrote in the introduction to *The Resurrection*, "with a certain myth that was itself a reply to a myth" (Ex, 392). The initial myth had been the nineteenth-century belief in progress; Yeats replaced it with one which was, at first, simply antinomial − the natural confronted by the supernatural −, then cyclical. But Yeats's myth was also a form of "personal utterance." He did not mean by it "a fiction, but one of those statements our nature is compelled to make and employ as a truth though there cannot be sufficient evidence" (Ex, 392), a statement of faith with which to explain the self and the world.

"Huddon, Duddon and Daniel O'Leary/Delighted me as a child," Yeats recalls in the poem which prefaces *Stories of Michael Robartes and His Friends:* "I put three persons in their place/That despair and keep the pace/And love wench Wisdom's cruel face" (VII, 32). The assertion claims continuity between his earliest imaginings and *A Vision.* But between the Robartes stories of the 1890s and those written for *A Vision,* Yeats has not only developed a philosophic system to account for the antinomies inherent in his occult belief, he has changed his attitude towards those antinomies. In "Rosa Alchemica," the narrator's fear that Robartes' vision is chiefly anarchic is well-founded. The seer thinks in terms of overthrowing one civilization for its opposite; his advocacy of pantheism, Yeats later suggested, was owing solely to the dominance of Christianity in the current civilization (Ex, 393). Robartes really promises order through power in "Rosa Alchemica."

He tells the narrator that in the spiritual world he can expect to become eternal substance rather than transitory shade; the *Splendor Solis* promises the control of the uninitiated through shaping power over divine forms. But between the Robartes stories of the 1890s and those written for *A Vision,* Yeats has recognized the ideas of order and power as in themselves futile and has actively embraced contraries, literally in the philosophy, and stylistically in the dialogues, in oxymorons like "wench Wisdom's cruel face" and in the development of his irony. The vision now transcends the opposites of the man of action and the man of dreams, of comedy and tragedy: "Hard-living men and men of thought/Burn their bodies up for nought/I mock at all so burning out" (VII, 32). Like the revived Robartes, Yeats too has become convinced that "Life is no series of emanations from divine reason such as the Cabalists imagine, but an irrational bitterness, no orderly descent from level to level, no waterfall but a whirlpool, a gyre" (VII, 40). Neither heroism nor mysticism consist any longer in a Unity based on the discovery of antinomy; instead both hero and mystic become like the dancer, between and beyond antinomies, making of life an art, indifferent to and mocking life and art. The system of *A Vision* is ultimately an ordered philosophy to explain the disorder of life, but the antinomy, Robartes points out, is not that of thought but of "life itself." The "whirling" and "bitterness" (VII, 52) of that life render irrelevant and absurd the very system which explains its chaos and which the poet "is compelled to make and employ as a truth." In Robartes' assessment of the system, Yeats's self-conscious irony is complete; the absolute seriousness and conviction behind *A Vision* is insisted upon while the system itself proves that its creation is a futile gesture. The gesture is all: the poet elaborates an order to account for disorder; recognizing the essential absurdity of the activity, he self-consciously, deliberately, assumes the Mask of a "foolish, passionate man" and so becomes wise.

VIII

The elaboration of a "philosophy" that Yeats achieved in *A Vision* and its fictional framework of *Michael Robartes and His Friends* he had first attempted in a novel. When he went to Coole Park in 1897, he was suffering nervous prostration which he attributed partly to "a novel that I could neither write nor cease to write which had Hodos Chameliontos for its theme" (A, 376). He had begun *The Speckled Bird* in 1896 while he was collecting the stories of *The Secret Rose* for publication and would rewrite it four times before abandoning it in 1902 or 1903.[65] In many respects this novel looks backwards to "Rosa Alchemica."[66] Its chief character, Michael Hearne, pursues occult knowledge and places himself for some time under the direction of one MacLagan[67] who, like Robartes, but in a manner even more rhetorical, prophesies that he and Hearne " 'shall see the streets run with blood, for no great spiritual change comes without political change too' " (SB, 58). Thinly disguised images of the trembling of the veil recur in all the versions with a notable analogue at the moment of revelation when Michael receives his "call": "Suddenly it was as if the grey waters had been torn away, it was as if they had been painted on paper which somebody was tearing, and he saw in their stead a sea of an intense brightness..." (SB, 37). But if some of its characterization and subject matter are reminiscent of earlier work, some of the detail of *The Speckled Bird* startlingly anticipates *A Vision*. In the "Island" Version, for example, Michael is reported as having asked "what happened to the moon when it had passed its last quarter" (SB, 118). In *Autobiographies* Yeats would enlarge the question to make it symbolic of the cultural decline he lamented: "what happens to the individual man whose moon has come to that fourth quarter, and what to the civilization...?" (A, 294). In *A Vision* he sets out to answer the question in terms of the individual personality and of history. The attributes Yeats would there assign to the full of the moon and the dark belong in *The Speckled Bird* to the Hearne household where all are absorbed "in that denial of life and affirmation of ideal beauty which comes to one as art, to another as religion" (SB, 116). At the end of the "Final" Version, rationalizing the place of Margaret in his thoughts, Michael also states sexual antinomy as the prototype for mysticism and art much as Yeats would have Robartes do at the beginning of *A Vision:* "All the arts sprang from sexual love and [therefore] they could only come again [in] the garb of [a] religion when that reconciliation had taken place" (SB, 106).

One could go on noting the parallels in detail between *The Speckled Bird* and Yeats's other occult writings, yet the fact remains that the "novel" was a rather radical departure for Yeats and one that failed him. It is essentially a *bildüngsroman* with Yeats himself so thinly disguised as his hero that a good deal of the criticism of the work has focused on the tracing of parallels between Hearne's life and Yeats's.[68] Even Hearne's visions are frequently the "vivid moments" Yeats records in *Autobiographies*. The Owl of Cwn Cawlwyd, for example, appears to tell Michael that " 'They covet the world' " (SB, 16); George Russell was probably one of the few people who would not have been startled to have a conversation Yeats recorded in "Ireland after Parnell" — " 'God possesses the heavens, but He covets the earth — He covets the earth' " (A, 249) — thus transformed. Michael's waking from a dream to hear a voice speaking through his lips and claiming to have made an image of him called Emmanuel (SB, 30) exactly parallels Yeats's account of the same dream in "The Stirring of the Bones" (A, 379). After abandoning this autobiographical novel, Yeats would not attempt prose fiction again for more than fifteen years. Then, working on

Stories of Michael Robartes and His Friends, A Vision and *The Trembling of the Veil,* he would assess the failure of *The Speckled Bird:* "My chief person was to see all the modern visionary sects pass before his bewildered eyes, as Flaubert's Saint Anthony saw the Christian sects, and I was as helpless to create artistic, as my chief person to create philosophic, order" (A, 376). Comparison of the aborted novel with *Stories of Michael Robartes* reveals that Yeats was helpless to create artistic order *because* he was helpless to create philosophic order. The novel contains some fine parody of occultists, particularly in the "de Burgh" Version, but Yeats can offer no real alternative to their manner of seeking wisdom. He ends the "Final" Version by having Michael, like so many contemplative heroes after him in the twentieth century, leaving for the East. What he will find there remains unnamed, unsuggested. Because he lacks any systematic thought, even if it be thought which, like *A Vision,* serves only to explain the disorder of the world, he also lacks perspective on himself. Yeats directs all his irony in the novel outwards at sects and personages who take themselves too seriously or behave too eccentrically while he treats Michael's adolescent yearning towards divine and sexual wisdom with a reverence and an effusion of lyricism it hardly deserves. Casting himself as hero of the *bildüngsroman,* Yeats failed to make biography and myth each other's doubles for lack of the self-conscious irony which later would distinguish the revived Robartes persona.

IX

Seriously as Yeats took himself as a member of The Order of the Golden Dawn and seriously as much of his writing presents that Order's mythic patterning of this world and the next, he always made the occultist in him serve the poet and the nationalist. In his attempt to smithy a Celtic mythology with which to wed the Irish to their own "rock and hill" (A, 194), he had turned for a time to a scheme to establish an order of Celtic Mysteries but, far more importantly, he also turned to the tradition of the gleeman for a persona who transformed biography into myth in his songs, myth into biography in the legends that grew up about his life. Among his first prose sketches in this tradition is "The Last Gleeman."[69] What interests about the story of Moran is its groping towards mythic suggestion within the limitations of the biographical sketch and its use of irony to mediate between biographical and mythic pattern. We literally get Moran's life from precisely located birth — "off Black Pitts, in the Liberties of Dublin, in Faddle Alley" (CT, 67) — to farcical funeral procession:

A good party of his admirers and friends got into the hearse with the coffin, for the day was wet and nasty. They had not gone far when one of them burst out with 'It's cruel cowld, isn't it?' 'Garra',' replied another, 'we'll all be as stiff as the corpse when we get to the berrin-ground.' 'Bad cess to him,' said a third; 'I wish he'd held

33

out another month until the weather got dacent.' A man called Carroll thereupon produced a half-pint of whiskey, and they all drank to the soul of the departed. Unhappily, however, the hearse was over-weighted, and they had not reached the cemetery before the spring broke, and the bottle with it. (CT, 78-79)

At the same time, epic suggestions which tend to make Moran a mythic type of all bards everywhere abound: shortly after birth he is afflicted with the blindness for which, presumably, the poet's vision is compensation; he once defends himself in court by comparing himself with Homer; he is successful in love and in war, defeating a usurper in a mock battle of words; he is cheered in death and a gratifying number of gleemen turn out to his wake. But Moran is also a self-mocker and his irony — and Yeats's — always anchors the mythic analogies. Going blind early, which precipitated his success as a poet, Yeats tells us, Moran also "became thereby a blessing to his parents" (CT, 67) who sent him out to beg. A similar ironic twist prevents the quasi-heroic bard's quite getting himself solemnly eulogized and buried. His farcical funeral does more than minimize the biographical sketch's tendencies to mythic pattern; it underlines our sense that the poet faces his difficulties with an almost savage joy which is the result of his own genuine passion, his mockery of others and of himself, his sense of his uniqueness, his awareness that gaiety and meaning in this life are self-wrought. His tragic stature grows from his solitariness, ironically conveyed by Yeats in his choice of incident and emphasis. Parodying his own recitations at first, in later life Moran sees himself denied by the crowd in favor of an impersonator. The final lines of the sketch, stressing the drunken mourners, the broken hearse and bottle to omission of any concern for coffin and corpse, powerfully intimate the poet's spiritual solitude and his disdain of the world's values.

The tone of "The Last Gleeman" remains anecdotal; Yeats implies Moran's aloneness by his choice of biographical incident rather than by explicit statement. Writing "The Crucifixion of the Outcast," he did not allow himself to be so constrained by the medieval Irish tale which was his source[70] but allegorically characterized his gleeman to emphasize his solitude. The crucifixion, in its typically Yeatsian inversion of the Christ myth, is clearly intended to name the Poet as the contemporary Saviour and to announce that he will accomplish his ends by overthrowing the current order. Cumhal is no meek Christ. His proficient cursing, " 'in rhyme, and with two assonances in every line of his curse' " (SR, 42), and his ruses for delaying his execution transfigure the passive acceptance of the Christian biography with a fierce energy. His final words, " 'Outcasts, ... have you also turned against the outcast?' ", echo the single moment when Christ feels himself to be solitary in His suffering but they are not followed by any redemptive prayer for forgiveness of his persecutors or by any sense of spiritual identity with them. Instead, Yeats stresses the extremity of the gleeman's isolation and suffering by the grotesque details of beggars throwing stones and of birds pecking at the head and wolves eating the feet of the crucified poet. He also makes it plain that the gleeman owes his suffering and his solitude to his spiritual superiority; " 'I am myself the poorest,' " Cumhal decides,

'and the tattered doublet of particoloured cloth upon my back and the torn pointed shoes upon my feet have ever irked me, because of the towered city full of noble raiment which was in my heart. And I have been the more alone... because I heard in my heart the rustling of the rose-bordered dress of her who is more subtle than Angus, the Subtle-Hearted, and more full of the beauty of laughter than Conan the Bald, and more full of the wisdom of tears than White-Breasted Deirdre, and more lovely than a bursting dawn to them that are lost in the darkness.' (SR, 50-51)

The myth of the Artist as an outcast Yeats undoubtedly owed to his self-confessed adolescent identification with "Manfred on his glacier," "Prince Athanase with his solitary lamp" and Alastor (A, 64).[71] Much of his life during the 1890s — the "extreme development" of "romantic doctrine" which governed his attachment to Maud Gonne (A, 399), the aloofness noted by his contemporaries which seems to have risen out of the feeling that he lacked self-possession (A, 93) and out of an intensity that must often have been without social grace — would have made this view of the artist attractive to him. In "The Crucifixion of the Outcast," the image of the Poet was probably also conditioned by the wit and aloofness of Wilde and Beardsley and the public's persecution of them; in *Autobiographies* Yeats would assess Beardsley's character in terms of victimage (A, 330-31).

Because it is so symbolic and so unexpectedly violent and because it concentrates on the gleeman's death, "The Crucifixion of the Outcast" is strongly evocative of a mythology of the poet; nonetheless its focus on the single culminating act of victimage and the rigid, nearly allegorical, nature of its symbolism prevent the coherence of biography and myth to even the extent of that of "The Last Gleeman." With the Hanrahan stories, Yeats returned to the idea of a biography with mythic implications, much expanded from "The Last Gleeman," to present a mythic type of the poet. While "The Devil's Book"[72] initially may have been written with no idea of the entire series, the chronological order of the periodical publication of the stories (1892-1896) suggests that Yeats soon saw the advantages to his mythologizing aims of creating an entire biography for Hanrahan. As he had for "The Last Gleeman," Yeats had an historical model for his bard, one Owen Roe O'Sullivan (1748-1784).[73] That model clearly lies behind the 1892 publication of "The Devil's Book" which Yeats is concerned in a note to identify as being basically biographical with the additional adornment of a folkloric fairy-mistress. But in the remaining five stories, published in periodicals between 1892 and 1896 and, the protagonist renamed, collected for *The Secret Rose* along with a considerably revised first story, fiction replaced legend and folklore as the narrative's controlling impulse. In the 1905 version of the stories, Yeats replaced this first story with "Red Hanrahan" (published in *The Independent Review* in 1903) so as to give the entire biographical cycle a more pronouncedly fictional shape and to increase its mythic symmetry. With the character of Hanrahan, Yeats made biography and myth each other's double by moving beyond historical confines; he later — accurately — declared that "I myself created Hanrahan" (Vpo, 411).

Yeats begins Hanrahan's biography at the point at which the *bildüngsroman* often ends, the moment when the protagonist is called to his vocation. All the versions of *Stories of Red Hanrahan* open with the protagonist's encounter with the supernatural. In a passage of "The Book of the Great Dhoul and Hanrahan the Red" (the first story of *The Secret Rose* sequence) which almost duplicates one in *Dhoya*, Cleena defines her love as a search for an anti-self: "'I love you,'" she declares herself, "'for you are fierce and passionate, and good and bad, and not dim and wave-like as are the people of the Shee' " (RH, 135). She also presents herself as the anti-self with which Hanrahan seeks union: " 'You have always loved me better than your own soul, and you have sought for me everywhere and in everything, though without knowing what you sought...' " (RH, 133). The encounter, Hanrahan's refusal of the proffered love,[74] the subsequent destruction of his house by the whirlwind of the Sidhe (RH, 134), and his beating and ostracism clearly follow the Romantic iconography typical of Yeats's earlier stories.

In 1919, looking back on the 1890s, Yeats described himself as having "three interests: interest in a form of literature, in a form of philosophy, and a belief in nationality." With "Red Hanrahan," the extensively rewritten story which replaced "The Book of the Great Dhoul and Hanrahan the Red," he began to " 'Hammer [those]... thoughts into unity' " (Ex, 263). Hanrahan confronts the occult powers who represent "a form of philosophy" but, in the rewritten story, the supernatural woman embodies not only a sexual and natural opposite and, therefore, an opportunity to complete himself, but nationalism as well. The imploring Cleena has given way to Echtge, wearing "the tired look of one that had been long waiting" (M, 220). The Hanrahan who had so vehemently rejected Cleena when she showed a mortal's desire, finds himself reduced to silence before the immortal Echtge's attendants who carry the four symbols of the Tuatha de Danaan, which Yeats linked with the Grail legend and with the four elements and their figurations on the Tarot cards.[75] As Cara Ackerman has demonstrated,[76] the substitution for Cleena of Echtge and the four women bearing the sacred treasures of Ireland — The Cauldron of the

Dagda, The Stone of Destiny, The Spear of Lug, and The Sword of Nuada — enlarges Hanrahan's bardic role to demand of him a knowledge of the supernatural and the salvation of Ireland. Rejecting Ireland and the occult, Hanrahan rejects a part of his calling and thereby condemns himself to remain spiritually incomplete and physically homeless and condemns Ireland, personified as the queen of Slieve Echtge, to go on awaiting her Saviour.

Hanrahan's adventures during his wandering record the results of his initial failure to accept his antithetical self and to serve Ireland. In "The Twisting of the Rope," he is denied the comfort of Oona in an ironically just counterpoint to his earlier failure to accept an immortal woman or to question her symbols. The first version of the story emphasizes alienation from mortal and immortal alike as his punishment; the spirits along the strand mock him by singing " 'Cast him out, cast him out, cast him out' " (RH, 145). Comfortably settled with Mary Gillis in the next story, he is yet troubled by " 'Ireland and the weight of grief that is on her' " and sings, as perhaps an eighteenth-century William O'Hanrahan did,[77] a song of mourning and of hope for "Cathleen, the daughter of Houlihan," a song in which the elements correspond to the four treasures and personify Yeats's Ireland. "Old brown thorn-trees," "black wind" and "noisy clouds," and "wet winds," "clinging air," and an "overflowed" "yellow pool" — earth, air and water — await the liberation of the fiery element of Cathleen whose eyes are "flame" and who stands "purer than a tall candle before the Holy Rood" (M, 237).[78] Hanrahan and his listeners are moved to tears by this song but he does not fare so well by his less patriotic compositions. Having called down a curse on his old age, on the three lesser elements (symbolized by the yew, the eagle, and the pike) and on his old neighbours, he suffers a fiery retribution wreaked by a crowd of those he has cursed. If he has been spared crucifixion, the outcast and chastened Hanrahan, calling this time on the protection of the four elements, has nonetheless again been sent wandering until he should gain the courage and wisdom he lacked when initially called.

He proves himself more worthy in "Hanrahan's Vision." Confronted again with the supernatural, this time he heeds the voice which bids him speak. The speaker identifies herself as Dervorgilla, doomed to be seen forever by her lover Diarmuid as a rotting corpse, symbolic Anglo-Norman rot at the heart of Ireland's culture. Hanrahan is not permitted to follow these spirits through the door into the mountain a second time but, by rejecting the traitorous lovers out of the nationalist senti-ment which should have made him question the treasure-bearing women of the first story,[79] he does move towards apotheosis.

That comes with his return to the villages and the lakes and woods about Slieve Echtge where he leads so contemplative a life he hears "a sound like the clashing of many swords" (M, 254) that, since his early

37

youth, Yeats had associated with the music of Heaven. Moving towards the supernatural, he encounters once again the four grey women. They play with the magic deck which had lured him out of doors in "Red Hanrahan" and begin a raucous quarrel which indirectly is over the fate of his soul after death. Hanrahan himself determines that fate. Recognizing the Cauldron, Stone, Spear and Sword, he asks the necessary questions: " 'What are they? Who do they belong to?' " Not only does he ask, but he acknowledges the error of his earlier silence: " 'And I have asked the question this time' " (M, 260).[80] In the resulting epiphany, Winny Byrne is revealed as young and supernatural, Hanrahan in death crosses the boundary between the worlds and the wedding wisps which suggest a mystic marriage include some "like a tall white candle for the dead" (M, 260), recalling Cathleen, the daughter of Houlihan, "purer than a tall candle before the Holy Rood."[81]

But it is the differences, as much as the parallels, between the encounters with the supernatural in "Red Hanrahan" and in "The Death of Hanrahan" which suggest the nature of the knowledge Hanrahan achieves. In the first story events are improbable by the standards of this world and are external to Hanrahan. He is led by magic to Slieve Echtge and he feels his dread of speaking because the queen and her four attendants are so clearly of another and grander world. In "The Death of Hanrahan," however, Hanrahan's vision and apotheosis are a function of his own perception and so are self-generated. The four grey women do not bear the treasures now. Instead, Hanrahan sees the treasures in the most quotidian of objects: Winny's cooking pot, hearthstone and knife and his own blackthorn stick. They, or their like, have been with him throughout his quest, their visible presence entirely a function of his visionary capability. Similarly, the immortal white-armed woman he has been seeking is no longer a throned vision apart from him, but is the previously invisible side of what is near at hand, the witless Winny with "her withered arms that were grey like crumbled earth" (M, 260). Hanrahan owes his apotheosis to his own transformative vision; when he begins "to see things double," to recognize that antitheses, the natural and the supernatural, are necessarily inherent in the same object, he discovers his self.

With the Hanrahan cycle, Yeats has accomplished what he had not been able to in his earlier fiction: he has been much more specific about the nature of Hanrahan's knowledge than he had been about that of the first Robartes persona or of Michael Hearne; he has unified his literary, occult and nationalist interests within a single bardic persona. For the first time in his fiction he has successfully used a "biography" not only to outline the particular, but to universalize it, to suggest through the pattern of one life the relationship of natural and supernatural and of both to the individual and to create a satisfactory type of the poet. He enlarges Hanrahan beyond biographical particularity in the direction of universal and mythic patterns and simultaneously reveals those patterns working themselves out in biographical detail. But the Hanrahan cycle is successful as more than the doubling of myth and biography. It is also audacious autobiographical gesture, not just because specific parallels can be traced between Hanrahan and Yeats[82] during the years he wrote and rewrote the stories, but because Hanrahan projects into the world the persona that was Yeats's ideal for himself and anticipates his final achievement of that ideal by many years.

X

The autobiographical significance of the Hanrahan stories rests, however, with the gesture itself. The years following the publication of *The Secret Rose* were particularly trying ones for Yeats; accounts of the period reveal him as far from achieving an integrated persona in either his personal or his professional life. As President of the '98 Centennial Association of Great Britain and France, he found himself marshalling factions far more often than advancing nationalism. Deciding (in retrospect, at least) that Irish politics were for him but the "temptation" of "creation without toil" (A, 202), less and less able to condone Maud Gonne's extremism, he withdrew from nationalist activities except where they touched on literary issues. Perhaps he already feared that, whatever turn political events took, Ireland would never create a Unity of Culture that completely emancipated her from England; Dervorgilla's description of hers and Diarmuid's purgatory and Hanrahan's refusal to pardon her by further speech suggest a pessimism at the heart of Yeats's nationalism. Active in the 1901 quarrels of The Order of the Golden Dawn, he lost a friend and mentor in MacGregor Mathers when he helped wrest Mathers' leadership from him.[83] At about the same time that he abandoned *The Speckled Bird,* he also abandoned his plans for The Celtic Mysteries, the rites of which he had worked on with Mathers.[84] In 1903, Maud Gonne married, proving the futility of the romantically ideal love Yeats had nurtured for fourteen years and on which he had allowed an affair with Olivia Shakespear to founder (Mem, 89). But however trying the turn of the century had been for Yeats, it had also brought tremendous excitement. He had seen his dream of a national theatre realized; the Irish Dramatic Society began to play with Irish actors. He was discovering that, in writing for the theatre, he could no longer use wavering rhythms to drop a veil between the delights of the faery-world and the hurly-burly of this; increasingly he learned to give his ideals and visions the concrete embodiment the stage demands. In that year, too, Yeats first read Nietzsche, "that strong enchanter" (L, 379), finding there a confirmation of the personal mythology he had been shaping from the Romantic poets, theosophy and the rituals of The Golden Dawn. He began to seek a new style that might embody these changes in his life and thought; his writing of this period is imbued with emotional astringency and sexual frankness, the first omens of the "tragic gaiety" of the late poems.

Yeats himself formulated the change in his writing from essays like "The Autumn of the Body" (1898) in Nietzschean terms: "The close of the last century was full of a strange desire to get out of form, to get to some kind of disembodied beauty, and now it seems to me the contrary impulse has come. I feel about me and in me an impulse to create form, to carry the realization of beauty as far as possible. The Greeks said that the Dionysiac enthusiasm preceded the Apollonic and that the Dionysiac was sad and desirous, but that the Apollonic was joyful and self sufficient" (L, 402).[85] Writing again to Russell in 1904, he condemns the "exaggeration of sentiment and sentimental beauty" in his early poetry and invokes "a mysterious command.... Let us have no emotions, however abstract, in which there is not an athletic joy" (L, 434-35).

Like much of Yeats's prose, these statements are emphatic about poetic ideals and evasive about the means to them. Writing to his father in 1913, however, he is more precise about the way to "athletic joy": "Of recent years instead of 'vision', meaning by vision the intense realization of a state of ecstatic emotion symbolized in a definite imagined region, I have tried for more self portraiture. I have tried to make my work convincing with a speech so natural and dramatic that the hearer would feel the presence of a man thinking and feeling" (L, 583). This definition of self-portraiture strongly resembles that of "personal utterance" which Yeats claimed to have arrived at as early as 1886 while reading the poem of the returned emigrant and which he recorded in a lecture, "Friends of My Youth,"[86] delivered March 9, 1910. Writing to his father while he was preparing the lecture series of which "Friends of My Youth" was a part, he described the series "as a plea for uniting literature once more to personality" (L, 548).[87] He moved in the direction of making the lectures themselves a stylistic paradigm of such unity by relying on personal experience to make his points; in the first draft of "Friends of My Youth," he confides, "I am going to be very personal in what I say, writing of other things by writing about my own mind" (FMY, 63).[88] "Personal utterance" demands a dramatic mode of speech but this statement makes self-dramatization the source, as well as the manner, of the utterance. In the letter written to his father three and one half years later in which Yeats defines " 'vision' " as "self portraiture," he is still more explicit about this: "It is in dramatic expression that English poetry is most lacking as compared with French poetry," the letter continues. "Villon always and Ronsard at times create a marvellous drama out of their own lives" (L, 583). This use of personal confidentiality in a lecture to explain convictions about poetry and the assessment of Villon's and Ronsard's poetry as drama wrought out of their own lives suggest that there is an equivalence between self and not-self, between art and life, and that art is a deliberately shaped and publicly projected version of one's autobiography. Latent in this is Yeats's doctrine of the Mask.

The idea of the Mask Yeats would have had from his earliest intellectual contacts. The "divided self" was by no means a new motif in European literature although, as Ellmann points out,[89] it became an extremely popular one towards the end of the nineteenth century, one which Yeats already had used very deliberately in *John Sherman.* We know that the poet confronted the idea of a consciously assumed Mask in a direct and elegant form on Christmas Day of, probably, 1889,[90] when he dined with Oscar Wilde. After dinner, Wilde read aloud what Yeats later termed " 'the most brilliant of his essays' " (IR, I, 93), "The Decay of Lying": "In point of fact what is interesting about people in good society...is the mask that each one of them wears, not the reality that lies behind the mask."[91] But in spite of Yeats's attempts, recorded in *Autobiographies,* to live imitatively, he was no quicker to find a theory by which to unite his life and his art than he was to find a narrative method of doing so. Only in 1902, when he read Nietzsche with his suggestions about the mask worn by the super-man and about a cyclical theory of history, did Yeats begin to use the word *mask* to unite life and art and to articulate the belief that the poet's as well as the mystic's knowledge was born of contraries. His marginal annotations of Thomas Common's *Nietzsche as Critic, Philosopher, Poet and Prophet* oppose the poet (Homer) to the philosopher-martyr (Socrates or Christ) and define him as one in whom there is an "affirmation of self — the soul turned from spirit to be its mask and instrument when it seeks life."[92] Add the "Lunar metaphor" (A, 331), and Yeats will have the basic doctrine of *A Vision.* In Nietzsche too, he would have found the union of individual artist and art expressed in terms of transcendency which he would have been familiar with from Madame Blavatsky's borrowings from the Indian tradition and which he would later elaborate in his own philosophy. The Dionysian man, Nietzsche writes in *The Birth of Tragedy,* "feels as if the veil of Mâyâ had been torn aside and were now merely fluttering in tatters before the mysterious Primordial Unity.... He is no longer an artist, he has become a work of art."[93]

While the aphorisms of the aesthetes and Nietzsche's superman both contributed to Yeats's doctrine of the Mask, his involvement with the occult tradition was certainly the most formative influence. His pre-occupation with the esoteric dated from at least 1884 when, in his last year at the High School in Dublin, another senior boy loaned him

41

A. P. Sinnett's *Esoteric Buddhism*.[94] "The mystical life," he would write to a sceptical John O'Leary in 1892, "is the centre of all that I do and all that I think and all that I write" (L, 211). By 1901, he was formulating the importance of "magic" in his life in terms of correspondences between imagined and lived experience; in a letter pleading for the resolution of one of the many crises of The Order of the Golden Dawn, he suggests that "whatever we build in the imagination will accomplish itself in the circumstance of our lives."[95] We can see in that special plea the seed, still dormant, of two of Yeats's deepest convictions: that the writer finds his true self by living a Mask, letting his thoughts and deeds be transfigured by a single lived myth, and that the poet must seek "equivalent expression" between his life and his art.

But only after 1907, and very slowly and laboriously, was Yeats able, by means of the concept of the Mask, to begin creating a *formal* system of " 'metaphors for poetry' " (VII, 8) out of the occult tradition. In the notes to *The Player Queen,* he recalled the play's genesis: "I began in, I think, 1907, a verse tragedy, but at that time the thought I have set forth in *Per Amica Silentia Lunae* was coming into my head, and I found examples of it everywhere. I wasted the best working months of several years in an attempt to write a poetical play where every character became an example of the finding or not finding of what I have called the Antithetical Self" (VP1, 761). In *Per Amica Silentia Lunae* itself, Yeats had already traced its philosophy to the writing of this play: "I began to believe...that the Middle Ages and the Renaissance were right to found...[their doctrine] upon the imitation of Christ or of some classic hero. Saint Francis and Caesar Borgia made themselves overmastering, creative persons by turning from the mirror to meditation upon a mask. When I had this thought I could see nothing else in life.... I was always thinking of the element of imitation in style and in life..." (M, 333-34). The first scenario for *The Player Queen,* which Curtis Bradford believes preceded any drafts[96] and which probably dates, therefore, from 1907, studies, according to Bradford's summary, "the effect of role-playing on character, the effect of the mask on the face beneath it."[97] Several of the early scenarios and drafts do show the Player Queen assuming the mask of the real queen and playing her role, even through a death scene, with more conviction than the real queen can muster because, through her queenly mask, the actress finds her true self. The third draft of the play, which was probably written before Spring, 1908,[98] has the Player Queen singing an early version of "The Mask."[99] In another draft which Yeats seems to have worked at over a considerable period and up to some time in 1910,[100] a version of the song appears which, if it is less effective as poetry than that he published in *The Green Helmet and Other Poems* (1910), is more explicit in its philosophy:

42

He.	"I would know what you are in yourself"
	My beloved said to me.
	"Put off that mask of burning gold
	With emerald [eyes]
	That I may know what you are."
[She.]	"I will not put away my mask.
	It is the mask of burning gold
	With emerald eyes that makes
	Your heart beat so quickly
	I would now [?] be praised by your beating heart."[101]

An intermediate version of the poem appears in a *Journal* entry of sometime after August 8, 1910 (Mem, 258-59). The same journal, in an August 2, 1910 entry, remarks that "I see always this one thing, that in practical life the mask is more than the face" (Mem, 254). During that same summer, Yeats worked on an essay published in *The Mask* in which he begins using the term in a systematic way, applying it to painting: "if we are painters, we shall express personal emotion through ideal form, a symbolism handled by the generations, a mask from whose eyes the disembodied looks..." (UP, II, 388). Although Yeats abandoned *The Player Queen* at about this time and did not resume work on it until 1915 when he turned it into prose farce, these early scenarios and drafts do show him developing and articulating the terms of his philosophy as he had been unable to do previously and anchoring it in the concrete demands of the stage. He did abandon the attempt to make *The Player Queen* poetic tragedy but meanwhile, in the fall of 1910, he worked closely with Edward Gordon Craig to design "a mask in the old Italian way" (L, 555) for the angel in a new production of *The Hour Glass.* "If the masks work right," Yeats enthusiastically projected, "I would put the fool and the blind man in *Baile's Strand* into masks" (L, 554).[102] Bearing with it significations from aestheticism, Nietzsche's aristocracy of the intellect, and the occult tradition, Yeats's symbol of the mask was becoming more and more concrete, ready for the extreme stylization to which Ezra Pound introduced him in the Noh drama.

XI

While these early drafts of *The Player Queen* do begin to articulate a daimonic philosophy and are preoccupied with the individual's discovery of his self by means of union with his opposite or mask, the fact remains that Yeats felt them to be literary failures. Perhaps searching for a form, perhaps only responding to the shape his experience assumed, he dramatized self and anti-self in another genre in an unpublished dialogue with "Leo Africanus." "Leo" was a spirit who, Yeats believed, spoke to him through the voice of a medium at a seance held in 1912 and who continued to make himself heard occasionally over the next several years.[103] Yeats wrote, in largely automatic script, [104] an exchange of letters between himself and "Leo" in which the spirit defined his role in the poet's life: "I am your opposite, your antithesis because I am all things furthest from your intellect & your will."[105] The letters are explicit too about "Leo's" function in Yeats's work; he does not bring revelation but instead articulates what the poet has known but been unable to formulate. Yeats assesses "Leo's" contribution to his thought in a final letter: "I am not convinced that in this letter [from Leo] there is one sentence that has come from beyond my own imagination.... I think there is no thought [in it] that has not occurred to me in some form or other for many years past; if you have influenced me, it has been but to arrange my thought."[106] The last phrase of this passage both anticipates his description of the revised *A Vision* as "stylistic arrangements of experience" and further clarifies the paradox central to "Leo's" appearance and to all of Yeats's mature thought: by providing the poet with a daimon or antithetical self, "Leo" has enabled Yeats to begin to understand his true self.

Yeats summarized his epistolary exchange with "Leo" as the arrangement of his thought a year after the appearance of "Swedenborg, Mediums, and the Desolate Places" (1914),[107] the first of his published essays to attempt to syncretize in a philosophy the tradition of the occult, literature, and Irish folklore. His narrative relation to his material in this essay is that of the "Leo Africanus" letters. "I shall write as if what I describe were everywhere established, everywhere accepted, and I had only to remind my reader of what he already knows" (Ex, 50), Yeats announces, thus placing the reader in the same relationship to the material as is Yeats himself. The effect is to create for the reader an hypothetical "double" in the life of the spirits for his own life, much as "Leo" did for Yeats. This not only obscures the boundary between the material and spiritual worlds, perhaps even draws aside the veil of matter, but leads to the assertion that it is in the imagination that one's biography finds its realization: "Sometimes our own minds shape that mysterious substance, which may be life itself, according to desire or constrained by memory, and the dead no longer remembering their own names become the characters in the drama we ourselves have invented" (Ex, 55). Many of the examples of belief in spirits that Yeats cites provide anecdotal "evidence" for this assertion: a stable boy is dismissed by his mistress for having told her dead husband to haunt a less populated place and a Japanese fable tells of a spirit whose purgatorial suffering goes on only because she believes in it. The assumption behind this rhetorical strategy is that of Yeats's 1901 adjuration to the members of The Order of the Golden Dawn: "whatever we build in the imagination will accomplish itself in the circumstance of our lives."

XII

While autobiographers are generally acknowledged seldom to tell the truth as another might perceive it,[108] Yeats's convictions that the dead might lose their identity and become figures in the imagined dramas of the living and that an imaginative reality can alter and determine material reality hold the possibility of radically transforming autobiographical statement. It was a possibility Yeats himself was slow to exploit. During a 1910 fund-raising campaign for the Abbey Theatre, he had delivered three lectures in London, the second of which, "Friends of My Youth," relied a good deal on personal reminiscence to distinguish between character and personality in a writer and to demonstrate that the poets of the 1890s aimed "To bring back the arts of personality," to write with an "emotional quality" which was the product of the cultivation of style and of "the deliberate creation of a great mask" (YP, 38-39). But in spite of its reminiscence, Yeats's account of his friends does not have a great deal of force as auto-biographical gesture; reminiscence is evoked only to prove a theoretical-historical point and the narrative lacks the schematic clarity and metaphoric intensity with which Yeats incorporated his fellow poets into his philosophic pattern in "The Tragic Generation." His motivations in giving the lectures may have had something to do with the haphazard nature of their reminiscence. They were essentially journalism and he had little use for his own or others' journalism. Joseph Ronsley suggests that these lectures "are notes, or even a first rough draft, for much of 'Four Years' and 'The Tragic Generation' " (FMY, 61). But Yeats himself seems to have used them, if he used them at all, as a source of facts rather than for their patterning of experience when he wrote *The Trembling of the Veil*, implying that, for him, they did not embody the public image he wished to cultivate of himself as completed by a daimonic opposite, or of his friends succeeding or failing as they found their daimons. The lectures seem to have been, for Yeats, in no way an autobiographical correlative of the preoccupation with the Mask which had run through the early drafts of *The Player Queen;* their autobiographical data remain merely illustrative material, aspiring neither to gesture nor genre.

Perhaps Yeats began thinking more seriously about the genre after Moore's publication of *Hail and Farewell,* which he characterized as "curiously honest, very inaccurate" (L, 564). Whatever the impulse, within a year of reading Moore and in notably conventional terms, he recommended autobiography to his father (1912). Two years later, he adopted the recommendation for himself with *Reveries over Childhood and Youth,* beginning a long period during which he wrote, along with his poetry, both autobiography and essays "discovering a philosophy" (Ex, 31). Published in 1915, his first autobiography had been written at the same time as "Swedenborg, Mediums, and the Desolate Places."

45

For the next twenty years, Yeats would spend much of his time writing autobiography and philosophic essays and would use each to inform the other (see Appendix). Personality in autobiography would become a microcosmic image of an universal and historical system; the philosophical system would find its explication in Yeats's own personality and experience. In *Per Amica Silentia Lunae*, Yeats acknowledges the autobiographical origin of his philosophic system: "I begin to study the only self that I can know, myself, and to wind the thread upon the pern again" (M, 364). He expands the concept of the Mask by repeatedly renaming it, by speaking of the "other self, the anti-self or the antithetical self, as one may choose to name it" (M, 331), or of "the Daimon" who "comes not as like to like but seeking its own opposite, for man and Daimon feed the hunger in one another's hearts" (M, 335). He finds cosmic equivalents of individual self and Mask in "Anima Hominum" and "Anima Mundi."

Later, in *A Vision*, Yeats would elaborate this opposition of self and anti-self and link the two in what he termed "Unity of Being," the harmony or balance transcending both. During the eight years it took him to write this second philosophic book, he began providing definitions of the Mask and alluding in other works to a harmony between it and the self. In *If I Were Four-and-Twenty*, an essay written in 1919, Yeats asserted the concept of "Unity of Being"[109] as the principle informing his life. Where in 1890 he had declared stridently that "There is no great literature without nationality, no great nationality without literature" (NI, 103-04), now he characterized his literature, philosophy and nationalism as the "discrete expression of a single conviction" (Ex, 263). In the continuation of his autobiography (1921, 1922), he re-expressed his "conviction" in terms of his developing philosophical system, of "Unity of Being" and the doctrine of the Mask:

I thought that in man and race alike there is something called 'Unity of Being', using that term as Dante used it when he compared beauty in the *Convito* to a perfectly proportioned human body.[110] My father, from whom I had learned the term, preferred a comparison to a musical instrument so strung that if we touch a string all the strings murmur faintly.... I thought that the enemy of this unity was abstraction, meaning by abstraction not the distinction but the isolation of occupation, or class or faculty.... (A, 190)

Of the Mask itself: it "delineates a being in all things the opposite to... [one's] natural state" (A, 247). At the same time, Yeats found doubles of personality in history and in culture. At the end of the essay *If I Were Four-and-Twenty*, in ironic self-effacement, he insisted on a national equivalent of Unity of Being, on what *Autobiographies* terms Unity of Culture: "... and if I were not four-and-fifty, with no settled habit but the writing of verse, rheumatic, indolent, discouraged, and about to move to the Far East, I would begin another epoch by

46

recommending to the Nation a new doctrine, that of unity of being" (Ex, 280).

These tensions and their suggested systematization and unity are but a more sophisticated formulation of those which had shaped Yeats's prose fiction; they have their prototype in the occult and, particularly, in the Rosicrucian tradition. In his criticism too, Yeats gathered his metaphors into the Rosicrucian symbol of unity. Thus, the 1907 essay, "Poetry and Tradition" (printed in 1908 as "Poetry and Patriotism")[111]: "the nobleness of the arts is in the mingling of contraries, the extremity of sorrow, the extremity of joy, perfection of personality, the perfection of its surrender, overflowing turbulent energy, and marmorean stillness; and its red rose opens at the meeting of the two beams of the cross, and at the trysting-place of mortal and immortal, time and eternity" (EI, 255). Yeats's delight in the symbol was in its "double meaning" (A, 254) which expressed itself in several contexts. To the rose of medieval Romances — the rose of sexual love and Rose of the Virgin —, he must have added Jenning's fusion of pagan and Christian myth (the Rosicrucians' "ideas concerning this emblematical red cross and red rose probably came from the fable of Adonis — who was the sun whom we have seen so often crucified — being changed into a red rose by Venus"[112]) and Waite's description of the rose as "symbol of sex spiritualised, for the name is applied to Shekinah," who rules over both sides of the cabbalistic Tree of Life, "in her desire after union with the King."[113] The visual representation of the Hermetic Rose Cross contains multiple symbols of the relationship of antithesis and unity. Each arm of the cross bears a pentagram whose five points are triangles. The two triangles on the left and on the right represent the four elements; the upper central triangle is topped with a wheel symbolizing their quintessence. These pentagrams are emblematic of the microcosm and are balanced by a hexagram, symbol of the macrocosm, placed on the lower limb of the cross. Uniting the four arms is the rose, its petals arranged to represent the twelve signs of the Zodiac, the seven planets pertinent to astrology and air, fire and water. This rosy cross configuration also signifies the macrocosm. At the center of the rose, the image is repeated — the beams of a smaller cross are united by a smaller rose — and this second rosy cross within the rose reiterates the idea of the microcosm.

The union of physical-mental, sexual-spiritual, microcosmic-macrocosmic antitheses which Yeats later outlined in *A Vision* is certainly contained in the Hermetic Rosy Cross. What made the image inadequate for Yeats after its final suggestion in the rose design for the cover of *Per Amica Silentia Lunae*, was, I suspect, its static quality. He sought a symbol which would establish an "equivalent expression" not only between macrocosm and microcosm but between historical moments, which would be dynamic and cyclic, in keeping with Madame

Blavatsky's theory of Nature. As a consequence, in *A Vision,* he translated his "mingling of contraries" into diagrams of opposing gyres. They originally represented Empedoclean Discord and Concord and turn, the tip of each touching the base of the other, in opposite directions, one expanding as the other contracts. Defining by analogy, Yeats identifies the first gyre as antithetical, realized by "conflict with its opposite" and separating man from man, the second as primary, treating of externals, uniting man with man (VII, 71-72). These gyres, with their opposed patterns of growth and diminishment, determine the nature of civilizations; when, for example, the antithetical cone waxes, it produces a corresponding antithetical culture. The gyres reveal the unity inherent in their opposed actions when the symbol is translated into a natural image: "The resolved antinomy appears...in the whirlpool's motionless centre, or beyond its edge" (VII, 195).[114] The image is apt in its energy and may have had one of its sources in Blake's symbol of the vortex for the manner in which man passed from the physical to the spiritual world.[115] To move closer to Yeats's contemporaries, it approximates the Lewis-Pound image of the Vortex, "patterned energy," "a circulation with a still center"[116]; Pound had first used the simile of two "great hollow cones...charged with a force like electricity" in an essay, published in 1912 in *The New Age,* on the "masterly use of words." I cannot prove that Yeats read Pound's essay when it appeared (although he had been closely associated with Orage, editor of *The New Age,* had answered the weekly's 1910 questionnaire on "The Art of the Theatre" [UP, II, 382-84], and had planned to give a lecture to the Leeds Art Club which revived the journal), but it seems very probable that Pound himself would have drawn the essay to Yeats's attention at some time during their close association. All the more so when one compares the action of Pound's metaphoric cones with Yeats's gyres: "the only way any two cones can be got to act without waste is for them to be so placed that their apexes and a line of surface meet exactly."[117]

Like all of Yeats's symbols, this of the gyres is highly synthetic. Whether or not he adopted his idea for his special arrangement of the interpenetrating cones from Pound, Yeats was familiar with the basic configuration from the cabbalistic hexagram, a macrocosmic unity formed by two intersecting triangles. The triangles represent a variety of opposites — fire and water, Father and Son, fire and air, earth and water, matter and spirit, sun and moon —, depending on whether one appeals to the Cabbala, Boehme, Blake or Yeats himself.[118] The impulse to set these triangles spinning Yeats also owed to theosophy and the doctrines of the Golden Dawn. Madame Blavatsky termed Fohat, "the dynamic energy of Cosmic Ideation,"[119] a " 'Fiery Whirl-wind' " which, she explained, "is the incandescent cosmic dust which only follows magnetically, as the iron filings follow the magnet, the directing thought of the 'Creative Forces.' "[120] The Golden Dawn's use of the hour-glass figure [121] as symbol of the transmission of forces from Malkuth (earth, physical body) to Kether (heaven, spirit) makes Blavatsky's dynamism more concrete. In one of the documents Mathers claimed to have received from the Order's "Hidden and Secret Chiefs," the transmission of forces is described: "in this case (seeing that Malkuth and Kether be in different planes and worlds) the lines of transmission of these forces are caught up and whirled about by the upper cone of the hour-glass symbol into the *vortex,* where and through passeth the thread of the unformulate – (i.e., Ain Soph [Infinity]. Etheric link). Hence they are projected in a whirling convolution (yet according to their nature) through the lower cone of the hour-glass symbol into Kether" (my italics).[122] Eager as always to find visual analogues which he could assimilate to his new symbol, Yeats would express these cones in terms of Dante's purgatorial mountain (and fuse them with its cabbalistic alternate, the *mons philosophorum),* his own tower and winding stair,[123] and a childhood memory of a pern-mill (VPo, 820).

Yeats's syncretic attitude towards his symbols carried him well beyond either specific literary associations or the force lines of Golden Dawn geomancy. Doubtlessly recalling Waite's analogy between the alchemical Venusian cross, the equal arms of which represented the four elements, and "the four parts of human personality – or body, mind, desire and will in purpose –,"[124] Yeats erected a personality theory on the revolutions of his gyres. Within them move what he termed "the *Four Faculties: Will* and *Mask, Creative Mind* and *Body of Fate"* (VII, 73; cf. VI, 138). The balance between these Faculties determines personality. In antithetical man, Will, the pragmatic aspect of personality, achieves self-knowledge only by imposing the Mask, its daimon or opposite, its desire or ideal, on the Body of Fate ("the series of events forced upon" the personality "from without") by means of transfiguring thought or the Creative Mind (VII, 83). The paradigm is one of dramatic conflict between opposites and Yeats found an allegory for his antithetical man or poet in the improvisation of *Commedia dell' Arte:* "The stage-manager, or *Daimon,* offers his actor an inherited scenario, the *Body of Fate,* and a *Mask* or rôle as unlike as possible to his natural ego or *Will,* and leaves him to improvise through his *Creative Mind* the dialogue and details of the plot. He must discover or reveal a being which only exists with extreme effort, when his muscles are as it were all taut and all his energies active" (VII, 84; cf. VI, 17-18).

Diagramming the pattern by which one or the other of these Faculties dominates in the interpenetration of the gyres, Yeats comes up with four cardinal points which he transfers to a circle. That circle he equates with the lunar cycle. In an elaborate development of an essentially astrological system, the different combinations of the Faculties determine the personality of each individual by identifying him with a certain lunar phase. The First Phase, the dark of the moon, represents totally primary man. Unity is possible only with that external to oneself, with God. Its persona cannot be found in this world but the saint most closely approximates it. The Fifteenth Phase, the full moon, represents totally antithetical man. Unity is with the self found through the Mask and, as it is in the Cabbala, can be considered analogous to the sexual act: "All these symbols can be thought of as the symbols of the relations of men and women and of the birth of children" (VII, 211).[125] Like the analogy with the theatre, the sexual symbol posits the "true self" as a quintessence born out of the union of opposites.

The artist or, mythologically, "Narcissus and his Pool" (A, 294) most closely approximates the unity born out of antithetical man's contemplation of his anti-self, his reversed image. Autobiography, gazing at oneself in literature, suggests itself as a genre natural to the antithetical phases but that autobiography will not aim at the revelation of what we often call character. Yeats described the individual whose phase is near that of the full moon as attaining to "personality, the breath of men's mouths" (S, No. 2 [1902], 9). That "personality" represents the achievement of Unity of Being through the assumption of the Mask and lets the artist express the *anima mundi*, the unconscious as well as the conscious life, the "general" as well as the particular mind (M, 343). "Character" he saw as belonging to the man who has not achieved Unity, to the fragmented consciousness. Hence Yeats can write that "my character is so little myself that all my life it has thwarted me. It has affected my poems, my true self, no more than the character of a dancer affects the movement of the dance" (Ex, 308). Literature, therefore, is opposed to character. The product of the "true self" discovered through the Mask, it belongs to personality, expresses that *anima mundi* the symbol of which is a garden or pool (M, 352)[126] or the dancer's relationship to the dance. Like Narcissus' pool, Yeatsian autobiography aims to reflect personality — a whole of mythic proportions establishing analogies between the individual life and the *anima mundi* — and not character — a fragment. Like Salomé dancing, the autobiographer must transform myth into biography, find myth in biography.

By visual analogy, Yeats goes on to equate his lunar circle with the Wheel of Being. This wheel functions as symbol of all cycles, individual, historical, and cosmic. Individuals as well as civilizations pass through all the phases and "Every phase is in itself a wheel; the individual soul is awakened by a violent oscillation (one thinks of Verlaine oscillating between the church and the brothel) until it sinks in on that Whole where the contraries are united, the antinomies resolved" (VII, 89;

cf. VI, 139: "Every gyre of every cone is...equal to an entire cone revolving through twenty-eight phases or their equivalent"). One thinks too of Yeats's own oscillation between antithetical and primary tinctures: "I am always, in all I do, driven to a moment which is the realisation of myself as unique and free, or to a moment which is the surrender to God of all that I am" (Ex, 305). In *Autobiographies,* antithetical man repeatedly gives way to primary man and then recovers himself again; the "Lunar parable" becomes a means of establishing correspondences between biography and myth or philosophy.

The process, like the movement of the gyres, is two-way, necessarily reversing itself. *Autobiographies* seeks to present as accomplished in the circumstances of the poet's life what he has built in his imagination, but so too has *A Vision* obviously been affected by the drama of "personal utterance" for, in it, a good deal of autobiographical material becomes evidence for theories of personality and history.

Yeats's biographers agree that he characterized himself as a man of Phase Seventeen, one to whom "Unity of Being...is now more easy than at any other phase" (VI, 75; VII, 141).[127] One can easily read back from the characteristics Yeats attributes to this phase to his own life and so see how the poet's conception of himself has in part shaped the attributes he assigns to the phases and has led him to make Phase Seventeen, where he places himself, along with Dante, Shelley and Landor, the creative apex of that system. In Phase Seventeen the ego or Will drives the individual to seek an antithetical self. His Mask is "Simplification through intensity," a simplification towards which Yeats's desire for "personal utterance" and self-imposed separateness led him. Creative Mind is "Creative imagination through *antithetical* emotion," the impulse to the Mask underlying Yeats's entire philosophical and autobiographical *oeuvre.* His Body of Fate is "Loss" (VII, 140-41; see also VI, 75-77), an allusion to Shelley's loss of wife and children, Dante's loss of Beatrice, Yeats's own loss of Maud Gonne. The man of Phase Seventeen characteristically uses autobiographical material to transmute the abstract as Yeats had been doing from *John Sherman* on. He finds his example "of the first victory of personality" in just such a use: "Dante in the *Convito* mourns for solitude, lost through poverty,[128] and writes the first sentence of modern autobiography, and in the *Divina Commedia* imposes his own personality upon a system and a phantasmagoria hitherto impersonal..." (VII, 289; VI, 199). His life becomes a metaphor for Yeats's own.

A good deal of the apparatus of *A Vision* involves a similar interchange between theory and autobiography and, occasionally, their fusion. In Yeats's introduction to the second edition, for example, the "communicators" who have explained the system to him, first through his wife's automatic writing, then through her speech while sleeping, no longer have an axiomatic existence apart from the Yeats couple:

"Much that has happened, much that has been said, suggests that the communicators are the personalities of a dream shared by my wife, by myself, occasionally by others... a dream that can take objective form in sounds, in hallucinations, in scents, in flashes of light, in movements of external objects" (VII, 22-23). The communicators belong to the tradition of the master's ghost, to be banished or welcomed and given corporeal form by the stable boy or the Yeats couple. Similarly, Yeats intended the portrait of Giraldus, commissioned from Edmund ·Dulac, to be a stylized medieval Mask of himself. In play, in high seriousness, the myth becomes biography, the biography a myth.

In *Autobiographies,* as in his poetry and his philosophical system, Yeats attempted to establish correspondences between personality and the nation, history, and myth. If in the poetry Maud Gonne could be "a Ledaean body," a Helen without "another Troy for her to burn," and Ireland could be his tower — "Is every modern nation like the tower,/ Half dead at the top?" —, so Yeats's striving towards Unity of Being might be his generation's striving to escape Victorian poetics, his nation's striving (or so he hoped) towards Unity of Culture. The man and his literature, the literature and the nation, become analogous in a larger metaphoric and philosophic construct: "Some will ask whether I believe in the actual existence of my circuits of sun and moon," Yeats concluded his introduction to *A Vision.* "To such a question I can but answer that... I regard them as stylistic arrangements of experience comparable to the cubes in the drawing of Wyndham Lewis and to the ovoids in the sculpture of Brancusi. They have helped me to hold in a single thought reality and justice" (VII, 24-25). The question, as does so much else in *A Vision,* appears in Mme. Blavatsky's writings. "Do the Occultists," she asks, "believe in all these 'Builders,' 'Lipika,' and 'Sons of Light,' as Entities, or are they merely imagery?" The responses of the poet and the theosophist to this problem of belief versus imagery indicate how closely Yeats had allied his philosophy, his life, and his poetry. While Blavatsky makes "due allowance for the imagery of personified Powers," she also firmly insists on literal belief.[129] Yeats's "stylistic arrangements of experience" are as firmly poetic; never denying his literal belief, he insists on the primary importance of the system as a "Lunar parable" which provides "metaphors for poetry." But not only does it provide metaphors, it also functions as a controlling metaphor itself, giving cohesive form to life and art.

In both his life and his art, Yeats consistently used the philosophical system as a mythic construct. In an early essay, he had recalled that the "Greeks... considered that myths are the activities of the Daimons, and that the Daimons shape our characters and our lives." The individual life becomes myth in this formulation and myth explains the life: "I have often had the fancy that there is some one myth for every man, which, if we but knew it, would make us understand all he did and thought" (EI, 107). Yeats attempts to shape his autobiography by means of the philosophy which he articulates in *A Vision* and which ultimately provides him with "some one myth." That philosophy becomes part of its own metaphor, existing in antithetical tension with the incohesiveness and inconclusiveness of life itself.

XIII

Yeats seems to have written his own autobiography with the encouragement of the genre he had given his father still in mind for the preface to *Reveries over Childhood and Youth* alludes to a remark of Oscar Wilde which he had cited to John Butler Yeats: "In any case, because one can always close a book, my friend need not be bored" (A, 3). Similarly, *The Trembling of the Veil* closes with a reference to the same historical value of reminiscence which he had earlier urged on his father: "I have written these words instead of leaving all to posterity... that young men, to whom recent events are often more obscure than those long past, may learn what debts they owe and to what creditor" (A, 381). But whatever the sincerity of the intention, its historical rather than literary bias is hardly sufficient to sustain a writer of Yeats's stylistic and introspective capabilities through twenty years of periodically writing autobiography, nor is it consistent with the auto-biographical impulse to nearly all his early prose.

The stylistic complexity of *Autobiographies* evolved gradually as Yeats moved beyond the genre's historical significance and considered its possibilities for the re-making of the self through the Mask and as he left the seemingly ingenuous narrative voice of *Reveries over Childhood and Youth* for the more analytic tone demanded by the portrayal of his activities and intellectual interests as a young man. Perhaps the first check and consequent moulding of the autobiographical "I" occurred even before he began writing in his desire for discretion. Curtis Bradford notes that Yeats carefully deleted from the typescript of *Reveries over Childhood and Youth* passages "that might give offense to his family."[130] His recollection of a deranged relation who trustingly appeared on their doorstep and whom they "betrayed" by returning to her asylum, even though she figures without her name in *Memoirs*, was deleted at Lily Yeats's insistence.[131] His account of his first orgasm was included in "First Draft" and again omitted in the use of that text for *The Trembling of the Veil*. References to his first auto-biography in letters to his father show much anxiety about the circumspection of his undertaking.[132] Continuing his memoirs, he writes that they "shall be for my own eye alone" (L, 603). And so much was. In his transmutation of "First Draft" into *The Trembling of the Veil*, Yeats omitted all reference to his affair with Olivia

Shakespear.[133] Manuscript fragments reveal him writing and rewriting the passages recounting Maud Gonne's visit to Bedford Park and his courtship of her. Constant throughout the drafts is the comparison of her complexion to the luminosity of the apple blossoms before which she stood, a comparison already used many years earlier in *The Speckled Bird* to describe Margaret. But it takes several successive drafts before Yeats can distance himself sufficiently from his subject to present her in the externalized terms of "a classical impersonation of the Spring" (A, 123) and of the birds and dogs she surrounded herself with, denying any contemporary knowledge of her mind, or before he can dismiss his unsuccessful courtship with a phrase: "being in love, and in no way lucky in that love, I had grown exceedingly puritanical" (A, 334). Perhaps in the interest of personal discretion, he suppressed the romantic motivation of his nationalism[134] in favour of the patriotic. Similarly he refused to respond directly and in kind to George Moore's *Hail and Farewell*[135] until he wrote *Dramatis Personae* after Moore's death.

If a predisposition to circumspection and what he probably regarded as good taste led Yeats to abandon the *tout dire* style with which he had begun "First Draft," other factors more germane to his life and work determined the mythopoeic form *Autobiographies* ultimately assumed. By the nineteen-twenties, Yeats's reading public knew him as a poet, a poet who by means of "personal utterance" fused the personal and the contemporary with the mythic and the traditional or historical. In relation to that public, Yeats concerned himself in *Autobiographies* not with the man, with what he termed "the bundle of accident and incoherence that sits down to breakfast," but with the author; he knew very well what critics of the genre have just begun to take into account, that the reader is interested in the literary autobiographer as a man consistent with his previous works.[136]

Because autobiography, skillfully used, is literature, not the confessional, because its chief persona is the author, not the quotidian man, it presents a "truth" of dual structural significance: it shapes the reader's literary experience and his perception of the author but it also molds the man behind the author. Author and man tend to fuse in the minds of both readers and writer. Autobiographical style, particularly if the work, like Rousseau's, aims at self-justification, is "une manière spécifique de se révéler à autrui." [137] As Rousseau's style, derived from his ensconcement in "sincerity," found first a modification in Stendhalian *égotisme*, then a counter-balance in the Decadents' creation of the self as literary artifice, authors began to realize that they clothed themselves with their work not so much for the observation of others as for their own self-definition. Paul Valéry, writing particularly of Stendhal and generally of those who choose to "déboutonner" [138] for themselves and their readers, suggests an inevitable self-reflexiveness in all literature: "L'Égotisme littéraire consiste finalement à jouer le rôle de *soi;* à se faire un peu plus *nature* que nature; un peu plus soi qu'on ne l'était quelques instants avant d'en avoir eu l'idée. Donnant à ses impulsions ou impressions un *suppôt* conscient qui. . .se dessine de plus en plus, et se *perfectionne* d'oeuvre en oeuvre *selon le progrès même le l'art de l'écrivain,* on se substitue un personnage d'invention que l'on arrive insensiblement à prendre pour modèle."[139] The writer, looking at himself through his literature until he takes the literary personage for a model, reverses the acknowledged direction of the literary enterprise: "l'oeuvre capitale d'un artiste, c'est l'artiste lui-même, — dont les ouvrages successifs. . . ne sont que les moyens et les effets extérieurs, — parfois accidentels." His own major work, the artist "se façonne et se modèle peu à peu, se déchiffre et se reconnaît; il devient un homme nouveau, celui qui fait enfin ce que lui seul peut faire."[140] When the writer simultaneously creates literature and is created by that literature, his autobiography becomes a reversible garment: it remains the expected portrait of the artist and, therefore, of the genesis of his works, but turned, it reveals the author shaping himself through his works and in their image.

No writer brought to autobiography a greater awareness of this reversibility of its supposed function than W. B. Yeats who, in his 1908 *Collected Works,* had chided those who criticized his penchant for revision:

> The friends that have it I do wrong
> When ever I remake a song,
> Should know what issue is at stake:
> It is myself that I remake. (VPo, 778)

In a 1909 *Journal* entry adapted for *Estrangement,* he altered the emphasis of the process, identifying (as would a more sceptical Sartre after him) the "imposture" with the self: "I thought myself loving neither vice nor virtue; but virtue has come upon me and given me a nation instead of a home. Has it left me any lyrical faculty? Whatever happens I must go on that there may be a man behind the lines already written; I cast the die long ago and must be true to the cast" (A, 485). "Now shall I make my soul" (VPo, 416): this from "The Tower," written the same year Yeats published *Estrangement.* The poet hammers his life into a shape compatible with his literary *oeuvre;* his autobiography is justified neither by logic nor by history but by the literary formula of "personal utterance": "I can no more justify my convictions in these brief chapters than Shakespeare could justify within the limits of a sonnet his conviction that the soul of the wide world dreams of things to come; and yet as I have set out to describe nature as I see it, I must not only describe events but those patterns into which they fall, when I am the looker-on" (A, 330). Those patterns act as mythic constructs uniting, with varying degrees of complexity, the poet and that "bundle of accident and incoherence," the private man; Yeats and Ireland; the personal and the universal; the present and the remembered life; the self and its Mask. Yeats's parable of the *Commedia dell' Arte* becomes apposite. In *Autobiographies,* he stage-manages his own life, and directs, in retrospect, an actor who is his earlier self. Given an "inherited scenario," the text of his life, and a Mask, a poet, philosopher and nationalist, a self-possessed, public, and antithetical man opposed to the quotidian self, Yeats as actor/stage-manager selects and improvises "the dialogue and details of the plot." His are literary and dramatic tools: imagination, gesture, and, above all, style, the "self-conquest of the writer who is not a man of action" (A, 516). With them he must transcend and transform the merely personal to reveal an essential being infused with tautness and energy. The extent to which he succeeds is the extent to which *Autobiographies* is literarily satisfying.

" . . .the memories of one's childhood are brittle things to lean upon"
(M, 96): so Yeats once excused some faulty recollection. *Reveries over
Childhood and Youth* never "leans upon" memories; instead it invokes
childhood experiences, as Henry James had just done, because they
"signified,"[1] or seem to have done so to the backward-looking autobiographer. Although its fragmented recollections present less complexity than does the organization of much of *Autobiographies,* it does
intimate from its opening lines the tendency to submit character and
incident to the demand for pattern which structures the collected work.
"My first memories," Yeats begins, "are fragmentary and isolated and
contemporaneous, as though one remembered some first moments of
the Seven Days. It seems as if time had not yet been created, for all
thoughts are connected with emotion and place without sequence"
(A, 5). More than a justification of the discontinuous narrative which
follows, the image places the poet at the centre of Creation [2] as does
Sturge Moore's cover design for the 1916 MacMillan edition of *Reveries
over Childhood and Youth.* That design, a "stylistic arrangement" of
rectangles and arcs, is vertically symmetrical around an abstractly
rendered tower. The strong vertical lines of the design are counterbalanced, at its top, by a horizontal band of two arcs and, at its
bottom, by a wider horizontal design of waves represented by stylized
curved lines. At the top of the tower, a recumbent baby clutches the
forefinger of the divine hand descending through the circles of heaven.
At its foot, a young man descends the tower stairs through a door he
holds half open. His posture—eyes downcast, hand gripping the door's
edge, left leg tentatively advanced towards the lower step—suggests
hesitancy, almost coyness,[3] while the figure's nudity conveys
defencelessness and an adolescent's innocent self-absorption and
reiterates the theme of birth. The journey down the tower stairs, from
earliest childhood to youth, coincides with the text of *Reveries over
Childhood and Youth;* the moment of Creation ends with the young
man's stepping into the world delineated in "Four Years." The waves
surrounding the tower's base present visually the metaphor of the time
of *Reveries* as a period of gestation for they recall both Porphyry's
"waters of generation" [4] and the Judeo-Christian creation myth. In the
Philosophus 4=7 ritual of The Order of the Golden Dawn, the
Hierophant invokes Genesis: "I arise in the place of the gathering of the
Waters, through the rolled-back clouds of night. From the Father of
Waters went forth the Spirit rending asunder the veils of darkness. . . ."[5]
By introducing himself both visually and verbally by allusion to the
Creation, Yeats directs us as to the manner in which he wishes his
autobiography to be read: he signals that his design is to be mythopoeic
rather than mimetic, he asserts his continuity with the "traditional

Cover design by Sturge Moore for the 1916 MacMillan edition of *Reveries over Childhood and Youth*.

knowledge" (Ex, 251) he deemed necessary to literature, he implies the Romantic conviction informing so much autobiography that the individual life and all of creation, the lived life and its reconstruction in art, can only be perceived and understood from the point of view of the individual consciousness and he intimates, by recalling The Golden Dawn ritual, that his autobiography will focus on the pursuit of a knowledge on the other side of the veil.

This "fragmentary and isolated and contemporaneous" narrative, this "reverie," Yeats defined as "the speech of the soul with itself" (EI, 333). Shaped by his father's theories of the unity of personality and of literature[6] and by his early admiration of Shelley, Yeats used reverie as the style necessary to the expression of the mystical experience. In an essay dated 1900, he had quoted Shelley on the nature of reverie and had gone on to define his own mystic ideology:

'Those who are subject to the state called reverie, feel as if their nature were resolved into the surrounding universe or as if the surrounding universe were resolved into their being,' and he [Shelley] must have expected to receive thoughts and images from beyond his own mind, just in so far as that mind transcended its preoccupation with particular time and place, . . . and he could hardly have helped perceiving that an image that has transcended particular time and place becomes a symbol, passes beyond death, as it were, and becomes a living soul. (EI, 79–80)

James Olney has analyzed the rhetoric of forgetfulness and evasion pervasive in Yeats's prose[7]; so too the rhetorical manoeuvring in this passage—the indirect use of a quotation from Shelley, Yeats's hypothesizing for him ("he must have expected," "he could hardly have helped"), the subjunctive "as it were"—simultaneously asserts Yeats's conviction and evades the question of literal belief. Nonetheless, the definition itself is important in a consideration of his autobiographical style.

Employed as autobiographical style, reverie shows affinities with several writers concerned to examine the "seed-time" of their "soul." But Yeats remains less concerned with "the history of a Poet's mind" and more preoccupied with detached images endowed with both personal and poetic significance than Wordsworth, his reverie lacks the subtle associativeness of Jamesian prolixness, the images with which he communes with himself have the altering effect but not the harshness of Henry Adams's "sudden strains that permanently warp the mind." Less psychological and "developmental"[8] than these autobiographers, enticed by the idea of shaping his life as he might shape a poem, Yeats reports that his first immersion in reverie occurred at puberty, attended by the romantic prop of a cave reminiscent of Shelley and by imaginative projections of his self into literary postures: "I began to play at being a sage, a magician or a poet. . . . as I climbed along the narrow ledge [to the cave] I was now Manfred on his glacier, and now Prince Athanase with his solitary lamp, but I soon chose Alastor for my chief of men and longed to share his melancholy . . ." (A, 64).

59

Nascent in this very serious play, this emerging conviction "that creation," even the creation of the self, "should be deliberate" (A, 83), is the doctrine of the anti-self Yeats would elaborate in the years following the writing of *Reveries*. As he muses over his earliest literary contacts, the poet insists on the motivating force of the doctrine he has not yet named; he sought in his narrative poetry, he tells us, "a landscape that is symbolical of some spiritual condition and awakens a hunger such as cats feel for valerian" (A, 74),[9] he "was about to learn that if a man is to write lyric poetry he must be shaped by nature and art to some one out of half a dozen traditional poses, and . . . this thought before it could be knowledge was an instinct" (A, 87). For a time Hamlet becomes an image of the unnamed anti-self, "an image of heroic self-possession for the poses of youth and childhood to copy, a combatant of the battle within myself" (A, 47). The youthful Yeats joins a debating club, "not from natural liking," but "to become self-possessed, to be able to play with hostile minds as Hamlet played" (A, 93), to begin to move towards his antithetical self. The emphasis on play, on action that involves spontaneous and deliberate choice, remains integral to the use of the Mask throughout *Autobiographies*: "Some day setting out to find knowledge, like some pilgrim to the Holy Land, he [the artist] . . . will play with all masks" (A, 470). In between the first intimations of the Mask in *Reveries over Childhood and Youth* and this statement in *Estrangement*, Yeats will explicitly use that doctrine as a metaphor with which to measure his successes and failures in forging a style and a personality for both himself and Ireland.

But in *Reveries over Childhood and Youth*, the idea of the Mask remains latent. Much of the success of the stylistic use of reverie in this book depends on its clarity as images,[10] on the absence of analytical complication. Yeats recalls the death of his brother[11] with the images an impressionable child retained—stories of the banshee's cry and his drawings of ships at half-mast—and not with adult expressions of mourning; he presents vivid memories of the behaviour of a particular schoolmaster never terming him a pederast because, as a boy, he had not understood the import of the man's behaviour.[12] Recollections invoked by reverie stand alone, without comment, without necessary connection with one another, because for Yeats they have seminal poetic value; they exist prior to any logical faculty.[13] "I was divided from all those boys," he tells us, "because our mental images were different" (A, 35). His particular images define his separateness in a manner simultaneously more naturalistic and more suggestive of mythopoeic values than that available to analytic discourse. Their fragmentation reflects the condition of their existence in his memory. A child perceiving "the broken corner of a tower with a winding stair" (A, 54) cannot foresee the man who would find in Virgil's *Aeneid* one of "the builders of my soul" (A, 58–59) and who would set Norman tower and Trojan ruins resonating against one another in his poetry. For Yeats as autobiographer of his childhood to do more than limn the "mental images" which originally "signified" would be to falsify the nature of his poetic development and experience, but for the reader, sharing the poet's retrospective vantage-point, the juxtaposition of those images is richly suggestive.

Reveries over Childhood and Youth, with its discontinuous narrative which is far richer as prophetic image than as literal fact, pre-figures both the themes and structure of much in the remainder of *Autobiographies* while never enunciating either. Yeats's family history not only illumines the characters who earliest people his imagination,[14] it endows him with a personal tradition: "All the well-known families had their grotesque or tragic or romantic legends, and I often said to myself how terrible it would be to go away and die where nobody would know my story" (A, 17–18). His relatives provide the necessary "double," the mirroring in "world history" of "personal history," and suggest the autobiographical impulse behind all of Yeats's writing, for, as he would write in his 1930 diary, "thoughts become more vivid when I find they were thought out in historical circumstances which affect those in which I live, or, which is perhaps the same thing, were thought first by men my ancestors may have known" (Ex, 293).

Each branch of the family brings a particular attribute to the poet and Yeats simplifies his family's history to emphasize those attributes. The sea-going Pollexfens suggest romantic adventure and, in their reticence and solitude, the note of tragedy, high, stern and lonely. "Even to-day," Yeats writes of his grandfather, William Pollexfen, "when I read *King Lear* his image is always before me, and I often wonder if the delight in passionate men in my plays and in my poetry is more than his memory" (A, 9).[15] The Middletons introduce him to faery stories, theme of much of his early work and premonition of his later systematization of the occult tradition. The Yeats branch provides him with an Irish history: "Now that I can look at their miniatures, turning them over to find the name of soldier, or lawyer, or Castle official, and wondering if they cared for good books or good music, I am delighted with all that joins my life to those who had power in Ireland. . ." (A, 21–22). The separate branches unite the contemplative and the active, the man of passion and the man of ideas. A Yeats says of them: "'We have ideas and no passions, but by marriage with a Pollexfen we have given a tongue to the sea cliffs.' " This, which W.B. Yeats termed "the only eulogy that turns my head" (A, 23),[16] brings the reader symbolically round to the Creation once again; the diverse family attributes—literature, the occult and nationalism—have achieved harmony in the birth of the poet.

61

Yeats never uses his doctrine of the Mask, of harmony as a balance achieved between self and antithetical self, overtly in *Reveries over Childhood and Youth* although he certainly had formulated it. [17] However, he does continue his early use of oppositions which thematically pre-figure his explicit references later in *Autobiographies* to the philosophic system of *A Vision*. As it was in *John Sherman,* Sligo is set against London and, by extension, Ireland against England; the natural study of birds' cries and moths with which Yeats occupies himself at Sligo becomes a source of poetic knowledge countering the barrenness of London schoolrooms. The first edition of *Reveries over Childhood and Youth* emphasized this contrast by its colour plate of Jack Yeats's "Memory Harbour" with the poet's accompanying explanation that the scene was "of Rosses Point." [18] Yeats further generalizes the conflict between the values represented by his two homes to a conflict between generations. The young poet counters his father's "mere reality" (A, 83)— "'I must paint what I see in front of me' " (A, 82)—with the occult: "It was only when I began to study psychical research and mystical philosophy that I broke away from my father's influence" (A, 89). [19] But he also minimizes this conflict between father and son in *Autobiographies,* suppressing mention, for example, of the incident with which he opens his first draft in which John Butler Yeats becomes so "enraged" by his son's "mysticism" and interest in Ruskin as to break a picture glass over his head (Mem, 19).

The central antithesis of *Reveries over Childhood and Youth* focuses not on the father-son conflict but on expressions of nationalism and particularly on John F. Taylor. Set against him is John O'Leary on whose gentle humility and unaffected "moral genius" (A, 95) Yeats dwells. O'Leary's role in *Autobiographies* is markedly and benevolently paternal. For a time Yeats lived with him, "the poet," he tells us, "in the presence of his theme" (A, 96). In retrospect, he identified all he had done as coming from O'Leary's conversation and library and from the debates of The Young Ireland Society to which both belonged (A, 101). [20] Most passionate among the debaters was John F. Taylor. Yeats opposes Taylor's ungainliness and tactlessness to O'Leary's gentle grace and good breeding, Taylor's deliberately dramatic oratory to O'Leary's "ignorance" of the "passionate value" of his statements (A, 96). In Yeats's scenario, however, Taylor functions as far more than a foil to O'Leary's self-effacing heroism; he also incorporates within himself the metaphor of the creator as antithetical man. In both *Reveries over Childhood and Youth* and "Ireland after Parnell," Yeats limns Taylor's "ungainly body in unsuitable, badly fitting clothes," his "excited voice speaking ill of this man or that other" (A, 214), but, declaring himself no "match" (A, 227) for Taylor in speech, he also dwells again and again on that speech:

his delivery . . . gave me a conviction of how great might be the effect of verse, spoken by a man almost rhythm-drunk, at some moment of intensity, the apex of long-mounting thought. Verses that seemed when one saw them upon the page flat and empty caught from that voice, whose beauty was half in its harsh strangeness, nobility and style. My father had always read verse with an equal intensity and a greater subtlety, but . . . it is Taylor's voice that has rung in my ears and awakens my longing when I have heard some player speak lines, 'so naturally', as a famous player said to me, 'that nobody can find out that it is verse at all'. (A,99)

Taylor's speech is that of "personal utterance" and, if before O'Leary Yeats had found himself "the poet in the presence of his theme," before Taylor he was the poet in the presence of his style. Taylor literally represents Yeats's anti-self. The poet faces the orator in debates because he feels such activity to be least natural to him, because he wishes to overcome his timidity and to cultivate "self-possession" (A, 99). As Yeats's ideal poet must find style by donning the Mask of his antithetical self, so Yeats himself found the image of his style in Taylor's oratory, an image of antithetical man in Taylor himself. The orator becomes, in his speech, model for the poet, in his conduct, warning. Yeats finds in him too the image of the tragic hero, shadowed by the futility of all he does. In "Ireland after Parnell," he is represented as a failed leader, one whose "temper" both "gave him genius" and alienated followers (A, 214) and one whose example suggests to the poet that politics but took him from his true self. "Did not Leonardo da Vinci," Yeats remarks in the context of Taylor's oblivion, "warn the imaginative man against preoccupation with arts that cannot survive his death?" (A, 216). If Taylor represents the man of action to the poet, his fall into oblivion serves as another cautionary tale.

These implied oppositions gain structural prominence in *The Trembling of the Veil. Reveries over Childhood and Youth* opens up images for experience; it does not impose order on them. The child strives to find himself in a variety of situations; the young man looks to shape himself and his writing, to clothe the nude figure opening the door onto the world with a philosophy and a literature. The tone of aspiration which informs much of the later narrative often emerges here, broken only in the last paragraphs by a second pattern which will gather force slowly throughout *Autobiographies* until it becomes dominant in *Estrangement* and *The Death of Synge* and undercuts the work's mythopoeic structure, a pattern of melancholy, of disillusion and defeat. Yeats links his first literary success, the publication of two books, within a single sentence with his grandmother's death. A few weeks later, he recalls, his grandfather also died, breaking the strongest of his links with Sligo. A traditional order crumbles in pettiness; servants begin to steal and people to quarrel over worthless ornaments. The tone is of an idyll broken.

The final paragraph intensifies the melancholy. In a coda to what has passed before, Yeats effects one of his entries into the work in an "editorial" capacity in order to comment from the perspective of his older self: "For some months now I have lived with my own youth and childhood . . . and I am sorrowful and disturbed . . . when I think of all the books I have read, and of the wise words I have heard spoken, and of the anxiety I have given to parents and grandparents, and of the hopes that I have had, all life weighed in the scales of my own life seems to me a preparation for something that never happens" (A, 106). In 1914, the personal and literary life remained unachieved. Yeats had not yet learned to "play with all masks," "to see things . . . doubled" in himself and the world; consequently, *Reveries over Childhood and Youth* contains but the promise of Unity of Being, not Unity itself. The the "old thought that life prepares for what never happens"[21] becomes "Among School Children" finally intimates the limitations inherent in using autobiography as a mythic construct. Cast in poetry, the "old thought" becomes Yeats's most famous and one of his most satisfyingly conclusive configurations of Unity of Being but the patterns of life, even if they can be extrapolated from daily experience for the mythologizing purposes of his autobiography, are never so satisfactorily climactic. When he redrafted the continuation of his memoirs, Yeats moved even further from the intimate and self-revelatory mode of autobiography and closer to the imposition of a completely external construct on his experience in order to prove of himself and his generation that the poet is one who "lives sincerely" and who "makes an experiment in life" (YP, 32).

While Yeats did use an antithetical structure, sometimes overt, often implied, in much of his early work, it took the long elaboration of *A Vision,* an elaboration which he made his major activity in the four years between his marriage and the publication of the first chapter of *The Trembling of the Veil,* to develop this antithetical structure, to name and define its attributes, so that it might simultaneously be a "philosophical system" and "metaphors for poetry." When he used the material of "First Draft" in writing *The Trembling of the Veil,* Yeats made two major structural revisions: he omitted, as we have seen, material of a personal nature, particularly that relating to Olivia Shakespear and Maud Gonne, and he imposed his new metaphor of antithesis on his reminiscences and characterizations. Where antithetical structure had been an undefined attitude rather than a system, an intuitive approach rather than an overt framework, in *Reveries over Childhood and Youth,* in this second autobiographical volume it becomes the controlling image.

The symmetry of Yeats's "Lunar parable" determines and explains much of the structure of the five chapters of *The Trembling of the Veil.* Yeats claims to have taken his title from Mallarmé's occult image for the moment of relevation so many *fin-de-siècle* writers felt to be near at hand and he thought that trembling of the veil characteristic of an age " 'seeking to bring forth a sacred book' " (A, 315).[1] Recalling his father's simile, Yeats had annotated Common's selections from Nietzsche's *The Antichrist* with the remark that "A sacred book is a work written by a man whose self has been *so* exalted (not by denial but by an intensity like that of the vibrating vanishing string) that it becomes one with the self of the race."[2] To write it, the poet must see through the "small tear" in Mallarmé's metaphoric veil to Unity of Being; having seen, his life and work become a "double," a mythological prototype, of the life of his people.

By the time he was writing *Autobiographies* and *A Vision,* nothing so confirmed Yeats in his convictions as the discovery of analogous symbols in different cultural and historical traditions. The concept of a veil of matter separating man from the spiritual world he had by now found at the heart of Platonism. But long before he began reading Thomas Taylor and Henry More, Yeats had come across the idea in what he characterized as "the only great prose in modern English" (A, 302): "just 'behind the veil,'" promises the Platonist Apuleius in *Marius the Epicurean,* lie truths which indicate "a world, wider, perhaps, in its possibilities than all possible fancies concerning it."[3] In the contexts both of Platonism and of Golden Dawn rituals, Yeats associated "the trembling of the veil" with the "trembling" horses in a Japanese painting, an image with which he questions the

"impassable barrier" (A, 187) between the physical and the supernatural worlds: "I had . . . read . . . of an animal painter so remarkable
that horses he had painted upon a temple wall had slipped down after
dark and trampled the neighbours' fields of rice. Somebody had come
into the temple in the early morning, had been startled by a shower of
water-drops, had looked up and seen painted horses still wet from the
dew-covered fields, but now 'trembling into stillness'" (A, 186). In
both the 1921 and 1922 editions of "Four Years," Yeats uses his
recollection of this painter to illustrate the nature of Mme. Blavatsky's
"masters." They were, he suggests by analogy with the horses of the
painting, "forms" that "could pass from Madame Blavatsky's mind to the
minds of others, and even acquire external reality," forms "born in the
imagination, where Blake had declared that all men live after
death. . . ."[4] By 1926, Yeats had pared down the account to align it
more closely with the system of *A Vision*. Both images, that of "the
trembling of the veil" and that of the horses made vital by the artist's
suggestive power, are used to intimate that the revelation of Art is the
revelation of that Unity of Being possible only to the antithetical man
contemplating his Mask. The autobiography, the images imply, will be
another attempt to achieve that Unity of Being, another art.

In *Autobiographies,* Yeats associates that Unity not only with
spiritualism but with Irish nationalism. But in *The Trembling of the
Veil,* he experiences both as abortive. *A Vision* had placed his era at
Phase Twenty-two, the point midway between Phase Fifteen, that of
antithetical civilization, and Phase One, that of primary civilization, of
the "body . . . completely absorbed in its supernatural environment"
(VI, 116; VII, 183). Phase Twenty-two represents a trough between
the antithetical and primary modes, the moment at which the
assumption of the Mask ceases to be the voluntary discipline of the
artist, and becomes "enforced," "character substituted for personality"
(VII, 86; cf. VI, 20). Such an age, Yeats thought, could produce no art
which fuses the opposites between which it stands; its possibilities must
remain unrealized: "Some of us thought that [sacred] book near
towards the end of [the] last century, but the tide sank again"
(A, 315).

Yeats's use of Mallarmé's image and his application of *A Vision* in
The Trembling of the Veil suggest a pattern of defeat, of promise and
its failure to be fulfilled, of a movement towards a moment of crisis and
a subsequent diminishment. This waxing and waning finds its analogy in
constructive images followed by destructive and in symbols of unity
succeeded by fragmented syntax. The central chapter, "Hodos
Chameliontos," figuratively charts that never fully realized moment
after which "the tide sank again," "Four Years" and "Ireland after
Parnell" the aspirations leading to it, "The Tragic Generation" and

"The Stirring of the Bones" disillusion, loss and fragmentation in both the personal and historical consciousness.

II

"Four Years" turns from the almost solipsist interest in "mental images" (A, 35, 186) which had characterized *Reveries over Childhood and Youth* to their manifestation in the external world. The chapter records Yeats's first acquaintance with the writers and occultists most nearly contemporaneous with him. Their treatment presents a complex instance of the autobiographer's double temporal perspective. With the possible exception of Oscar Wilde, whose greater age, wealth, wit and notoriety—even before his trial—made him more visible than others of Yeats's friends of the period, the autobiographer seems to present the painters and writers of his "generation" (A, 164) in terms of his youthful perception of their relative merits. But if Todhunter and Nettleship rank as equally with Henley and Morris in *Autobiographies* as they did in the attention of the youthful Yeats, they are nonetheless subjected to a scrutiny of which the poet, at twenty, would have been incapable. The mature Yeats erects antithetical images into the basis of a characterology in which each person seeks an image, the opposite of his quotidian self, which he then tries to shape into his "true self." William Henley's powerful torso belies his amputated leg: "half inarticulate . . . beset with personal quarrels, [he] built up an image of power and magnanimity till it became . . . . his true self" (A, 125–26). With what he considered to be "the antithesis that is the foundation of human nature" (A, 128) governing his account, Yeats opposes Wilde's charm, "acquired and systematized," to R.A.M. Stevenson's more natural charm which "belonged to him like the colour of his hair" (A, 132). With the anecdotal virtuosity which makes for much of the charm of *Autobiographies,* he chooses to explain Wilde as the antithesis of his "dirty, untidy, daring" family in Dublin, as performing "a play which was in all things the opposite of all that he had known in childhood and early youth" (A, 138). He sets Wilde in his white dining-room—"perhaps too perfect in its unity, his past of a few years before had gone too completely" (A, 134–35)—against his mother's household—"there is an old story still current in Dublin of Lady Wilde saying to a servant, 'Why do you put the plates on the coal-scuttle? What are the chairs meant for?'"(A, 137). From the vantage-point of thirty years, Yeats similarly describes the shortcomings of his early contemporaries—Florence Farr, Edwin Ellis, Jack Nettleship—, shortcomings visible to the youthful poet but not thus explicable by him, in terms of the inability of each to find or, having found, to conform with "his simplifying image" (A, 159). Since it is only the man of Phase Seventeen who, in the characterology of *A Vision,* finds his Mask through

67

"simplification," metaphorically at least Yeats is condemning his contemporaries for not being himself. As he did in *Reveries over Childhood and Youth,* he here implicitly asserts that his "mental images were different" from theirs. By describing his contemporaries, Yeats attempts to define what he was not or what he transcended.

But when he "described what image—always opposite to the natural self or the natural world—" (A, 171), his contemporaries copied, Yeats did not entirely mould his youthful perceptions to the more sophisticated classifications of the mature poet. The terminology and the clarity of the antithetical metaphor belong to the autobiographer but the antithetical impulse, as yet undefined, belonged to his subject also: "My mind began drifting vaguely towards that doctrine of 'the mask' which has convinced me that every passionate man . . . is, as it were, linked with another age, historical or imaginary, where alone he finds images that rouse his energy" (A, 152).[5] The "mental images" of the occult replace those of his earlier "reveries" in this search; the doctrines of Mme. Blavatsky and MacGregor Mathers supplement the Pre-Raphaelite movement, Pater's aestheticism and Symons's symbolism. Against the "conviction that the world was now but a bundle of fragments" (A, 189), a conviction to which *The Trembling of the Veil* in its turning from one activity to another bears eloquent testimony, Yeats began to adapt his father's doctrine of Unity of Being, imbuing it with historical and literary tradition.

It is this aspiration to Unity of Being which lends all the characters in *Autobiographies* a mythopoeic tincture. Yeats's acquaintances possess more than historical or dramatic significance; they are both symbols of the fragmentation against which he reacted and images of a striving—a notably unsuccessful striving—to overcome that fragmentation. They created much of the ambience in which the youthful Yeats moved; by later classifying them in terms of self and Mask, he gives that ambience the value of a mythos.

At the point in his narrative at which Yeats explicitly turns to the occult, to an acceptance of correspondences between worlds, he also begins establishing reverberations between his prose account and his poetry. Previously he had quoted his own poetry as the syntactic completion of a prose thought or that of others as illustrative of some statement in his text; he reproduces, for example, a long passage from Shelley to indicate the strength of his early identity with Ahasuerus and to mark the literary origins of his interest in the cultivation of the mythic attributes of the self. But in the context of self, anti-self and Unity of Being, he lets his own poetry resonate against his prose rather than illustrate it. Lines from "The Second Coming" form an apposition to what "I did not forsee . . . the growing murderousness of the world" (A, 192). Naming "abstraction, . . . the isolation of occupation, or class or faculty" (A, 190), as the enemy of Unity of Being, Yeats apposes to that definition lines from "The Hawk" published some forty years after

68

the time of which he is speaking:

> Call down the hawk from the air,
> Let him be hooded or caged
> Till the yellow eye has grown mild,
> For larder and spit are bare,
> The old cook enraged,
> The scullion gone wild. (A, 190-91)

Such a juxtaposition forces us to unite statement and poem in a context larger than either. The apposition remains meaningless until we treat the hawk as emblematic of the abstraction Yeats believed inherent in logical thought unmodulated by emotion,[6] the empty larder, the cook and the scullion as physical manifestations of the spiritual famine resulting from such abstraction. This done, we have created a space between prose and poem in which we momentarily situate the autobiographer. Yeats has suffused the ostensibly historical and "developmental" autobiography with the imaginative world from which his current writing springs and has anchored that imaginative world in autobiographical circumstance; self and anti-self, biography and myth, each becomes its opposite and generates.

III

Yeats makes another such image from his poetry the axis of the second chapter of *The Trembling of the Veil*. If "Four Years," dealing as it preponderantly does with literature, evokes the stirrings of Yeats's aspirations to Unity of Being, "Ireland after Parnell" might be said to portray his search for an anti-self through which to realize it. As he ends "Four Years," Yeats begins to specifically associate Ireland with both the fragmentation he finds in the world and the possibility of vanquishing it through Unity of Being: "a nation or an individual with great emotional intensity might . . . give to all those separated elements, and to all that abstract love and melancholy, a symbolical, a mythological coherence" (A, 193).[7] "I had begun to hope, or to half hope, that we might be the first in Europe to seek unity as deliberately as it had been sought by theologian, poet, sculptor, architect, from the eleventh to the thirteenth century" (A, 195). He confesses to "the wildest hopes" of creating an Irish *Prometheus Unbound,*[8] of unifying his country "by an image, or bundle of related images" which "might move of themselves and with some powerful, even turbulent life, like those painted horses that trampled the rice-fields of Japan" (A, 194). The ideal nation might see "behind the veil" and become the ontological equivalent of the work of art.

But Yeats's account in "Ireland after Parnell" of his attempt to effect a transmutation of Ireland, to arouse in her that Unity of Culture, based on enlightened patriotism and myth, which would be analogous to the individual's Unity of Being, is brief and bitter, a record of personal animosities and petty quarrels. The entire chapter reveals the extent of Yeats's editorializing in *Autobiographies* for it exactly reverses the judgment of the young man who had sought to create a literary revival through political action. Writing in 1899 about the creation of a national literature, Yeats had thought that the "fall of Parnell and the wreck of his party and of the organisations that supported it were the symbols, if not the causes, of a sudden change. They were followed by movements and organisations that brought the ideas and the ideals which are the expression of personalities alike into politics, economics, and literature . . . a new kind of Ireland . . . was rising up amid the wreck of the old kind, and . . . the national life was finding a new utterance" (UP, II, 185–86). In *Autobiographies,* Yeats remains faithful to this view of Ireland only insofar as he continues to see Parnell's fall as a catalyst. But in terms of the nation's failure to achieve Unity of Culture which patterns *The Trembling of the Veil,* the fallen hero symbolizes a Unity of Being which Ireland has spurned; Parnell remains solitary in his exhibition "of power over self, and so of the expression of the self" (A, 233). His legendary silence and rigid self-control confront the quarrels and vain rhetoric of the politicians who remain after him. Their parties are equivalents of self and anti-self failing to achieve unity. In such an environment, Yeats would decide in retrospect, participation in any nationalist organization could only be an error. "I had surrendered myself to the chief temptation of the artist, creation without toil" (A, 202).

Still editorializing about the past from the vantage-point of nearly thirty years, Yeats suggests that, although he has not served his own writing by fighting the "rancour" (A, 206) of Ireland's melodramatic reconstruction of its history, he has unknowingly eased the way for Synge. The very characteristics which made his political work so personally useless become one-half of a new view of Ireland, summed up in an antinomic image central to *The Trembling of the Veil:*

I had . . . a conviction that we should satirize rather than praise, that original virtue arises from the discovery of evil. If we were, as I had dreaded, declamatory, loose, and bragging, we were but the better fitted—that declared and measured—to create unyielding personality, manner at once cold and passionate, daring long-premeditated act; and if bitter beyond all the people of the world, we might yet lie—that too declared and measured—nearest the honeycomb:—

> Like the clangour of a bell
> Sweet and harsh, harsh and sweet,
> That is how he learnt so well
> To take the roses for his meat. (A, 207)

Some pages later in *Autobiographies,* Yeats again uses this antithesis of "bitterness" and "honeyed comb," this time with reference to Parnell: "he might have brought the imagination of Ireland nearer the Image and the honeycomb" (A, 221).[9] If the image and the lines from

"Another Song of a Fool" *(The Wild Swans at Coole,* 1919) only slightly anticipate the composition of *The Trembling of the Veil,* Yeats's characterization of Ireland as a nation of extreme antinomies dates from his earliest youth,[10] and the specific antithesis of harshness and sweetness for a powerful nation from a 1904 address celebrating the birth of Robert Emmet.[11]

As he so often does, Yeats has fused several contexts in this image for an antithesis which had long been in his thought. He himself explained something of its origins when he later cited, in a note to "Among School Children," Porphyry's *Concerning the Cave of the Nymphs* as the source of the phrase "honey of generation" (VPo, 828).[12] Porphyry traces three symbolical uses of honey: it "is assumed in purgations, and as an antidote to putrefaction, and aptly represents the pleasure and delight of descending into the fascinating realms of generation."[13] Yeats uses the first signification in the phrase "nearer the Image and the honeycomb"; he fuses the second with an allusion to Samson's riddle in the last stanza of "Vacillation" and in *Autobiographies.* The connotation of "delight of descending into . . . generation" Yeats unites with other sources and generalizes well beyond its original significance. It already appears in the early epithet "Baille Honeymouth," perhaps echoing Venus' promise in *Marius the Epicurean* of a kiss "full of the inmost honey of her throat."[14] It reappears in the sexual metaphor for Unity of Being which controls several of the later poems[15] and, having assumed the additional context of Coventry Patmore's "The Precursor," becomes the image underlying the lunar symbolism of *A Vision.* Patmore had drawn an analogy between St. John the Baptist and Christ, between "natural love" and "supernatural love" (VII, 212),[16] defining honey as the signifier of that "natural love,"[17] St. John as " *'Precursor'* "[18] of "Divine Love."[19] Yeats defines "natural love" more explicitly as "sexual love," used by antithetical man as a method and symbol of self-transcendence, by drawing attention to Patmore's "pleasure" in the similarities of Leonardo's figures of St. John and Dionysus and asserting that identification as the basis of his own philosophical system: "all the symbolism of this book applies to begetting and birth, for all things are a single form which has divided and multiplied in time and space" (VII, 212). If Yeats's use of "the honeyed comb" in *Autobiographies* owes something to all these contexts, his antithesis between it and bitterness he draws specifically from Porphyry who notes that the ancients also considered honey "as a symbol of death, in the same manner as gall is of life," signifying "that death is the end of evils, but that the present life is laborious and bitter."[20] That antithesis he had already paraphrased in "Swedenborg, Mediums, and the Desolate

71

Places" where he represents the spirits as telling us that "The sorrow of death . . . is not so bitter as the sorrow of birth" (Ex, 48). "The full soul loatheth an honeycomb; but to the hungry soul every bitter thing is sweet" (Proverbs, 27, v. 7): that formulation of the antithesis takes us back to the occult for it heads the first plate of *The Secret Symbols of the Rosicrucians.* [21] In Rosicrucian doctrine, the beehive—and, by metonymy, the honeycomb—is a symbol of Unity recalling, in its pyramidal shape, the tower, in its layers, the winding path around the *mons philosophorum.* That association had doubtless been the source of John Sherman's pleasure at finding a house with "a row of beehives under a hedge" (JS&D, 103) on his return to Ballah and of the youthful poet's oft-quoted desire to have "a hive for the honey-bee,/ And live alone in the bee-loud glade."

In *Autobiographies,* Yeats further complicates his allusion to the honeycomb by quoting from "Another Song of a Fool," the song of the schoolmaster metamorphosed into a butterfly. Schoolmaster and butterfly long represented for Yeats the straight and generally arid path of logic and the more indirect and creative way of intuition. The bell of these lines not only tolls time—baptism, marriage, and death—, but its tones—"Sweet and harsh, harsh and sweet"—duplicate the bitterness and the honeycomb. This reference to the honey moves beyond the original sexual or "natural" signification of the image; it becomes the honey which, in Samson's riddle, symbolizes spiritual sweetness preventing bodily corruption, meat out of the devourer, sweetness out of strength, through God's miracle or, in Yeatsian terms, Unity of Being: "The lion and the honeycomb, what has Scripture said?" (VPo, 503). The final reference to "Roses for his meat" recalls Yeats's and Patmore's "Precursor" of "Divine Love" and self-transcendence. Substituting roses for "wild honey," Yeats brings a large body of new allusion to bear on the rose, the symbol of unity he had already used so extensively in his earlier poetry, and reinforces his emphasis on Unity of Being as means of personal and national salvation in an increasingly fragmented world.

But the Irish have not "declared and measured" themselves and Synge as this hoped for embodiment in a writer of Ireland's Unity of Being remains some fifteen years in the future of the events Yeats narrates in "Ireland after Parnell." Faced with the contemporary failure of nationalism as a cohesive force, Yeats can only change direction once again. In the "one house where nobody thought or talked politics" (A, 236) he finds a group of Theosophists with whom he develops his interest in the occult. The antithetical structure with which he sets himself as artist against George Russell, [22] saint or primary man, both rationalizes his defection from politics and foreshadows his failure to find Unity of Being through the study of theosophy. "I thought there could be no aim for poet or artist except expression of a

'Unity of Being' like that of a 'perfectly proportioned human body'"
(A, 246), he writes of himself. But Russell belongs to that group of
men—the saint, "the man of science, the moralist, the humanitarian, the
politician,"—who must seek no anti-self, "no image of desire, but await
that which lies beyond their mind—unities not of the mind, but unities
of Nature, unities of God" (A, 247). Yeats's unity must be with his self,
theirs with a form outside the self. Politics suffers in this contrast,
dealing as it does with mere power, whereas Art, through artifice,
embodies the instinctual, the innate tradition passed from generation to
generation as birds pass on the skill of nest-building: "politics, for a
vision-seeking man, can be but half achievement, a choice of an almost
easy kind of skill instead of that kind which is, of all those not
impossible, the most difficult. Is it not certain that the Creator yawns
in earthquake and thunder and other popular displays, but toils in
rounding the delicate spiral of a shell?" (A, 249). [23] Not only are
power—"brute blood"— and artifice opposed in this metaphor, but the
shell's spiral is synonymous with Yeats's symbol of unity out of
conflicting forces, expanding and contracting gyres. The image places
the poet at "A new beginning, a new turn of the wheel" (Ex, 337), and
the characterization of Russell's vision as antithetical to Yeats's suggests
that if the poet has found an image of his anti-self in the house at Ely
Place, he has not yet transcended opposites to achieve the Unity of
Being he desires.

IV

As was Yeats's earlier change of direction, so this turning from political
nationalism to the occult is accompanied by the "wildest hopes"
"that this philosophy would find its manuals of devotion in all
imaginative literature, and set before Irishmen for special manual an
Irish literature which, though made by many minds, would seem the
work of a single mind, and turn our places of beauty or legendary association into holy symbols" (A, 254). [24] However, in "Hodos
Chameliontos," Yeats recalls neither himself nor Ireland as on the way
to Unity of Being but as overwhelmed by the multiplicity and fragmentation of the images he pursues. Obsessive questions which go un-
answered the better to represent the youthful Yeats's confusion, fill the
narrative and all his evidence of Unity of Being is represented as merely
having increased his personal sense of fragmentation: "To that
multiplicity of interest and opinion, of arts and sciences, which had
driven me to conceive a Unity of Culture defined and evoked by Unity
of Image, I had but added a multiplicity of images . . ." (A, 269); "I
was . . . astray upon the Path of the Chameleon" (A, 270). That sense of
fragmentation Yeats reflects in the style and structure of the chapter;
anecdotes and questions are often brief, seemingly unrelated,

juxtaposed without transitions as they are in the narrative of Michael's quest among the various occult groups in *The Speckled Bird.*

Sections VIII and IX of "Hodos Chameliontos" contrast strongly with the increasing fragmentation evident throughout *The Trembling of the Veil,* first in the failure of artists and writers to achieve harmony between their self and anti-self, then in Ireland's refusal to accept her Image or Mask, and finally in the outright chaos of the occult in which "image called up image in an endless procession" (A, 270). Against this confusion experienced by his autobiographical subject, the young man, Yeats sets the more composed image of the "settled man" (A, 270) writing that autobiography. The passages that follow constitute a most marked intrusion of the authorial present—"the canaries have just hatched out five nestlings" (A, 270)—to reverse the direction of *The Trembling of the Veil.* The mature Yeats explains both his "ungovernable craving" (A, 264) and his youthful mistaking of the proper method by which to seek its satisfaction by reference to innate learning. His canaries' building of a nest when he has placed the requisite materials in their cage, his small daughter's sexual and maternal instincts: these now constitute his evidence of *anima mundi,* of a "knowledge or power," both primal and universal from "beyond" the mind (A, 272), which informs creative action. "An image"—the grass he gave his canaries, the felt movements of the foetus—evokes the creative response "but our images must be given to us," as he gave the canaries their nest-building materials, "we cannot choose them deliberately" (A, 272). The poet becomes "lost" through striving to choose, through attempting to create a false mythology.

The images of the mating canaries and their nestlings, of his young daughter already sexually and maternally responsive, are emblematic of the sexual union, in both its orgasmic and procreative aspects, as the basic metaphor of Yeats's pattern of dualities and their resolution through the generation of the self. In the long passage which follows his examples, Yeats re-expresses that pattern, citing analogues from literary tradition: "I know now that revelation is from the self, but from that age-long memoried self, that shapes the elaborate shell of the mollusc and the child in the womb, that teaches the birds to make their nest; and that genius is a crisis that joins that buried self for certain moments to our trivial daily mind . . . . Dante and Villon . . . through passion become conjoint to their buried selves, turn all to Mask and Image . . ." (A, 272-73).[25] Applying the imagery of union and subsequent rebirth which informs *The Trembling of the Veil,* Yeats continues, "We gaze at such men in awe, because we gaze not at a work of art, but at the re-creation of the man through that art, the birth of a new species of man" (A, 273). Keats, he quotes himself, "coarse-bred son of a livery-stable keeper," makes "Luxuriant song" (A, 275). Pivotal within the structure of *The Trembling of the Veil,* the passage marks a turning from optimism, "wildest hopes," always to be scattered, to necessary pessimism, the conviction that Unity of Being can be achieved only at the price of a Body of Fate productive of personal crisis and loss: "Had not Dante and Villon understood that their fate wrecked what life could not rebuild, had they lacked their Vision of Evil, had they cherished any species of optimism, they could but have found a false beauty, or some momentary instinctive beauty, and suffered no change at all . . ." (A, 273). Yeats's philosophical statements inevitably arise from the need to explain himself and this anagogic interpretation of Renaissance literature is no exception. The analogy between literary tradition and Yeats's personal and nationalistic interests follows directly: "And these things are true also of nations . . . . And as I look backward upon my own writing, I take pleasure alone in those verses where it seems to me I have found something hard and cold, some articulation of the Image which is the opposite of all that I am in my daily life, and all that my country is . . ." (A, 274). The juxtaposition suggests that Unity of Being will be born of the confrontation of auto-biography and myth. For the birth to take place a transformative pessimism is as necessary to the contemporary nation and its poet as it was to the transfiguring vision of a Dante or Villon.[26] Where the first two chapters of *The Trembling of the Veil* recorded the hope of synthesis, the last two record this necessary disillusion, failure and fatalistic despair, culminating in a moment of rebirth.

V

> Acquaintance; companion;
> One dear brilliant woman;
> The best-endowed, the elect,
> All by their youth undone,
> All, all, by that inhuman
> Bitter glory wrecked.
> But I have straightened out
> Ruin, wreck and wrack;
> I toiled long years and at length
> Came to so deep a thought
> I can summon back
> All their wholesome strength. (VPo, 504-05)

Written in 1931, "The Results of Thought" aptly summarizes "The Tragic Generation" which consistently presents its personae as "by their youth undone" and by "that inhuman/Bitter glory wrecked." And if *Autobiographies* hardly leaves us with an impression of "their whole-some strength," it certainly does reveal Yeats casting himself as a "deep considering mind," shaping his subject matter, straightening it out, distorting, condensing, omitting, exaggerating facts to impose pattern on what he now chose to see as "Ruin, wreck and wrack."[27]

Ian Fletcher has remarked Yeats's over-dramatization in "Four

75

Years" of his role in the founding of The Rhymers' Club and his failure to list members other than those that he knew well.[28] Fletcher does not choose between "stylisation" or "simple forgetfulness" (and Olney[29] suggests that forgetfulness is a stylistic mode in Yeats) as motive for Yeats's "inaccuracies" but, whatever the cause, they result in the identification of The Rhymers with "The Tragic Generation."[30] Where "Four Years" and "Ireland after Parnell" have traced aspirations, never successfully realized, to find through literary and political organization a Unity of Culture in Ireland comparable to Unity of Being in the individual, "The Tragic Generation" and "The Stirring of the Bones" mark both Yeats's realization of his failure and his intimations of a new path to Unity. Thus "The Tragic Generation" formulates a response to his earlier characterization of The Rhymers: "'The only thing certain about us is that we are too many'" (A, 171). In recording the disintegration of both this democratic assemblage and the remainder of the youthful Yeats's circle, it begins to postulate an aristocracy of the arts, to intensify the transcendence of the quotidian self, to mythologize the "true self" which Yeats aimed at in poetry and autobiography.

Yeats structures the central sections of "The Tragic Generation" with analogies between anecdote or literary gossip and his lunar "symbolism" (A, 293), each illustrating the other and both pointing to the failure to attain that Unity of Culture which had been the goal, even if not always so precisely formulated, of the young poet. Wilde's downfall, described in Section II, is explained in Section III by reference to Yeats's lunar system. He belongs to Phase Nineteen, the phase which marks "a sudden change" from the more completely antithetical minds closer to the full of the moon, but which has not yet achieved the "professional and abstract" (A, 293) climax of the age. His nature belongs to just that point where "no mind made like 'a perfectly proportioned human body' shall sway the public" (A, 293) again. Out of phase with his time, just past those phases where men can attain to complete immersion in the self, his posing or seeking after an Image becomes self-caricature. He divides the stage with Shaw, a man in phase with the age, a man "quite content to exchange Narcissus and his Pool for the signal-box at a railway junction, where goods and travellers pass perpetually upon their logical glittering road" (A, 294).

Yeats finds an analogue for the two dramatists in two portraits. In Strozzi's portrait of a Venetian gentleman he sees subjective predominance, man living in and through "his whole body" (A, 292). Strozzi's portrait epitomizes the artist's transcendence of his everyday self through a completely antithetical nature, a transcendence which remained just of of Wilde's reach. In contrast, Sargent's portrait of President Wilson, mechanical and dead in all except the eyes, explores the abstraction characterizing Shavian rhetoric. Nonetheless it is Shaw and Sargent who are one with their time and that reflection

Bernardo Strozzi: *Portrait of a Gentleman*. Oil on Canvas. Courtesy of the National Gallery of Ireland.

introduces the pattern of defeat, disintegration and self-defense which pervades the last two chapters of *The Trembling of the Veil*. The age, Yeats felt, stood on the edge of a void, on the verge of complete abstraction and superficiality, of the individual's absolute divorce from the self: "Neither his crowd nor he [Shaw] have yet made a discovery . . . that the moon draws to its fourth quarter. But what happens to the individual man whose moon has come to that fourth quarter, and what to the civilization . . . ?" (A, 294). This is no mere rhetorical question. Much of the despair of "The Tragic Generation" lies in the fact that, editorializing the past as he is at this moment, Yeats implies the answer in ethereal and half-remembered pipe music which gives way to a single certainty, that "the dream of my early manhood, that a modern nation can return to Unity of Culture, is false" (A, 295). Lines from "The Phases of the Moon" signal the change and introduce a certain Stoic despair and resignation to the individual, rather than the nation, as the unit of modern consciousness and activity.

The absence of Unity of Being in Yeats's contemporaries personifies the fragmented nature of the time. The "disorder" of The Rhymers' lives is the expression of an " 'age of transition' "; they "lacked coherence" as the result of that age (A, 304). Pater symbolizes the tragedy of the transition: *"Marius the Epicurean* . . . taught us to walk upon a rope tightly stretched through serene air, and we were left to keep our feet upon a swaying rope in a storm" (A, 302-03). Yeats's fellow poets fall off that rope in "The Tragic Generation," always illustrating his antithetical structure as they do so. Johnson and Dowson represent saint and sexual sinner, pre-figuring the Martyn-Moore antithesis of *Dramatis Personae;* Johnson's "spiritual ecstasy," Yeats hypothesizes, heightened "the Vision of Evil" (A, 310) he appreciated in Villon and Dante; Dowson, idealistically and romantically in love, copulates with whores. Saint and sinner are united in the characterization of Beardsley whom Yeats explains as having come to see with "a kind of frozen passion, the virginity of the intellect" (A, 332), the erotic and vicious apparitions moving before his eyes.

The ironies of the failure to achieve Unity of Being multiply in "The Tragic Generation" until its characters become not so much tragic as forlorn. Their masks fall. Fascinated as many of these men may have been a Vision of Evil and by a tragic purpose, in fact they attained to nothing so absolute. Theirs was neither the Unity of Being nor the transfiguring gaiety (VPo, 565) of tragedy. Instead their wavering indirection and lack of Unity, the sordidness of much of their activity, typify the incohesiveness and inconclusiveness of the age. One of Yeats's seemingly disordered memories reiterates this misdirection with a mordant wit and demonstrates the effectiveness of his anecdotes in

John Singer Sargent: *Woodrow Wilson*. Oil on Canvas. Courtesy of the National Gallery of Ireland.

"The Tragic Generation." The sexual union which is the metaphor behind his concept of Unity of Being and which is parodied or degenerate in "The Tragic Generation" is made ironically revelatory of the time in a story about MacGregor Mathers: "Mathers is much troubled by ladies who seek spiritual advice, and one has called to ask his help against phantoms who have the appearance of decayed corpses, and try to get into bed with her at night. He has driven her away with one furious sentence, 'Very bad taste on both sides'" (A, 346).

The fragmented memories with which this chapter ends, as have the others, reflect the incoherence among his fellows and in his country and historical period. As he did in "Ireland after Parnell," Yeats turns to the historic present tense. His use of the tense in *Reveries over Childhood and Youth* is attributable to the discontinuousness of early memories and to the vividness of their recollection. But in *The Trembling of the Veil,* although Yeats does use the historic present in many anecdotal fragments, both the tense and those fragments suggest something beyond mere discontinuity or the attempt of the Romantic historians to create an impression of action by use of the present which Fletcher cites as Yeats's model.[31] The Romantics derive their use of the historic present from its similar use in moments of intense action or excitement in epic literature. However, Yeats, in his reading of these epics, seems to have responded as markedly to the fall of Troy as to the battles preceding it, to consequences which assumed mythic proportions as to the particular actions causing them, to cyclic rather than individual history. While his use of the historic present undoubtedly owes a good deal to its Romantic adaptation to create a sense of action, it also derives from its epic use in moments of despair, defeat and crumbling civilizations to create a pathos and poignancy that yet does not lack sublimity. It is the historic present of those moments in the *Aeneid* when images of defeat overpower historic fact, when the historic present takes over from the perfect in the reiteration of that fact: "ceciditque superbum/Ilium et omnis humo fumat Neptunia Troja." Moreover Yeats relies heavily on the copulative in his use of the historic present, both at the end of "The Tragic Generation," where he records images for the lack of coherence in a literary movement, and in "The Stirring of the Bones," where he presents events as discrete, unrelated to one another by style or logic, to record a similar lack of cohesiveness in Irish political movements. Yeats himself is minimally active in these memories: "I am at Stuart Merrill's" (A, 347), he tells us, or "at Maud Gonne's hotel" (A, 370), at "the Mansion House Banquet" (A, 366) or "sitting in a café" (A, 347). The copulative diminishes his action, transforms him into a passive register of what goes on around him: " I am walking . . . when Synge . . . says" (A, 346), he begins; he does not *feel* sad but tells us that "I am very sad" (A, 348). At the same time, the passive voice and the linking verb consistently leave him present at his own memories as an observer rather than a participant: "It is eight or nine at night" (A, 367); "The meeting is held in College Green" (A, 367); "Mathers is much troubled" (A, 346) and "I am told" (A, 371); "French sympathizers have been brought" (A, 369). He turns himself and others into surfaces on which the record of fragmentation inscribes itself; "I notice" (A, 346, 371) introduces his observations. This historic present tense with its strong associations with epic and heroic poetry, combined as it is with the copulative verb and the passive voice, assumes ironic nuances in *The Trembling of the Veil* where it reflects the crumbling of a cultural and national unity that are never quite achieved, that never quite reach heroic proportions or produce a " 'sacred book.' "

The last two of the fragmented memories concluding "The Tragic Generation" concern the theatre and indeed the theatrical metaphor[32] has been almost as dominant as the "Lunar parable" throughout the chapter. The collapse of The Rhymers' Club, the chapter's central event, finds its metaphor in the stage: "The Rhymers had begun to break up in tragedy, though we did not know that till the play had finished" (A, 300). Both the plays of Ibsen and Shaw which open the chapter and that which closes it, framing it, as it were, in a metaphor of drama, personify the abstraction and lack of coherence for which Yeats blamed his time. Ibsen and Shaw both hit at Yeats's "enemies" (A, 279, 283) but with methods he cannot accept. Their "inorganic, logical straightness," memorably imaged as a clicking, shining, perpetually smiling sewing machine, is far removed from his own mythic approach to literature and from "the crooked road of life" (A, 283). The performance of *Ubu Roi* which closes the chapter is another harbinger of "objectivity." Père Ubu, wielding power with a murderous autocracy that quickly becomes absurd, coining innumerable oaths out of Rabelasian archaisms and cloacal, ranarian imagery—"if it be life to pitch/Into the frog-spawn of a blind man's ditch"—throwing a toilet-brush across the stage, moving like a puppet, [33] behaves and speaks in a style characterized by emotional and intellectual falsity: "comedy, objectivity, has displayed its growing power once more. I say: 'After Stéphane Mallarmé, after Paul Verlaine, after Gustave Moreau, after Puvis de Chavannes, after our own verse, after all our subtle colour and nervous rhythm, after the faint mixed tints of Conder, what is more possible? After us the Savage God' " (A, 348-49).

Between these productions which open and close "The Tragic Generation, " Yeats places two references to the drama which point a way out of the abstractionist void. One, an analysis of Synge in terms of his lunar characterology, looks ahead to the long meditation on that playwright which underlies much of the rest of *Autobiographies*. Synge, unlike Wilde who suffers in an age moving into abstraction through

81

being too close to the antithetical mode of self-realization, or Shaw whom Yeats considers to be completely in step with his age, has passed the moment of crisis when abstraction begins to dominate. Rather than seek union with an Image of the self, he moves towards disinterested union with that outside himself: he "had to take the first plunge into the world beyond himself, the first plunge away from himself that is always pure technique, the delight in doing, not because one would or should, but merely because one can do" (A, 344). Hence Yeats's praise of his use of dialect; it enables him to "escape self-expression" and to "see all that he did from without, allow his intellect to judge the images of his mind as if they had been created by some other mind" (A, 345). He uses the primary mode of creation as Yeats uses the antithetical, to create the passionate moment.

The central dramatic image of "The Tragic Generation," however, involves "some Herodiade of our theatre" and piles metaphor upon metaphor of Unity of Being. A remembrance of Symons' reading to Yeats from Mallarmé's "Hérodiade" evokes the Salomé passage. In the lines quoted from Mallarmé,[34] Salomé ostensibly speaks to her nurse; actually she addresses the moon, Yeatsian symbol of the antithetical self's having attained to complete Unity of Being. Yeats repeats the symbol by equating the circle of the spotlight, another full moon, with that Unity: "Yet I am certain that there was something in myself compelling me to attempt creation of an art as separate from everything heterogeneous and casual, from all character and circumstance, as some Herodiade of our theatre, dancing seemingly alone in her narrow moving luminous circle" (A, 321).

His use of Salomé as embodiment of both virginity and Vision of Evil, as the instrument by which the self transcends itself and this world, is not particular to Yeats in the nineteenth century. He would have known the myth in its dualistic aspect from Flaubert's "Hérodias" in which Salomé, the tool of her mother's evil, makes her terrible request with a child's lisping naiveté. Much else would have forced it on his attention: Wilde's *Salomé,* two paintings by Gustave Moreau—*La Danse de Salomé* and *L'Apparition—*, Huysmans' detailed description of both these pictures in *A Rebours*[35] and his association of them with lines he quotes from Mallarmé's "Hérodiade."[36] In a note to "The Hosting of the Sidhe" Yeats recalls that the Sidhe "journey in whirling winds, the winds that were called the dance of the daughters of Herodias in the Middle Ages" (VPo, 800)[37] and in "Nineteen Hundred and Nineteen" he had used "Herodias' daughters," blind now and whirled "in the labyrinth of the wind" (VPo, 433), as image of chaotic violence. The metaphor is rich with the ambiguity Yeats liked best. Salomé as whirlwind embodies the conflicting opposites of his gyres; Salomé as single dancer, both in her person and in the moon-like circle of light in which she moves, embodies the Unity to which the conflict gives rise. Thus, in his *Journal,* Yeats finds "a visionary beauty" (Mem, 284) in Beardsley's *Salomé with the Head of John the Baptist,* and, in one of the scenarios of *The Player Queen,* the actress clearly becomes a Salomé figure. " 'If I did not love him [Martin] better than my own soul would I do him so much evil? ' " she rhetorically asks, then goes on to desire the part of Hérodias, for " 'When I dance . . . I wish to make my soul greater, I wish to be something I have only dreamt of, I wish to hit the moon with my head, I wish to become a flame that men can warm themselves by and light themselves by.' " [38] In three of his late plays,[39] Yeats would alter the myth to make his Salomé figure the equivalent of "the veil of the temple"; "A screen between the living and the dead" (VPl, 993), she dances before a severed head, attaining to Unity of Being, symbolized by a sexual embrace, through adoration of her opposite, life dancing to death, royalty dancing to minstrel or swineherd, in an ecstasy of commingled attraction and repulsion. Dancer and dance, for both Yeats and Symons, [40] had long been images of Unity of Being and, in *A Vision,* Yeats equates the dance with the Great Wheel itself (VII, 80). He intensifies his metaphor for antithetical man completely immersed in self by making his dancers single; one recalls all these Salomé figures and the indistinguishable dancer and dance from the end of "Among School Children." The whirling dancer, like her association with whirlwinds, provides another visual synonym for the Yeatsian gyre; in *A Vision* Yeats refers to the gyres touching the sides of "the ascending cone" of a particular civilization as creating "the horizontal dance" (VII, 270; cf. VI, 182: "the horizontal movement").

Yeats's evocation of "Herodiade" presents a possibility of Unity of Being through art in its images of moon and spotlight, dance and dancer, the dancer being associated in this case with St. John the Baptist and, therefore, with the earlier symbol of the honeycomb. But by citing this "Herodiade" in her "luminous circle," Yeats not only creates a visual analogue to his moon symbol and alludes to a multiplicity of other images of Unity of Being, he also lends the myth dramatic life, extends it in space and time. He transfigures it to make it simultaneously myth, and, acted out, biography. On the philosophical plane, this literal "revelation" corresponds to the moment of "revelation" within a culture when the gyres reverse their directions, the moment within an individual life or within the rise and fall of a civilization when all cycles—biographical, historical and mythic—become analogues of all others. Within the context of autobiography, the desire to create "an art as separate from everything heterogeneous and casual, from all character and circumstance, as some Herodiade of our theatre" suggests a resonance among the personal striving towards Unity of Being, the moment of historic change, and mythic cycles of change and recurrence.

VI

Because, in Yeats's metaphor, his age belonged to a descending gyre, the possibilities inherent in the moment of change prove abortive at the historical level. In the structure of *The Trembling of the Veil*, "The Stirring of the Bones" stands to "Ireland after Parnell" as "The Tragic Generation" stood to "Four Years." It traces the disillusion and disintegration which reverse the "wildest hopes" of the earlier chapter; it acknowledges that the "deliberately chosen experiences" (A, 354) meant to lead to Unity of Being have led instead to a path of personal error.

An imagery of destruction clings to the discussion of Ireland throughout this chapter, an imagery counterbalanced by one of personal rebirth. Recognizing the impossibility of Unity of Culture in Ireland, the young man has persisted in hoping against hope for the nation's spiritual regeneration: "Seeing that only the individual soul can attain to its spiritual opposite, a nation in tumult must needs pass to and fro between mechanical opposites, but one hopes always that those opposites may acquire sex and engender" (A, 360). However, in "The Stirring of the Bones," the participants, as well as the movement, reveal self and anti-self, unreconciled opposites, destroying one another, never engendering Unity of Culture.

In his narrative of the procession to the Wolfe Tone Memorial and the dedication of its corner-stone—an occasion that should be symbolic of national unity—, Yeats once again abandons his more connected narrative for short fragments in which the historic present dominates and ellipses replace transition. These ellipses indicate fragmentation of personality and culture as well as discontinuity of visual images. Redmond's overheard remark reveals Unity dissolved in petty pushing for "place and precedence" (A, 366) in the procession and Yeats himself gives way to the crowd's "abstract passion" (A, 366) while listening to Dillon's speech. Recollections of Victoria's Jubilee are associated, in the same fragmented style, with James Connolly, prefiguring the Easter Uprising and "the growing murderousness of the world." The evening of the Jubilee, Yeats once again loses himself in the violence of the crowd. Unable to raise his voice above a whisper because, he suggests, of the day of public speaking he has just ended, he can do nothing; he feels himself "freed from responsibility" and can "share the emotion of the crowd" (A, 367-68). The suggestion that the inability to speak frees one from responsibility is less than convincing but, whether or not one accepts Yeats's explanation, he clearly presents us, in his involvement with the crowd, with a crisis of conscience existing at both the national and the personal levels.

Yeats's account here differs considerably from that in *Memoirs*. There, having "resigned" himself, he feels "the excitement of the moment, that joyous irresponsibility and sense of power." The emphasis lies on his restraint of Maud Gonne and the conflict between them; his inability to speak remains more incidental. The return of conscience is more dramatic: "That night I went to all the newspaper offices and took responsibility for my action." Yeats deleted from the manuscript of "First Draft" the phrases, "and asked the editors not to attack the police. I had an idea that the police could be won over" (Mem, 113). The deletion suggests that he successively modified his accounts of the event in order to present an image of himself as self-possessed. In *Autobiographies,* the next morning's newspaper accounts of damage and injury induce a poetic statement of returned conscience: "I count the links in the chain of responsibility, run them across my fingers, and wonder if any link there is from my workshop" (A, 368). Clearly Yeats moves from a relatively detailed and "truthful" account of his role in the riots to one that is designed to transform autobiographical fact so that it might mesh with the larger pattern of tragic failure to achieve Unity of Culture.

In the 1926 and all subsequent editions of *Autobiographies* [41] a complex vision shared among several people effects the transition from national to personal breakdown: Yeats sees, "between sleeping and waking, as in a kinematograph, a galloping centaur, and a moment later a naked woman of incredible beauty, standing upon a pedestal and shooting an arrow at a star" (A, 372). Symons has a sympathetic vision and very soon after receives a story recording the same vision from Fiona MacLeod (William Sharp): "Some one in the story had a vision of a woman shooting an arrow into the sky and later of an arrow shot at a faun that pierced the faun's body and remained, the faun's heart torn out and clinging to it, embedded in a tree" (A, 373). Within a short time, two children unknown to Yeats have similar visions. With considerable credulity, he chose to regard this shared vision as an instance of thought transference [42]; as such it seemed to promise an archetypal knowledge. In the text of *Autobiographies,* Yeats interprets the vision in terms of the cabbalistic Tree of Life. The arrow represents the straight path of "'deliberate effort'" through the tree as opposed to the path of the serpent, "the winding path of nature or of instinct" (A, 375), a distinction Yeats knew from the Ritual Opening of the O=O Grade of The Order of The Golden Dawn. It is the path of the sage or primary man and seems to promise "'a wisdom older than the serpent'" (A, 375) through the "'deliberate effort'" involved in the study of magic. [43] The star is analogous to the "'golden heart [which] is the central point upon the cabbalistic Tree of Life'" (A, 374); it corresponds to the sun. In Cabbalism, the sphere attributed to the sun is joined to that attributed to the moon "by a straight line called the path Samekh" (A, 375), a line that again opposes the winding of the serpent. The vision would seem, then, to promise the wisdom of the sage through the cultivation of magic.

In this representation of the dream, Yeats has been faithful to his experience of it, to what he learned about it at the time it occurred and to his own error in believing Unity of Being could be achieved through a consciously chosen Mask; he has not stepped outside the temporal scheme of the autobiography. However, in notes to the vision, he provides a second interpretation made with the advantage of more recently gained knowledge.[44] The vision, he claims, explains a sentence uttered by a woman in a trance: "'live near water and avoid woods because they concentrate the solar ray'" (A, 371). Water is associated in occult and astrological systems with the moon; Yeats thought the sun, by association with the Tree of Life, symbolized the star at which the woman of the vision had shot the arrow. The medium's sentence is thus explained: "my invocation had for its object the killing or overcoming in some way of a 'solar influence'" (A, 578). The poet's path is not that of Samekh, of the straight line of the arrow shot at the sun, but that of the serpent.[45] Yeats has finally found an answer to his dilemma in "Hodos Chameliontos," for to follow the path of Samekh, according to Golden Dawn doctrine, the initiate must "have a perfect and absolute knowledge of the Bow" that shoots the arrow. "But the Bow is of brilliant and perfect colour whose analysis and synthesis yield others of the same scale"[46]; the path of its arrow is the Path of the Chameleon. Only by abandoning that path, the path of the philosopher-sage, will Yeats achieve Unity. For him, Unity of Being is with the self, not with some force external to that self; life and imagination must become one.

In this initial presentation of the dream, Yeats had noted that the Cabbalists "attributed" the path Samekh, the straight line joining the spheres of sun and moon, "to the constellation Sagittarius" (A, 375). In his notes to the vision, he quotes a definition of the constellation Sagittarius: "'The symbol is an arrow shot into the unknown. It is a sign of Initiation and Rebirth'" (A, 579). With the introduction of "Initiation and Rebirth" and in the context of the notes, the dream assumes an interpretation from two myths: that of Cybele slaying her lover (in some versions her son), Attis, or having him slain, with an arrow and that of the slain Dionysus whose heart was saved by his sister Minerva and was enclosed by Jupiter in an image of the boy. In both cases, elaborate rites mimicked and celebrated the sacrificial death and rebirth of the god. Yeats elsewhere uses the Dionysian version in specific references to seasonal rebirth: the opening song of *The Resurrection* draws an analogy between the yearly event and the larger cycle of "Magnus Annus." In "Parnell's Funeral" and songs in *A Full Moon in March,* he fused the two variations of the myth. Yeats's notes to "Parnell's Funeral" tell us that he thought of the shot star of the poem as symbol of "accepted sacrifice" and that he linked it particularly with the notes he provided in *Autobiographies* to the archer vision (VPo, 834).

Yeats's self-effacement in *The Trembling of the Veil* in favour of "The Tragic Generation" has been frequently remarked[47] and a letter he wrote to Olivia Shakespear as he completed "Four Years" (Dec. 22, 1921) has served to reinforce the impression that this self-effacement was part of the deliberate patterning of *Autobiographies:* "I study every man I meet at some moment of crisis—I alone have no crisis" (L, 675). But the introduction into the 1926 edition of *The Trembling of the Veil* of the archer vision belies this earlier statement of intention. Where the initial version of *The Trembling of the Veil* had showed Yeats's acquaintances each approaching a moment of crisis and each ultimately failing to find his simplifying image, the interpolated vision serves to show Yeats himself at a similar moment of crisis, to show him faced with the antithetical choice his contemporaries failed to make in their own best interests: he may continue to pursue the path of the arrow, to seek out deliberately his Mask as does the philosopher, or he may follow the path of the serpent, of instinct, and accept his Mask as it is given him.

Drafting the lecture "Friends of My Youth," Yeats had summarized his survival of "The Tragic Generation": "I can understand that generation, for I was of it. I almost shared its curse without any excess to help the strain of the emotion which was the foundation of our work. The only thing in life that we valued [lyric emotion] left me at last worn out with a nervous excitement. I renounced a lyrical mood that I might remake myself" (FMY, 69). This personal note Yeats excised before delivering the lecture nor did it ever find its way as direct statement into *Autobiographies;* however, it does accurately describe the pattern of "crisis" behind his interpolation of the archer vision into the second vision of "The Stirring of the Bones." His renunciation of the lyrical mood of the 1890s is the necessary sacrifice which leads to the rebirth intimated in the analogies between his vision and myth; the acceptance of the import of the vision—and, indeed, the extreme credulity with which he accepted William Sharp/Fiona Macleod's tardy report of his sympathetic experience—suggests his willingness to accept his Mask as it is given him. His visit to Coole Park and the consequent founding of an Irish Theatre will make that acceptance emphatic. The correct choice having been made, the closing passages of *The Trembling of the Veil* see the poet and nascent dramatist rewarded with revelation.

Yeats separates the account of the archer vision from that of the beginning of his work with Lady Gregory by ellipsis rather than by beginning a new section, another signal in *Autobiographies* that the two events are not strictly related through logical transition, but are meant to resonate in a manner suggesting the operations of Fate. The link between the two is made stronger by his explicit temporal association of the dream and his first visit to Coole and the dream's associations with death and rebirth are reiterated in his relations with Lady Gregory: their mutual interest in the occult assumes the role of Cybele, slayer and saviour. Yeats represents himself as on the verge of physical and mental collapse when he first goes to Coole: "I was in poor health," he confesses, made incapable of sustained work by "the strain of youth . . . and I had lost myself besides . . . upon Hodos Chameliontos . . . . I had got there through a novel [*The Speckled Bird*] that I could neither write nor cease to write which had Hodos Chameliontos for its theme . . . . It is not so much that I choose too many elements, as that the possible unities themselves seem without number . . ." (A, 376). In this passage, Yeats again deliberately altered the emphasis on certain experiences to stress the significance of antithetical pattern in *The Trembling of the Veil*. A manuscript of the account of his work with Lady Gregory gives his unhappy love for Maud Gonne as a source of his nervousness[48]; *Memoirs* suggests that both Maud Gonne and his political activities contributed to it; "Friends of My Youth" blames the nervous energy behind the lyricism of The Rhymers. But all these are minimized in *Autobiographies* in favour of the occult. Within the framework of the occult, Yeats's dissipation of his own energies in a deliberate seeking of a Mask has led to the dissolution of Unity of Being just as the dissipation of emotional intensity and mythological tradition has led Ireland to fragmentation. But if the occult has led to a death of the spirit, it also becomes the instrument of its rebirth. Through his and Lady Gregory's collection of "folk-belief" (A, 377), a far more instinctual and less convoluted application of the occult tradition than Cabbalism, Yeats formulates the "first few simple thoughts" (A, 378) that become the philosophical system of *A Vision* and finds the doctrine of the Mask latent in a peasant's account of seasons out of joint.[49] Philosophical systematization, the ordering of the occult through analogies to "explain the world" (A, 378), begins to replace the numberless unities, the chaos of over-active logic, of "Hodos Chameliontos."

Two specific experiences involving religious imagery expressive of spiritual rebirth and revelation reinforce his new discoveries about the self. In the first, which occurs in the middle of the poet's step across a stream at Coole Park, the emotion is of transcendence of the self in its surrender to some larger divine power and is, therefore, analogous to the import of the archer vision. The second projects the birth of a god, associated in Yeatsian mythology not only with personal rebirth, but with the cataclysmic moment when an old civilization begins to die and a new one to grow: "I woke one night to find myself lying upon my back with all my limbs rigid, and to hear a ceremonial measured voice, which did not seem to be mine, speaking through my lips. 'We make an image of him who sleeps', it said, 'and it is not he who sleeps, and we call it Emmanuel.' After many years that thought, others often found as strangely being added to it, became the thought of the Mask, which I have used in these memoirs to explain men's characters" (A, 379). [50] Having understood that it is indeed a *Mask* he has been seeking, having been given it, Yeats becomes free to channel his activity in directions more appropriate to him. The association with Lady Gregory turns him to the drama, a means of creating Mask, of fusing myth, at least within the confines of art, and biography, of projecting himself as a *dramatis persona.*

In terms of the structure of the 1926 edition of *Autobiographies (Reveries over Childhood and Youth* and *The Trembling of the Veil),* a revolution of the wheel has been completed, a spiritual birth analogous to the physical Creation announced in the initial imagery of *Reveries* has finally come round. When Yeats collected all the volumes of *Autobiographies* in 1938, these visions would not only complete the cycle, bring the wheel around again, but would open into the new phase described in *Dramatis Personae.*

FOUR: *DRAMATIS PERSONAE*

Dramatis Personae was the last book of *Autobiographies* to be written. Yeats conceived it ambitiously, then, in its execution, restricted its scope considerably. In 1926, he writes of his project: "My new Autobiography—1900 to 1926—may be the final test of my intellect, my last great effort" (L, 721). What he meant to include in the "last great effort," how he intended to structure it, we can only guess. When he finally wrote it in 1934, twenty-six years had been reduced to four years; *Dramatis Personae* covers only the years of the Irish Literary Theatre, until Irish actors began to play in what had become the Irish National Dramatic Society (1902) and well before the beginning of Annie Horniman's patronage in 1904. The conversation leading to the theatre's early support by Lady Gregory (1897) with which Yeats had concluded *The Trembling of the Veil* and to which he reverts in this book (A, 397) marks one boundary of this narrative, Zola's death and Yeats's quarrel with Moore about their proposed collaboration on *Where There is Nothing* (1902), the other.

The reader, armed with Yeats's statements in letters about his intentions, is left to speculate on his reasons for abbreviating his original project. It may well be that, when he actually began to write, he found himself unwilling to re-traverse the difficult years following Maud Gonne's marriage in 1903 and so stopped short of them. That he would have found it difficult to narrate this portion of his life with the same reticence and detachment with which he alluded to Maud Gonne earlier in *Autobiographies* is perhaps evident in a reference to her in *Dramatis Personae:* "I must have spent the summer of 1897 at Coole. I was involved in a miserable love affair . . . . My devotion might as well have been offered to an image in a milliner's window, or to a statue in a museum, but romantic doctrine had reached its extreme development . . . . My health was giving way, my nerves had been wrecked" (A, 399). Alluding to Dowson's palliative seeking after whores as a response to unrequited romantic love, he creates, in the implicit analogy with his own case and comparison with his response, a bitterness he had not yet revealed in *Autobiographies.*

More importantly, the nature of Yeats's autobiographical material itself would have tended to weaken the book's structure had he extended *Dramatis Personae* beyond 1902. The formation of the Irish National Dramatic Society can be taken as marking the success of the Irish Literary Revival and the account of the various quarrels, alliances and misalliances of the Abbey's early years, compelling in themselves, would be repetitive and something of a dénouement in terms of Yeats's role as chief protagonist of the literary revival. A middle-aged theatre manager makes a less legendary figure than a youthful and romantic nationalist poet. Moreover, as the successes of Irish Nationalism went beyond the achieved literary revival to the fight for political independence, Yeats's role as nationalist became increasingly peripheral. Assuming no active political role again until he became Senator, he could only have presented himself as an involved spectator of the 1916 Rebellion and the Civil War; an autobiographical account of this period would necessarily demand a shift in tone and point-of-view which—magnificent and strong as it is in the poems—would have weakened the overall structure of *Dramatis Personae*.

Whether one wishes to attribute Yeats's decision to end *Dramatis Personae* with the events of 1902 to his painful involvement with Maud Gonne or to his diminishing political role, whether one defines the state of his "nerves" by reference to an extreme Romantic melancholy or to a more prosaic twentieth-century nervous breakdown, one does admit the narrative integrity of the small enclosure of time he recreated. In keeping with the dramatic focus of the book, Yeats cites his first visit to Coole as a new "act," a new commencement in his life: "When I went to Coole the curtain had fallen upon the first act of my drama" (A, 395). [1] The phrase, and the association in *Autobiographies* of this first visit to Coole with moments of vision, is reminiscent of *The Speckled Bird,* in which, after the vision of himself as Emmanuel, Michael Hearne speculates,

The vision first and then this news of Margaret, what greater proof of supernatural guidance? He was told to work and was brought without delay to his fellow-worker. The voices at the other end of the boat were raised with anger now, but he did not hear them. He was thinking of his life which had but just begun. (SB, 42)

The new beginning of *Dramatis Personae* carries connotations of spiritual rebirth, of a new attempt on the part of antithetical man to find his Mask as a man of action. Within Yeats's system, no metaphor could be more apt than that of the theatre, self-expression externalized, given objective embodiment by actors. In keeping with this new beginning, he places both his organization of the Irish Literary Society and the National Literary Society and his work for the Irish Nationalists firmly in the past. Having concluded that "if Ireland would not read literature it might listen to it, for politics and the Church had created listeners" (A, 396), having "withdrawn from politics because I could not bear perplexing, by what I said about books, the simple patriotic men whose confidence I had gained by what I said about nationality" (A, 448), he turns to drama as the new mode of action which will unite literature, the occult and nationalism. That *Dramatis Personae* should begin with a second reference to Yeats's and Lady Gregory's collection of "folk-belief" and to their plans for a theatre and that it should terminate at the point at which the initial phase of that theatre was approaching an end and at which two of its principal dramatists, Moore and Yeats, began to quarrel lends the work chronological and thematic shapeliness.

Yeats seems first to have thought of this autobiography as a "drama" extending the tribute to Lady Gregory he had begun in "The Stirring of the Bones"; in February, 1934, in its incipient stages, he refers to it as "my *Lady Gregory.*" At this point, Moore and Martyn, as participants in the Irish Literary Theatre, share the "scene" (L, 820) with her, although Yeats also emphasizes that he is picturing "for the first time this preposterous person" (L, 820), Moore. Two and one-half months after this letter, Yeats tells his correspondent that "I am still busy writing about George Moore, and in reading him that I may write" (L, 822); the portrait of Moore had taken over *Dramatis Personae.*

Where previously in *Autobiographies,* he had juxtaposed the philosophical system of the present man on the memory of the past to create an autobiographical reverie which could only have suffered at the intrusion of documentation, now, in *Dramatis Personae,* Yeats explicitly constructs his narrative by reference to aids external to his own memory. He re-read Moore that he might outdo him in his own manner[2]; he refers to letters to Lady Gergory as his source of information about the events of which he writes (A, 407) and he quotes extensively from them that his account might seem well documented and uncoloured by Moore's *Hail and Farewell.* This imitation of Moore and use of quasi-documentation operates at more than one level of significance in *Dramatis Personae.* Most obviously it is a technique for indirectly refuting Moore. It enables Yeats to respond to Moore, using Moore's style, all the while discrediting it.

While Yeats seems to have abandoned the metaphoric and philosophical implications of his earlier style in *Autobiographies,* closer examination reveals him making a moral statement about what he sees as Moore's baseness of vision, a statement that resonates against the metaphoric structure informing the rest of *Autobiographies.* Any number of parallels can be traced between *Hail and Farewell* and *Dramatis Personae.*[3] Moore had described Yeats as "an Irish parody of the poetry that I had seen all my life strutting its rhythmic way in the alleys of the Luxembourg Gardens, preening its rhymes by the fountains, excessive in habit and gait"[4]; Yeats limns Moore as "a man carved out of a turnip, looking out of astonished eyes" and cites "Manet's caricature" (A, 405) of him as proof that his French circle saw him in the same way. He dismisses Moore's nationalism by parenthetically remarking of one of his picayune quarrels with his neighbours, hilariously and unreasonably absorbing and prolonged, that "he had but wrapped the green flag around him" (A, 444). In *Ave,* Moore had assessed Yeats as "thinner in his writings than in his talk,"[5] but had already mocked the talk: "and he [Yeats] continued to drone out his little tales in his own incomparable fashion, muttering after each one of them, like an oracle that has spent itself—'a beautiful story, a beautiful story!' When he had muttered these words his mind seemed

Edouard Manet. *George Moore.* Pastel on Fine Canvas. The Metropolitan Museum of Art, The H.Q. Havemeyer Collection. Bequest of Mrs. H.O. Havemeyer, 1929.

to fade away, and I could not but think that he was tired and would be happier tucked up in bed."[6] Yeats responds to the general charge about his talk that he "disliked Moore's now sentimental, now promiscuous amours, the main matter of his talk" (A, 431) and quotes several particularly brutal examples of his wit where women were concerned. Moore's specific example he turns against him by quoting Moore's "eloquence" on looking at proofs of the Yeats-Ellis *Blake:* "His 'How beautiful, how beautiful!' is all I can remember" (A, 403). Moore had amused himself by telling how Martyn, a Palestrina enthusiast, had mistakenly taken the *Adeste Fideles* sung by a woman for plain-chant sung by a boy soprano[7] ; Yeats responds with an anecdote in which Martyn reveals Moore's "coarse palate" (A, 443) and with quotations from letters about Moore's endless succession of much-abused cooks.

While such parallels attempt to outdo Moore in his own seemingly ingenuous style of satire, Yeats carries them still further, with the "documentary" support of letters as testimony to his veracity, to impugn Moore's motives and honesty. Yeats's reference to the letters and his quotations from them in Section IX of *Dramatis Personae* are far from innocuously placed. He has devoted one section of his narrative to Moore when he tells us that he is consulting the letters he had written Lady Gregory in order to "remind myself of these and other events" (A, 407). He proceeds to quote these letters extensively in a series of anecdotes that, at first, have nothing to do with Moore. These letters, since they are his own, are, of course, as "subjective" as any autobiographical narrative but Yeats's use of them lends his narrative the air of a man recounting the eccentricities of his acquaintances for a friend's amusement rather than that of one who has long brooded on retaliation for offenses given. When he does turn again to Moore, it is to recount his part in the first productions of the Irish Theatre, still documenting the narrative with quotations from the letters. By the time the account of the Moore-Martyn-Yeats cooperative effort to write plays ends and Yeats moves on to the heart of his attack on Moore, his documentation has had its effect; he has dignified his animus with a tone of historical veracity that persists long after he ceases to quote letters in support of his statements.

Yeats's tone not only creates his own veracity but impugns Moore's. Offhand and frequently snobbish allusions to Moore's family are intended to mark his lack of cultivation and, by extension, artistic discernment. "Lady Gregory once told me what marriage coarsened the Moore blood, but I have forgotten," Yeats begins (A, 402), then goes on to deny Moore necessary cultivation: "He had gone to Paris straight from his father's racing stables, from a house where there was no culture" (A, 404). Keats, "The coarse-bred son of a livery-stable keeper," may make "Luxuriant song" through the discovery of Mask, but Yeats never grants Moore, who is presented as continuing to debase

94

an inherited tradition rather than as discovering the tradition he lacks, the compensatory joy of "song." Not only is Moore presented as lacking the tradition which Yeats increasingly felt to be necessary to literature, he lacks, except where the visual arts are concerned, the most rudimentary acquired knowledge or manners: "He spoke badly and much in a foreign tongue, read nothing, and was never to attain the discipline of style" (A, 405). Having discredited Moore's pretensions to cultivation and knowledge, Yeats goes on to attribute his stories and, again by implied extension, much of *Hail and Farewell* to an enthusiasm for a witticism that could often override the truth. "All his friends suffered in some way," Yeats comments of one of Moore's remarks abut a mistress; "good behaviour was no protection, for it was all chance whether the facts he pursued were in actual life or in some story that amused him" (A, 403). Moore's egomania, he implies, overrules all considerations of taste, veracity and integrity: "He was all self and yet had so little self that he would destroy his reputation, or that of some friend, to make his audience believe that the story running in his head at the moment had happened, had only just happened" (A, 434). Establishing, as he does, so many implicit parallels with the stories of *Hail and Farewell,* Yeats gains strength for these suggestions through Moore's own ingenuous tone when he acknoweledges his "self-consciousness" which creates for him "comedy after comedy": "All my friends are actors in these unwritten plays; and almost any event is sufficient for a theme on which I can improvise."[8]

Yeats's slow accumulation of suggestions of Moore's untrustworth-iness, through allusions first to his family and his lack of education and then to his propensity for situating himself as centre or originator of brilliant or witty dialogues which never took place, culminates in a characterization of Moore as plagiarist. Moore has made an enemy by claiming for himself the perverse exploitation of an adolescent's poverty that is but a "plagiarism" (A, 434) from *A Rebours;* Yeats recounts the anecdote without comment but also without recollection of Huysmans' "influence" on his own "Rosa Alchemica." In the controversy over the "plagiarisms" in Moore's *Modern Painting,* Moore's frankness becomes, in Yeats's narrative, an insolence which the reader is meant to contrast with Lady Gregory's integrity: "'The man I object to', said Moore, 'is the man who plagiarizes without knowing it; I I always know; I took ten pages.' To Lady Gregory he said, 'We both quote well, but you always put inverted commas, I never do'," (A, 449). This choice of "evidence" is both selective and obviously aimed at furthering an impression of objectivity; Yeats suppresses, for example, Moore's tongue-in-cheek acknowledgement that he had made use of passages Yeats had suggested to improve the characterization of Ulick Dean in *Evelyn Innes* and his request that Yeats keep silent about the source of the revisions.[9] Discrediting Moore with much the same pose of frankness that Moore had used in *Hail and Farewell,* leaving an impression of "objectivity" through the passing use of letters as documentation, through anecdotes provided by Moore himself or by persons in whom Yeats is disinterested, and through his occasional magnanimity,[10] Yeats creates a tone of credibility if not of graciousness for his main autobiographical concern in *Dramatis Personae:* the development of style.

If the tone of Moore's *Hail and Farewell* had initially made it seem inoffensive although indiscreet,[11] Yeats did not remain charitable in his assessment of it; he soon spoke of it as a "disfiguring glass" (L, 586). A letter written by Lennox Robinson to Yeats some six weeks after Hardy's death suggests that the satirical possiblities of Yeats's reciprocating Moore's autobiographical interest had been entertained frequently among his friends and that discretion—motivated by taste? or by tact in the face of Moore's litigous nature?—had restrained Yeats. "George Moore has been moving heaven and earth to get Hardy's O.M.," Robinson writes. "Lady Cunard was worked hardest, finally the government referred the matter to Gosse who pondered . . . and said . . . 'No.' So poor George was carried to hospital where he lies a-dying—they say—and *now* can't we have—not all the autobiography—but just a little book all about him by you?" (L—WBY, 483). In his reassessment of *Hail and Farewell,* Yeats must have found particularly painful the passage in which Moore feels "sorry for Yeats and for his inspiration which did not seem to have survived his youth," predicts that he will write little more because he is "always talking about style,"[12] and asserts that Yeats has "very little [ear] for folk idiom."[13] For the real crux of the diatribe against Moore is style. After the 1898 Centennial, Yeats withdrew from political activity except when repressive commercial or clerical factions threatened the Abbey Theatre. The political aspect of the "man of action" lapsed into quiescence until the convulsion of 1916 gave an opportunity for poetic and personal statement of tragic and visionary intensity. Yeats needed some new force to shape his Image or anti-self. That force, he decided, must be style. In a *Journal* entry of 1909 which he later included in *Estrangement,* he associates style with Mask or personality: "Style, personality—deliberately adopted and therefore a mask—is the only escape from the hot-faced bargainers and the money-changers" (A, 461). Or again: "The self-conquest of the writer who is not a man of action is style" (A, 516). Most of the characterization of Moore in *Dramatis Personae* points to his lack of style and, sometimes implicitly, sometimes directly, to Yeats's possession of it. "Moore for all his toil had never style" (A, 424); "He did not know that style existed until he returned to Ireland in middle life" (A, 405); "ambition made him in later life prefer sentences a Dublin critic has compared to ribbons of tooth-paste squeezed out of a tube" (A, 406). An allusion to their correspondence about *Diarmuid and Grania,* one letter of which has Yeats asserting that his superior judgment in matters of style must be accepted by Moore if their collaboration on the play is to continue, [14] reiterates the point. Yeats, granting Moore a certain capability for dramatic construction, intensifies his criticism and consolidates the impression of his own gifts by suggesting that Moore not only could not discover his own style but could not imitate his, Yeats's: "Our worst quarrels, however, were when he tried to be poetical, to write in what he considered my style. He made the dying Diarmuid say to Finn: 'I will kick you down the stairway of the stars'. My letters to Lady Gregory show that we made peace at last, Moore accepting my judgment upon words, I his upon construction" (A, 435). In Yeats's view, Moore's real failure lay in his unrealizable desire to be Yeats; style became "his growing obsession, he would point out all the errors of some silly experiment of mine, then copy it" (A, 438). Their collaboration on plays for the Irish Literary Theatre "was unmixed misfortune for Moore, it set him upon a pursuit of style that made barren his later years" (A, 437).

Ultimately, Yeats suggests that Moore's failure to find a style places him outside the Irish literary tradition and in the English camp. In the twentieth century, "England had turned from style, as it has been understood from the translators of the Bible to Walter Pater, sought mere clarity in statement and debate, a journalistic effectiveness, at the moment when Irish men of letters began to quote the saying of Sainte-Beuve: 'There is nothing immortal in literature except style'" (A, 437). Moore, Yeats tells us, could find "no escape" in Ireland from style: "the difficulties of modern Irish literature, from the loose, romantic, legendary stories of Standish O'Grady to James Joyce and Synge, had been in the formation of a style . . . . His nature, bitter, violent, discordant, did not fit him to write the sentences men murmur again and again for years. Charm and rhythm had been denied him" (A, 438). Moore's nature, in Yeats's account, is irrevocably English, his identification with Ireland which *Hail and Farewell* chronicles, an enthusiasm based on a false understanding of himself.

Yeats underlines Moore's lack of a literary style at the personal level. He sets Moore outside the Irish attitude once again by impugning his morality in a comparison of his posture and that of the orator Taylor. Taylor's "body was angular, often rigid with suppressed rage, his gaze fixed upon some object . . . , his erect attitude suggesting a firm base. Moore's body was insinuating, upflowing, circulative, curvicular, pop-eyed" (A, 422). The physical solidity of the Nationalist orator opposed to the piscine adjectives applied to Moore sets the moral erectness of the first against the implied moral slipperiness of the second.[15] "Violent and coarse of temper" (A, 428), Moore betrays ill-breeding and a lack of style and culture time and again, both in his quarrels and in the stories he invents. His practical ineptitude reinforces the absurdity. He dresses the part of a "country gentleman" (A, 443) but does not know how to attach his braces so as to keep his pants from falling down; he is depressed because, having propositioned a woman by telling her, " 'I was clean and healthy and she could not do better'" (A, 403–04), he has been refused. Although Yeats mitigates his portrait of Moore with occasional touches of magnanimity which lend it an air of credibility, its cumulative effect is one of baseness or vulgarity, baseness of birth, up-bringing, conversation, motives, literary style and personal conduct. Yeats subtly emphasizes this baseness in his initial presentation of Moore when he employs the expression "the root facts of life" (A, 403). "Root facts," it turns out, are most often economic, and to them Moore would sacrifice "all that seemed to other men good breeding, honour, friendship" (A, 403).

What Yeats sees as Moore's natural predilection in both personal and literary matters for such "root facts" over style is, in his terms, a moral fault. Style, Yeats often explained, is the literary equivalent of morals in life. A passage in his *Journal* speaks of "that thing which is to life what style is to letters: moral radiance, a personal quality of universal meaning in action and in thought" (Mem, 258). He iterates the equivalence in an entry included in *The Death of Synge:* "The element which in men of action corresponds to style in literature is the moral element.[16] Books live almost entirely because of their style, and the men of action who inspire movements after they are dead are those whose hold upon impersonal emotion and law lifts them out of immediate circumstance" (A, 515–16). That correspondence Yeats had allied to the tradition of the poet as courtier and made central to the 1907 essay "Poetry and Tradition": "In life courtesy and self-possession, and in the arts style, are the sensible impressions of the free mind, for both arise out of a deliberate shaping of all things, and from never being swept away, whatever the emotion, into confusion or dullness . . . . a writer . . . should never be without style, which is but high breeding in words and in argument" (EI, 253). In *Dramatis Personae,* the admixture of anecdotes about Moore's personal inadequacies and of analysis of his literary defects is a negative equivalent of Yeats's analogy between style and morals. The absence of the one implies the absence of the other; Yeats has given us a Moore conspicuously lacking "high breeding."

Yeats's attempt to characterize Moore in the latter's own manner and his occasional references to letters so as to seem to verify that characterization by documentation, lead him away from the reverie and the elaborate allusions and metaphors which structured the earlier volumes of *Autobiographies.* The prose of *Dramatis Personae* has a directness which contributes to the forcefulness of both the attack on Moore and the tribute to Lady Gregory. But while Yeats no longer specifically alludes to the philosophical system or "metaphor" which provided him with the antithetical structure of *The Trembling of the Veil*, that structure, transformed from explanation into style, also governs *Dramatis Personae*. One can see it, as always in Yeats, controlling the choice of detail and metaphor.[17] Martyn, with his "subconscious hatred of women" (A, 386), finds his antithesis in Moore, whose conversation is a series of amorous anecdotes. Moore and Martyn are "peasant sinner" and "peasant saint" (A, 402). Most of the original Tulira Castle, Martyn's home, had burned, "as though fate had deliberately prepared for an abstract mind that would see nothing in life but its vulgarity and tempations" (A, 386); Coole House, on the contrary, was one in which "Every generation had left its memorial" (A, 389). Martyn and Moore come from stock coarsened by mésalliances but Yeats links Lady Gregory's maiden name with a variation found in Shakespeare and traces her ancestors to "some Duke of Northumberland" (A, 392), their Irish holdings to the seventeenth century. Yeats implicitly and occasionally explicitly sets up his own transcendence of the self, his seeking of a Mask in style, against Moore's failure to achieve style and extends this antithetical structure by a reference to Douglas Hyde where it expresses itself in terms of English versus Gaelic.

Ultimately, Yeats uses this antithetical structure in *Dramatis Personae* to exalt Lady Gregory. In *Hail and Farewell*, Moore had gone on from his pity for the end of Yeats's "inspiration" to dispraise Lady Gregory and her work. He had represented her as lacking in social tact and her family as "undistinguished . . . in love, in war, or in politics, never having indulged in anything except a taste for Bible reading in the cottages."[18] Her collection of folk-belief seems, in Moore's juxtaposition of the two, but a variation of the proselytizing visits of her mother and sisters to their tenants, her re-telling of it, but a "patchwork" of European translations made with no real ear for "the idiom of the Galway peasant."[19] Responding from the elitist position in politics and culture he had adopted in middle age, Yeats uses Martyn and Moore as a foil to the cultural values he represents by Coole Park and Lady Gregory. He justifies the proselytizing of the Persse women—it "expressed their love" (A, 394)—and ascribes Lady Gregory's refusal to participate in it to the moral sensitivity of a "born student of the great literature of the world" (A, 394). Her values are feudal values, the concomitant in the social order of the Renaissance in the arts: "She knew Ireland always in its permanent relationships, associations . . . , never lost her sense of feudal responsibility, not of duty as the word is generally understood, but of burdens laid upon her by her station and her character, a choice constantly renewed in solitude" (A, 395). This view of Lady Gregory as combining the best of the feudal chatelaine and the contemplative artist enables Yeats to present her as governing her life, not by "root facts," but by the credo that the "'only wrong

99

act that matters is not doing one's best work'" (A, 408). The essence of his tribute to her is that she provided the environment, the Irish equivalent of Urbino, in which he could begin to move towards his own "best work." Yeats represents her own plays and folk-tales as the product of such an environment, of a long culture with its roots in the English and Celtic Renaissance; "they were made possible by her past; semi-feudal Roxborough, her inherited sense of caste, her knowledge of that top of the world where men and women are valued for their manhood and their charm, not for their opinions, her long study of Scottish Ballads, of Percy's *Reliques,* of the *Morte d'Arthur.* If she had not found those tales, or finding them had not found the dialect of Kiltartan, that past could not, as it were, have drawn itself together, come to birth as present personality" (A, 456).

This imagery of poetic rebirth, of self and Mask creatively revealing the "true self," exalts Lady Gregory and simultaneously ostracizes George Moore. Pointing the moral to his portraits, Yeats defines the Mask by which each of his *dramatis personae* have achieved "personality":

A writer must die every day he lives, be reborn, as it is said in the Burial Service, an incorruptible self, that self opposite of all that he has named 'himself'. George Moore, dreading the annihilation of an impersonal bleak realism, used life like a mediaeval ghost making a body for itself out of drifting dust and vapour; and have I not sung in describing guests at Coole—'There one that ruffled in a manly pose, For all his timid heart'—that one myself? Synge was a sick man picturing energy, a doomed man picturing gaiety; Lady Gregory, in her life much artifice, in her nature much pride, was born to see the glory of the world in a peasant mirror. (A, 457).

Moore, along with the others, seems to have discovered an antithetical self. But its nature serves finally to dismiss him. Yeats shows himself finding a Mask as the man of action, the aristocratic Lady Gregory as recorder of folk-belief, the dying Synge as a writer vibrant with energy; these Masks are solid, fleshed. Not so Moore's. A body of "drifting dust and vapour" does not cohere; indeed it characterizes one of John Butler Yeats's definitions, in a letter to his poet-son, of what a poet is *not:* "I like a poet to be a little reactionary .... a true poet ... is local .... Out of vapour you can make a background or an atmosphere, not the *body* of poetry . . ." (L—WBY, 329). Drifting dust and vapour as the non-substance of a personality from which no literature will emerge say little for Moore; the image of his using life like a medieval ghost—Yeats had relished a description of Moore as a "'boiled ghost'" (L, 315)— implies the necessary dismissal of his realism; Yeats's choice of a quotation to end the chapter removes him altogether from the stage. Yeats marks the tribute he wishes to pay Lady Gregory by ending his chapter with lines from her folk translation in *Gods and Fighting Men* of the legend of Diarmuid and Grania, lines which apotheosize her. The choice of text and of Lady Gregory's version over his own and Moore's dramatic version makes it plain that, if in Ireland " 'The stag to the East is not asleep . . .; the bog lark is not asleep to-night on the high stormy bogs' " (A, 458), it is no fault of Moore's. His *dramatis personae* characterized, their works presented, Yeats makes plain his view that he, Synge, and Lady Gregory gave birth to the Irish Literary Revival by virtue of breeding, style, Irishness and inner conviction, that Moore but adopted it, wrapped, for a time, a conspicuous green flag about him.

FIVE: *ESTRANGEMENT* AND *THE DEATH OF SYNGE*

In *Estrangement* and *The Death of Synge,* Yeats selected from and rearranged sections of a *Journal* he kept with some regularity in 1909 and with increasing irregularity thereafter. [1] He moved to the opening of *Estrangement* an entry which suggests the *journal intime* tradition: "To keep these notes natural and useful to me I must keep one note from leading on to another, that I may not surrender myself to literature. Every note must come as a casual thought, then it will be my life. Neither Christ nor Buddha nor Socrates wrote a book, for to do that is to exchange life for a logical process" (A, 461). Although Yeats has ascribed certain characteristics of the *intimistes*—introspection, timidity, a searching for unity [2] —to himself throughout *Autobiographies,* the principles of selection and organization which shape *Estrangement* diverge much farther from that tradition than his statement of intention seems to suggest.

Selection, even in a journal the avowed aim of which is *tout dire,* is inevitable; no writer can possibly record every fluctuation of his thought. But Yeats, by omitting in *Estrangement* large sections of the original *Journal* and by re-ordering many of those remaining, considerably intensifies certain concerns of the original documents and gives them a thematic and stylistic coherence they had not previously possessed. He actively intervenes as writer to emphasize and structure the latent thematic possibilities of the *Journal,* to transform life into literature. His *intimiste* statement is not only unveracious as a declaration of intention for *Estrangement,* it functions as a deliberately misleading signpost. It enables Yeats to juxtapose certain thematic and cultural concerns, gaining for them an intensity born of a cumulative effect, without using the more connected discourse of the philosophical essay or novel. The individual entries tend toward mythic rather than logical significance. They accumulate their force of conviction by reverberating one against the other, by suggesting equivalencies, and not by closely reasoned connections.

By structuring his themes so that they seem but impressions of the moment, by claiming an *intimiste* motivation which his careful selection and arrangement invalidates, Yeats presents an elitist political position and passes harsh judgment on Ireland and its writers in a form more palatable and, therefore, probably initially more convincing, than would have been a more connected statement. He gives his reader the raw material of autobiography, shows his opinions taking shape as responses in specific contexts. Remaining attached, within the literary frame of the journal, to the personal situation, these opinions assume a credibility which those of the more overtly political *On the Boiler,* for example, lack. A personal context, the presence of a mind musing over its own observations and operations, saves them from the dogmatism characterizing the political testament in which personal anecdote provides illustrations rather than motivations. Yeats's statement of an *intimiste* intention, however untrue to the actual structure of *Estrangement,* insists on that personal context with which to deal with impersonal themes.

His themes emerge from those of the rest of *Autobiographies.* Generally they are the three interests, literature, the philosophy of the occult, and nationalism, which he claimed as central to his life. They manifest themselves specifically in his evolving concept of the Mask, in his consideration of the artist as carrier of traditional culture and in his indictment of Ireland for her failure to fulfill the nation's obligation to the artist. Even though Yeats had selected the entries which open *Estrangement* from the *Journal* before writing *Dramatis Personae,* they follow naturally from the preoccupation with style which characterizes his response to Moore. A debate on a political question lets Yeats once again contrast logic (Moore's realism) and the style (personality, Mask) which creates the series of equivalencies typical of his mature use of myth and symbols. "Logic," he observes in the context of the debate,

is a machine, one can leave it to itself; unhelped it will force those present to exhaust the subject, the fool is as likely as the sage to speak the appropriate answer to any statement, and if an answer is forgotten somebody will go home miserable. You throw your money on the table and you receive so much change.

Style, personality—deliberately adopted and therefore a mask—is the only escape from the hot-faced bargainers and the money-changers. (A, 461)

His next entry extends the contrast to the world of nationalism. It arises from a conversation with "a man typical of a class . . . new in Ireland" (A, 461), a man "with the ill-breeding of the mind, every thought made in some manufactory and with the mark upon it of its wholesale origin—thoughts never really thought out in their current form in any individual mind, but the creation of impersonal mechanism—of schools, of text-books, of newspapers, these above all" (A, 462).[3] While the suggestion of mechanism links Irish culture and Yeats's original opposition of logic and style or Mask, his further observation of such men as intellectual "parvenus"—they object to the word *shift* and wish to substitute *tapers* for *candles* (A, 462–63)— extends the second term of the antithesis, the Mask, to a sense of tradition, to what becomes the Urbino symbol in his writings:

This ill-breeding of the mind is a far worse thing than the mere bad manners that spit on the floor. Is not all charm inherited, whether of the intellect, of the manners, of the character, or of literature? A great lady is as simple as a good poet. Neither possesses anything that is not ancient and their own, and both are full of uncertainty about everything except themselves . . . . They assume convictions as if they were a fashion in clothes and remould all slightly. (A, 462)

Paralleling the rhetorical question of this passage, Yeats outlines the artist's response to the absence of Unity of Culture and intimates the grounds of his personal "estrangement" from Ireland: "To oppose the new ill-breeding of Ireland . . .I can only set up a secondary or interior personality created out of the tradition of myself, and this personality (alas, only possible to me in my writings) must . . . have that slight separation from interests which makes charm possible while remaining near enough for passion. Is not charm what it is because an escape from mechanism?" (A, 463). Much of the remainder of *Estrangement* bears on this divergence of Ireland's increasing "ill-breeding" or "mechanism" from an inherited tradition while much of Yeats's bitterness arises from the conviction that the only tradition possible to the poet in such circumstances is this secondary "tradition of myself." But this tradition and the necessity for it also constitute his "estrangement": an estrangement from the contemporary culture of his own country, an estrangement from his own personality at moments when he participates in that culture instead of in the tradition of his own writings.

The linking of personality and tradition fostered the romantic appreciation of feudalism which had been latent in Yeats's exaltation of the Renaissance and developed, in his long association with Lady Gregory, into a symbolic vision of Coole Park as an Irish Urbino,[4] himself as its Castiglione. She had "brought to my wavering thoughts steadfast nobility"; in the midst of his fear that she is dying, grief finds expression in "Castiglione's phrase ringing in my memory, 'Never be it spoken without tears, the Duchess, too, is dead'" (A, 478).[5] Her planting of trees that will not reach maturity for some fifty years leads to an elaborate metaphor of the artist as an aristocrat: "We artists, do not we also plant trees and it is only after some fifty years that we are of much value? Every day I notice some new analogy between the long-established life of the well-born and the artists' life. We come from the permanent things and create them, and instead of old blood we have old emotions and we carry in our heads always that form of society aristocracies create now and again for some brief moment at Urbino or Versailles" (A, 473–74).

The identification of the artist and the cultured aristocrat results in a position similar to that Wyndham Lewis, whose "energy" (L, 733) Yeats praised, termed "The Politics of the Intellect."[6] Lewis specifically repudiates the class consciousness of Yeats's politics, but the divergence lies in different connotations of the word *aristocracy* rather than in any fundamental disagreement. Aristocracy, Lewis argues, is based on "a *difference* that is not a reality."[7] Aristocrats are, in fact, of the same stuff as their servants; they erect artificial class barriers, isolating themselves as a privileged enclave, to disguise this fact. "The intellect," however, "is more removed from the crowd than is anything: but it is not a snobbish withdrawal, but a going aside for the purposes of work, of work not without its utility for the crowd."[8] In Yeats's formulation, "Culture is the sanctity of the intellect" (A, 489). Yeats—whose ideal aristocrat obviously approximates the cultured

Medici family much more closely than it does the antics of those who gathered around the Sitwells or Harold Acton, and who much admired Lewis's work [9]—expressed the latter's idea of artistic withdrawal in order to produce work relevant to the society at large in his seemingly paradoxical desire to retreat into another Urbino that he might write in a "common" speech untainted by journalism and raised by the poet to passionate intensity, "the emotion of multitude" (EI, 215), a speech in which image begets analogous images.

In *Estrangement,* this concept of an aristocracy of the intellect becomes the new prism through which Yeats refracts all his preoccupations. Relating it to the Mask, he finds analogies for it in the courtly "discipline" of love and in the drama. In the "discipline" of "true love," Yeats theorizes with reference to Solomon and Sheba, each "divines the secret self of the other, and refusing to believe in the mere daily self, creates a mirror where the lover or the beloved sees an image to copy in daily life; for love also creates the Mask" (A, 464).[10] The beloved represents the antithetical self, "a group of stellar influences in the radical horoscope" (A, 480), the "external expression" of "an element in his [the lover's] character, and his destiny" (A, 481). [11]

Most pervasive in *Estrangement,* however, is the metaphor of the drama for the assumption of the Mask. Drama, Yeats suggests once again, is philosophy purged of the abstract by action (action, we must remember, is the equivalent in life of style in literature), the myth become biography. The movement from philosophy to drama he saw as the natural evolution towards Christianity and so as the natural expression of our civilization:

In Christianity what was philosophy in Eastern Asia became life, biography and drama. A play passes through the same process in being written. At first, if it has psychological depth, there is a bundle of ideas, something that can be stated in philosophical terms; my *Countess Cathleen,* for instance, was once the moral question, may a soul sacrifice itself for a good end? but gradually philosophy is eliminated until at last the only philosophy audible, if there is even that, is the mere expression of one character or another. When it is completely life it seems to the hasty reader a mere story. (A, 468)

If we turn again to Yeats's system of lunar analogies, we recall that the saint personifies the completely primary self while the artist embodies total absorption in the antithetical self. The saint exteriorizes myth in biographical circumstance, the artist deliberately shapes biography by mythic standards. The drama, therefore, because it is biographic in seeming form—a mere story—, philosophic, psychological or mythic in the initial impulse to it and in its essence, becomes Yeats's prototype of artistic "discipline": "There is a relation between discipline and the theatrical sense. If we cannot imagine ourselves as different from what we are and assume that second self, we cannot impose a discipline upon ourselves, though we may accept one from others. Active virtue as distinguished from the passive acceptance of a current code is therefore theatrical, consciously dramatic, the wearing of a mask. It is the condition of arduous full life" (A, 469). The theatrical metaphor makes artistic discipline a mode of action and so resolves Yeats's youthful conflict between contemplative man and the man of action; the artist becomes one who would "play with all masks" (A, 470).

Having cast his antithetical doctrine in theatrical terms, Yeats combines it with the ideal of Urbino to indict the contentious forms Irish nationalism had taken. The decrial of factionalism, of false rhetoric and hatred in institutions and in individuals, which had formed the substance of his attack on Ireland in *The Trembling of the Veil* is generalized in *Estrangement* to a meditation on the national soul. Yeats opposes the peasant's nationalism, exemplified by Allingham's spontaneous and emotional love of the soil, to the artificial "ideas of Ireland" and the "conscious patriotism" of Davis (A, 472) and commonplace men. The peasant and the artist Yeats saw as sharing in "emotion of multitude," with the artist's superiority lying in his possession of a richer tradition of that emotion: "Supreme art is a traditional statement of certain heroic and religious truths, passed on from age to age, modified by individual genius, but never abandoned" (A, 490). In between peasant and artist Yeats saw the object of his attack: the Irish middle class. Whether religious or political in their pursuits, they are characterized as "empty souls" (A, 469) longing "for popularity that they may believe in themselves" (A, 466). Opinion extirpates creative emotion, "mechanical logic and commonplace eloquence" crush "all that is organic" (A, 488) in the individual or the culture, the most fanatic versions of the primary phases destroy the antithetical self. In *Estrangement*, the result is an intellectual and emotional castration which makes Unity of Being impossible:

The root of it all is that the political class in Ireland—the lower-middle class from whom the patriotic associations have drawn their journalists and their leaders for the last ten years—have suffered through the cultivation of hatred as the one energy of their movement, a deprivation which is the intellectual equivalent to a certain surgical operation. Hence the shrillness of their voices. They contemplate all creative power as the eunuchs contemplate Don Juan as he passes through Hell on the white horse. (A, 486)[12]

In *Estrangement* Yeats always circles back from Ireland's political and cultural hatreds and his own nationalist aspirations and work for the Abbey to the context of feudal authority, of the benefits he saw accruing from a society unlike Ireland's which made an Urbino possible. Authority in government is the Yeatsian analogue to theatrical "discipline" in the individual life; it provides a means to a Unity of Culture equivalent to individual Unity of Being. In *Estrangement*, that authority provides the antithesis to Irish culture and politics and the failure of its means dominates Yeats's meditations. He hypothesizes

106

that the arts rule and produce Unity only when conjoined with an authority which values them. Yeats reveals this conviction by the vatic nature of his rhetoric as much as by any overt statement. Denunciations of Ireland's refusal of Unity of Culture mix with prophecies that a necessary authority is about to be "rediscovered": "Anarchic revolt is coming to an end, and the arts are about to restate the traditional morality" (A, 490). But "No art can conquer the people alone—the people are conquered by an ideal of life upheld by authority. As this ideal is rediscovered, the arts, music and poetry, painting and literature, will draw closer together" (A, 491). Then the oracular see-saw of *Estrangement* immediately reverses itself in predictions of failure: "The Abbey Theatre will fail to do its full work because there is no accepted authority to explain why the more difficult pleasure is the nobler pleasure. The fascination of the National Movement for me in my youth was, I think, that it seemed to promise such authority" (A, 491). Whatever the personal reasons for Yeats's bitterness in *Estrangement*, he attributes the "failure" not only of the Abbey but of the entire Nationalist movement to a democratic propensity for hatred and to his state's distance from the traditional order of an Urbino:

Ireland has grown sterile, because power has passed to men who lack the training which requires a certain amount of wealth to ensure continuity from generation to generation, and to free the mind in part from other tasks. A gentleman is a man whose principal ideas are not connected with his personal needs and his personal success. In old days he was a clerk or a noble, that is to say, he had freedom because of inherited wealth and position, or because of a personal renunciation. The names are different to-day, and I would put the artist and the scholar in the category of the clerk, yet personal renunciation is not now sufficient . . . or perhaps it is sufficient but is impossible without inherited culture. For without culture or holiness, which are always the gift of a very few, a man may renounce wealth or any other external thing, but he cannot renounce hatred, envy, jealousy, revenge. Culture is the sanctity of the intellect. (A, 489)

His remedy for the national dilemma is a form of power politics in the hands of a cultured elite, a fusion of literature, inherited values and nationalism: "We require a new statement of moral doctrine, which shall be accepted by the average man, but be at the same time beyond his power in practice . . . . A true system of morals is from the first a weapon in the hands of the most distinguished" (A, 492). Yeats's own hatred in *Estrangement* is partly conditioned by the knowledge that no such moral doctrine is about to become authoritative.

In one of the book's last entries, he seeks to explain once again, more calmly this time, both the failure of political and cultural nationalism in Ireland and his own goals for his country in terms of the need of an Image, an antithetical self or Mask: "There is a dying-out of national feeling very simple in its origin. You cannot keep the idea of a nation alive where there are no national institutions to reverence, no national success to admire, without a model of it in the mind of the people. . . . for the general purposes of life you must have a complex mass of images, something like an architect's model" (A, 493). The Young Ireland poets bequeathed a rudimentary model; they "created a mass of obvious images that filled the minds of the young . . . . Our own movement thought to do the same thing in a more profound and therefore more enduring way" (A, 493). The final passages of *Estrangement* return us to the rearranged journal's opening attack. The Abbey and the Irish Literary Revival erred in overestimating the cultural capabilities of the middle class, in refusing to recognize their "ill-breeding":

> . . . I did not see, until Synge began to write, that we must renounce the deliberate creation of a kind of Holy City in the imagination, and express the individual. The Irish people were not educated enough to accept images more profound, more true to human nature, than the schoolboy thoughts of Young Ireland. You can only create a model of a race to inspire the action of that race as a whole, apart from exceptional individuals, when you and it share the same simple moral understanding of life . . . . Having no understanding of life that we can teach to others, we must not seek to create a school. (A, 493-94)

Yeats finally defines his "estrangement" by the extent to which artists in Ireland and he in particular have failed to shape the personality of the nation. The only remedy he can suggest lies in compromise, in the adaptation of the ideas of the artist to the medium the ill-educated understand, journalism: "Yet in the work of Lady Gregory, of Synge, of O'Grady, of Lionel Johnson, in my own work, a school of journalists with simple moral ideas could find right building material to create a historical and literary nationalism as powerful as the old and nobler. That done, they could bid the people love and not hate" (A, 494).

Once again the hope goes unrealized and *Estrangement* ends with two short and anti-climactic passages. One seems to have the point of much of Yeats's anecdotal material; the divergent accounts of a certain haunted house given by Catholics and Protestants illustrate the triviality of much Irish dissension and the basis of most of it, measure the untraversable distance between Yeats's ideal of another Urbino and the Irish reality. The other provides the epitaph for his hopes for Ireland: "Nobody running at full speed has either a head or a heart" (A, 495).

The dislocation of the passage from its original place in the *Journal* and the omission of a prefatory statement—"There is no wisdom without indolence" (Mem, 168)—increase its overtones of doom. Ireland has refused to accept a traditional authority which would foster the intelligent leisure of an Urbino and "creative power," indeed can very likely see no authority but England's, no court but the legacy of Victoria's. "Running at full speed," she remains mechanized and will not attain to Unity of Culture.

Estrangement, with its denunciation of Irish politics, Irish culture, Irish hatred, seems hardly to belong in an autobiography; actual events often serve as a merely fortuitous impulse towards a rhetoric of bitterness. The book is obviously not autobiographical in terms of the intensely psychological and confessional connotations we often give that word in the twentieth century. While the form of the journal does provide a personal context and the bitterness of Yeats's rhetoric introduces a subjective element, he directly tells us little of the nuances of thought which lead to particular actions or opinions, little of the self conceived as ego. But by presenting himself as a poet with a correlative political Mask instead of displaying "the bundle of accident and incoherence that sits down to breakfast," he does write a form of autobiography which his own literary aesthetic pemits. And while he abandons the mimetic form towards which autobiography had tended throughout the Victorian period, Yeats adapts an equally influential autobiographical tradition, that of Montaigne's *Essays.* Selecting and arranging passages from a *Journal* that, even in its original form contained much less that was merely personal than such journals generally do, Yeats reveals a mind musing much as does Montaigne's in his thematic essays. The interest of the passages as autobiography lies in their revealing, as Montaigne claimed of his writings, not only the man making his work, but the work shaping the man, a very bitter man in the case of *Estrangement.* The autobiography becomes "consubstantial" with its author[13] and the journal is a particularly apt genre to chart the final transition from the optimism of his youth to the energetic pessimism of his middle years.

The Death of Synge opens with a question symptomatic of a change of tone in the journal entries: "Why does the struggle to come at truth take away our pity, and the struggle to overcome our passions restore it again?" (A, 499). Pity in the usual sense of the word formed but a small part of Yeats's literary stock of emotions. Both his poetry and his prose generally aim at a more astringent emotion, one more magnificently knowing and accepting of the nature of man in the world and his possibilities of its transcendence, an emotion "that looks beyond mankind and asks no pity, not even of God" (A, 524). But Yeats's rhetorical question effects a movement from the savage bitterness which characterized *Estrangement* towards a less impassioned utterence than that of the man who had written, "I cry continually against my life" (A, 491).

He immediately takes up the final suggestion of *Estrangement's* denunciation of Ireland that, appropriately tailored to the limitations of the uncultured, an historical and literary nationalism might yet revivify the country and save it from hatred. The tone is more controlled and the question of the mis-education of the Irish, the substitution of "pedantry" for a "sense of style or feeling for life" (A, 500), opens up into Yeats's basic antitheses: character and personality, primary and antithetical self, the "powerful but prosaic art, celebrating the 'fall into division,'" of the modern period (the art of Augustus John) and art with "that energy which seems measureless and

109

hates all that is not itself" (the art of Botticelli and Giorgione) celebrating "the 'resurrection into unity'" (A, 502). This series of entries culminates in one of Yeats's clearest statements about the moment of ecstasy concomitant with the complete assumption of the Mask and analogous to the mythic moment of rebirth into knowledge: "I think that all happiness depends on the energy to assume the mask of some other self; that all joyous or creative life is a rebirth as something not oneself, something which has no memory and is created in a moment and perpetually renewed" (A, 503).

Towards the end of *The Death of Synge,* Yeats returns to this statement in two passages. One places it in the context of sixteenth-century Venetian costumes " pictured in *The Mask* [14] —all fantastic; bodily form hidden or disguised . . . . Life had become so learned and courtly that men and women dressed with no thought of bodily activity . . . . Does not the same happen to our passions when we grow contemplative and so liberate them from use? They also become fantastic and create the strange lives of poets and artists" (A, 522-23). The second discusses the response in the appreciation of art which corresponds to the joy of creation through the Mask, a transformation of the audience which the drama, perhaps because it mediates more literally between myth and biography than other art forms, can evoke: "All creation requires one mind to make and one mind of enjoyment. The theatre can at rare moments create this one mind of enjoyment, and once created, it is like the mind of an individual in solitude, immeasurably bold—all is possible to it" (A, 519). In between the opening theoretic formulations of *The Death of Synge* and these later ones, the entries become more personal, more rooted in daily activity and individual tragedy. If their personal nature permits the entrance of pity, the mythological boldness they assume lifts them beyond it once more.

In *Estrangement* Yeats's acquaintance with Synge marked the beginning of his conviction that Ireland would fail to achieve Unity of Culture—"I did not see, until Synge began to write, that we must renounce the deliberate creation of a kind of Holy City in the imagination" [15]—; in this book Synge's death becomes the new symbol of Ireland's loss of Unity of Culture. The statement "Synge is dead" (A, 507) gains implacability as Yeats goes on to intimate an identification of the playwright with what Ireland might have become. The vision of Tir-nan-Oge, of Synge's having "gone upward out of his ailing body into the heroical fountains" (A, 511), elevates him into the type of the hero-poet, cursed with physical infirmity and gifted with poetic insight. Even the ostensibly objective listing of "Celebrations" and "Detractions" transforms Synge's faults into poetic virtue, into the antithesis "necessary to the full expression of himself" (A, 512). Yeats's tribute identifies Synge with Homer, calls him "'blind old man of Scio's rocky isle'" (A, 512). He had designated the prototypical poet with a similar reference: "'When any stranger asks who is the sweetest of singers, answer with one voice: "A blind man; he dwells upon rocky Chios; his songs shall be the most beautiful for ever" ' " (A, 151). [16] When we recall that Yeats took Homer as his own symbol— "Homer is my example and his unchristened heart"—and that his own weak eyesight doubtless increased his empathy with the blind poet, a tentative identification is established between Yeats and Synge.

Interspersed with recollections of the events surrounding Synge's death are reflections on two Abbey plays, intimations of the way the theatre might have gone, towards "'resurrection into unity,'" had Synge lived and been understood, and of the way it is going, towards "the 'fall into division.'" Predictably, Yeats establishes once again his obsessive structure of the antithetical versus the primary, Urbino versus "a democracy like this" (A, 513):

I see that between *Time*, suggestion and *Cross-roads*, logic, lies a difference of civilization. The literature of suggestion belongs to a social order when life conquered by being itself and the most living was the most powerful . . . . Leisure, wealth, privilege were created to be a soil for the most living. The literature of logic, the most powerful and the most empty, conquering all in the service of one metallic premise, is for those who have forgotten everything but books and yet have only just learnt to read . . . . I . . . think that the French and Irish democracies follow . . . a logical deduction to its end, no matter what suffering it brings, . . . because they have broken from the past, from the self-evident truths, from 'naked beauty displayed'. (A, 514) [17]

The comparison of plays effects what political and cultural analysis had in *Estrangement;* it laments that democratic mechanism, as always in Yeats's assessments of his own time, is winning the day.

In the context of the two plays and of Yeats's hypothesis that the theatre is in a privileged position to create in an audience a transcendent joy analogous to that of the artist, Synge's death becomes productive of an "equivalent expression" in more than one world. The passage immediately preceding the statement of his death provides a bridge from the personal to the national, another suggestion of Synge as an Irish Homer, and a link with Yeats's initial question about pity: "One does not feel that death is evil when one meets it,—evil, I mean, for the one who dies . . . . The wildest sorrow that comes at the thought of death is, I think, 'Ages will pass over and no one ever again look on that nobleness or that beauty'. What is this but to pity the living and to praise the dead?" (A, 507). The passage echoes one from Homer which Yeats had remembered in connection with Wilde's death: "I thought of Homer's description of the captive women weeping in seeming for Patroclus yet each weeping for her own sorrow because he was ever kind" (L, 347). The Homeric allusion serves to increase the passage's mourning until *The Death of Synge* becomes both a eulogy for the dead dramatist and an elegy for Ireland. Synge represents the Mask of Ireland, its true self, which it has refused; this is the point of Yeats's comparison of him with yet another national poet, Burns,[18] in the outburst against the man

111

"with a look of a wood-kern"(A, 519), a representative of uncultured or "outlaw" Ireland:

At last I said, 'When a country produces a man of genius he never is what it wants or believes it wants; he is always unlike its idea of itself. In the eighteenth century Scotland believed itself religious, moral and gloomy, and its national poet Burns came not to speak of these things but to speak of lust and drink and drunken gaiety. Ireland, since the Young Irelanders, has given itself up to apologetics. Every impression of life or impulse of imagination has been examined to see if it helped or hurt the glory of Ireland or the political claim of Ireland. . . . There was no longer an impartial imagination, delighting in whatever is naturally exciting. Synge was the rushing up of the buried fire, an explosion of all that had been denied or refused, a furious impartiality, an indifferent turbulent sorrow. His work, like that of Burns, was to say all the people did not want to have said. . . .' (A, 520)

Ireland's rejection of Synge's work is a rejection of its creative self, his death, the death of the Unity of Culture for which Yeats had hoped and worked. Yeats's pity, if indeed it is pity and not a resigned despair, is not for Synge, but for the nation denounced with so much passion in *Estrangement*.

He follows his comparison with a thought from a dream: "'Why should we complain if men ill-treat our Muses, when all that they gave to Helen while she still lived was a song and a jest?'" (A, 521). [19] The thought suggests Yeats's abandonment of what he had initially conceived to be the Irish cause, a retreat into the artist's isolation that had been so much a part of the tradition of Romantic sensibility and that had persisted in the twentieth century in such formulations as Wyndham Lewis's in which the artist is necessarily isolated from the "crowd" by virtue of the superiority of his intellect. For Yeats the writer is a writer because he intensifies the life around him with a passion beyond the reach of others; he concludes *The Death of Synge* with the single aphorism, "A good writer should be so simple that he has no faults, only sins" (A, 527). In the context of eulogy, the aphorism clearly points to the essence of Synge's nature and achievement; in the context of the Mask of the man of Phase 17, "Simplification through intensity," it reasserts Yeats's standard for himself.

Appealing to biographical accuracy, we recognize that Yeats's retreat consequent upon his re-evaluation of what was possible in Ireland was neither complete nor enduring but, in terms of the structure of *Autobiographies,* it does complete his estrangement and ultimately marks his failure to achieve Unity of Being. Synge set up as hero, Yeats allusively identified with him, the necessity of the writer's finding a Mask and the nature of Yeats's own Mask obsessively re-asserted, the autobiography should surely go on to mark a phase of increasing personal, spiritual and literary fulfillment, a phase where Unity of Being if not Unity of Culture is realized. The shift in genre from the memoir of *Dramatis Personae* to the journal entries has intimated that this will not be the case, that fragmentation rules; Yeats's failure to account autobiographically for the years between Synge's death and his own Nobel Prize makes the case plain. In *The Bounty of Sweden* Yeats is finally honoured for personal achievement and as representative of his country. Yet the tribute of the book is to what he, Lady Gregory and John Synge *tried* to achieve and to what Sweden *has* achieved. As such it provides a poignant coda to *Autobiographies,* one whose very dignity and restraint underline both the possibilities and the limitations of the mythic tendency to Unity of Being which had dictated the structure and the style of earlier portions of the book.

SIX: *THE BOUNTY OF SWEDEN*

Yeats opens *The Bounty of Sweden* with yet another disingenuous disclaimer. He recalls Mathers' words to him on his first visit to Paris— " 'Write your impressions at once, for you will never see Paris clearly again' " (A, 531)—, and concludes with a remark of Synge's and a statement of his own intentions:

'Is not style', as Synge once said to me, 'born out of the shock of new material?'
    I am about to write, as in a kind of diary, impressions of Stockholm which must get whatever value they have from excitement, from the presence before the eyes of what is strange, mobile and disconnected. (A, 531)

Style, Yeats has often told us, is the deliberate assumption of the Mask. The use of Synge's statement here is no contradictory credo but a way of rendering impertinent possible criticisms of the lack of obvious architectonics in these passages of "reverie" over Sweden.[1] Yeats pursues the illusion of immediacy by using the present tense and by first recording the things travellers always report: conversations, itinerary details, observations of architecture. But, in fact, the "Stockholm impressions" were written rather deliberately after Yeats's return as "a sort of 'bread and butter letter' to Sweden, and at last a part of my autobiography" (L, 701).

The advantage of an aesthetic theory which posits that the artist "will play with all masks" is that he can assume a tone appropriate to the occasion. The modesty of Yeats's disclaimer, his confession that in writing his poetry, "though the labour is very great, I seem to have used no faculty peculiar to myself, certainly no special gift" (A, 532–33), the pervasive tone of dignity in *The Bounty of Sweden* are far from the "fanatic heart" which shaped so much of the "personal utterance" of the later poems and which had revealed itself in *Estrangement*. In *The Bounty of Sweden*, the Mask is that of the courtier, and Yeats later took great pleasure in a compliment paid his wife to the effect that the Swedish Royal Family thought he had " 'the manners of a Courtier' " (L, 827). In the Royal Court, he finds a contemporary Urbino and an example of much that he had elaborated theoretically in earlier books of *Autobiographies*. That it is appropriate for Yeats to adopt the mask of Castiglione in this court where it seemed but affectation in modern Ireland makes for much of the difference between the stridency of *Estrangement* and the graciousness of *The Bounty of Sweden*.

From the first impression he records of them, Yeats images the Swedish royalty as belonging to the traditionally cultured and leisured class whom he apotheosized in his frequent allusions to Urbino. The pastoral-seeming king has a face "like some country gentleman who can quote Horace and Catullus" (A, 539) and Yeats links Princess Margaretha even more firmly with such a tradition, the greatest achievement of which he believed was the mind of the poet and the perfect beauty, spiritual and physical, of a few women. For her he resurrects the image of the shell he had used to characterize Margaret in *The Speckled Bird*,[2] image of the most subtle and enduring beauty and of the exercise of creative power, and visual equivalent of the gyres themselves; her face was "full of subtle beauty, emotional and precise, and impassive with a still intensity suggesting that final consummate strength which rounds the spiral of a shell" (A, 540).

Joseph Ronsley has listed the contrasts Yeats draws between Ireland and Sweden[3]; he uses these contrasts to identify himself with the tradition of the Courtier. The firing of cannon in Dublin is the sign of civil war and raises an "instinctive alarm"; in Stockholm it forms part of a ritual "of gaiety and goodwill" (A, 543). In the rituals of the reception at the palace, Yeats finds "it is Life herself that is praised" (A, 544); through a doctrine of courtly love he identifies himself with those rituals. In Ireland, the analogue of the service of a court, service of a woman, has been perverted; the woman has become the nationalist abstraction of Cathleen Ni Houlihan: "I had thought how we Irish had served famous men and famous families, and had been, so long as our nation had intellect enough to shape anything of itself, good lovers of women, but had never served any abstract cause, except the one, and that we personified by a woman, and I wondered if the service of woman could be so different from that of a Court." His reverie leads him to think "that there were men living . . . who had served a woman through all folly, because they had found no Court to serve" (A, 545). One recalls his earlier reference to the "extreme development" of his Romantic idealism which had prolonged his "miserable love affair" with Maud Gonne; Yeats manages to imply that, in this substitute service both to Maud Gonne and to Ireland (Cathleen Ni Houlihan), he too is a Courtier, remembering the Urbino to which he immediately alludes. That Urbino, evoked by the Court ceremonies, stands opposed to any "equivalent gathering . . . called together by the heads of some State where every democratic dream had been fulfilled," a gathering in which the conversation would be governed by "sarcasm" (A, 546) and none but the very old would be comfortable.

All Yeats's observations of the arts in Stockholm tend in this same direction. Swedish Impressionism shows not only in the French absorption with the empirical fact of light but a profound familiarity with and love of the place painted; it possesses "an emotion held in common" (A, 551) which both administers and creates tradition. The Town Hall, a Ruskinian Utopia decorated by craftsmen working in "seeming perfect freedom" yet in harmony with a larger design, embodies Unity of Culture: "These myth-makers and mask-makers worked as if they belonged to one family . . .; all that suggestion of novelty and of an immeasurable past; all that multitude and unity, could hardly have been possible, had not love of Stockholm and belief in its future so

115

filled men of different minds, classes, and occupations that they almost attained the supreme miracle, the dream that has haunted all religions, and loved one another. No work comparable in method or achievement has been accomplished since the Italian cities felt the excitement of the Rennaissance . . ." (A, 555–56).

This meditation on Sweden and Yeats's lecture on "The Irish Dramatic Movement" which concludes the volume were written as separate exercises and combined to make a volume for the Cuala Press. In the Preface to the 1925 Cuala edition (omitted from later editions), Yeats accounts for the volume's structure:

> Every winner of a Nobel Prize for Literature is invited to deliver a lecture before the Royal Swedish Academy and to send a copy to be printed in the proceedings of that body. I spoke at my own choice about our theatre, and a couple of months ago dictated to a friend as many of my words as I could remember . . . & added there to [sic] certain explanatory notes. But immediately upon my return from Stockholm I had written a meditation called 'The Bounty of Sweden' which pleases me better, because it has a newer theme; and now I have put both into this little book, adding nothing new but a couple of notes.[4]

Yeats's reproduction of his lecture to the Royal Academy underlines both his sense of himself as recreator of the *anima mundi* and his tribute to a Sweden which he saw as having achieved Unity of Culture where Ireland had failed: "I think as I speak these words of how deep down we [himself, Lady Gregory and Synge] have gone, below all that is individual, modern and restless, seeking foundations for an Ireland that can only come into existence in a Europe that is still but a dream" (A, 554). The conclusion to the lecture itself encapsulates much of *Autobiographies:* Yeats's tribute to Lady Gregory and Synge, his literary aims, the defeat of those aims at the national level in Ireland.

> . . . when I received from the hands of your King the great honour your Academy has conferred upon me, I felt that a young man's ghost should have stood upon one side of me and at the other a living woman sinking into the infirmity of age. Indeed I have seen little in the last week that would not have been memorable and exciting to Synge and to Lady Gregory, for Sweden has achieved more than we have hoped for our own country.[5] I think most of all, perhaps, of that splendid spectacle of your Court, a family beloved and able that has gathered about it not the rank only but the intellect of its country. No like spectacle will in Ireland show its work of discipline and of taste, though it might satisfy a need of the race no institution created under the influence of English or American democracy can satisfy. (A, 571–72)

"Consciousness is conflict" (Ex, 331); the other face of a personal triumph is the defeat of his hopes for a literary nationalism that might weld the Irish into one.

But if Ireland's growing "abstraction" points up the defeat of Yeats's particular version of nationalism, the placing of *The Bounty of Sweden* at the end of *Autobiographies,* the reproduction of the lecture as a coda reciting once more his ideals, his metaphoric position between Lady Gregory, mistress of an Irish Urbino, and John Synge, the tragic poet-hero with whom he had identified himself, attempt to establish a personal victory of mythic proportions. The Nobel Prize would make a fitting and dignified end to many autobiographies but, given the long meditation on the theory of the Mask which has pervaded *Autobiographies,* the many Masks with their corresponding rhetoric which Yeats has revealed himself adopting since he first "chose Alastor" as his "chief of men," his subjection of his friends to the scheme of self and anti-self, his hopes and disillusions begin to suggest the mythic context of the poet as hero. In the scheme of *A Vision,* the hero, exemplified by Nietzsche, and the poet most easily achieve Unity of Being through the Mask. Only the way to the Mask differs: "The poet finds and makes his mask in disappointment, the hero in defeat" (M, 337). The hero's function is heroic action, the poet's "Heroic reverie" (VPo, 619).

Although Yeats does not explicitly insist on it, many of the central visions, meditations and events which structure *Autobiographies* have analogues in heroic patterns, particularly if we transpose those patterns from physical to psychological configurations, something Yeats had done since youth ("It is a natural conviction for a painter's son to believe that there may be a landscape that is symbolical of some spiritual condition" [A, 74]). One might cite among heroic motifs the "Emmanuel" dream which calls Yeats to rebirth through the Image; his spiritual trial, "lost upon the path of Hodos Chameliontos"; his apprehension of Unity of Being, a unity that in the hero cycle manifests itself either in spiritual union with a god or sexual union with an unusually beautiful woman; his attempt to "save" Ireland by showing her the way to Unity of Culture, analogous to the hero's bringing back of knowledge from another world. On the cosmic level, his lunar model of individual reincarnations and historic cycles parallels that of the hero's circular journey from waking to sleep to waking, from the conscious to the unconscious and back to the conscious, from natural to supernatural to natural again, from separation to initiation and return.[6] Yeats's modernity lies precisely in his use of autobiography to suggest aspects of this heroic journey. Unlike earlier mythographers, he does not need the physical apparatus of a *Divine Comedy* or a God, external to the self, with which the saint strives to be reunited. In his poetic mapping of the subjective self, the journey is inward into the soul and back again and the nation's journey must be similarly inward into its own tradition; the union is with the self.

Heroic action and the hero's ultimate defeat often transcend in tragic ecstasy the confusion of the world; nonetheless both have their original impulse in that world, and often too, the world clings to the hero to the last, an irony Yeats had appreciated in the earliest prose piece of his we have: "Congal when he has accomplished deeds of marvellous valour is slain by the hand of an idiot boy who carries a sickle for sword, and the lid of a cauldron for shield. Ah, strange irony of the Celt" (UP, I, 85). Yeats's own heroes also find it difficult to remain unmitigatedly sublime; "the best of our moments are marred by a little vulgarity" (M, 105). Perhaps Naoise comes closest. But Cuchulain dies once in the magnificent futility of fighting waves; resurrected, he dies again, heroically upright, at the hands of a blind beggar who has been paid twelve pennies. Yeats's King Congal averts a similar fate by suicide only to be reincarnated by the Great Herne as an ass. The Cuchulain cycle especially never loses its tragic sublimity, yet the hero is touched with an ironic futility not unrelated to farce.

A similar sense of ironic futility—directed inward by the structure of *Autobiographies* itself and directed outward in rhetoric against Ireland—modulates Yeats's mythic pattern of himself as the poet-hero. The personal victory—his emergence out of "The Tragic Generation," his Nobel Prize, his forging of a style—is a victory, even an heroic victory, but a victory which in the context of the structure of *Autobiographies* is incomplete. Yeats everywhere in *The Bounty of Sweden* presents himself as a simple man, one who feasts on sausages to celebrate the news of the Prize, one who has difficulty walking backwards up the stairs from the royal throne, and a gracious man, one who is "conscious of that sympathy which makes a speaker forget all but his own thoughts, and soliloquize aloud" (A, 553). The autobiographical posture seems that of one who has found Unity of Being, yet even its intimacy has a formal quality which makes us realize that we are seeing the public figure. Yeats does sometimes treat himself with irony,[7] he admits a touch of vulgarity as one possible antithesis to the occasion's formality and his own heroic position: he retreats backwards to his place and examines his medal to conclude that, old though he is, his Muse is moving perpetually with Swedenborg's Angels " ' " towards the day-spring of her youth" ' " (A, 541); he catches himself telling a woman whose "smiling road" of courtesy has centuries of ritual behind it that he is "going to change the thought of the world" (A, 541–42). But even that irony acts as a check on the public image alone. We do not see the true self, the personality that has achieved Unity of Being through adoption of the Mask except as emblematic figure: Irish Senator, Irish poet, courtier, each in his public role. The narrative strategy has the same effect as did that of Yeats's move from the tight structure of *The Trembling of the Veil* to the seemingly fragmented journal of *Estrangement* and *The Death of Synge;* it leaves the same impression of lacunae as did his decision to exclude the years between Synge's death and his Nobel Prize. In *Autobiographies* Yeats gives us Unity of Being as a theory and a mythic structure, as a personal myth and then as a personal choice which estranges him from his nation, finally as an accomplished fact. But like a postulant in The Order of The Golden Dawn, the reader is asked to accept the end on faith. In

The Bounty of Sweden Yeats presents himself as having moved from fragmentation of personality, from his estrangement from Ireland and from the rhetorical bitterness which in varying degrees characterized the earlier books to the Unity of Being those books image, in doctrine and structure, as the ideal. The reader can contemplate the personality that has attained this Unity, and he may even leave his contemplation with the satisfaction one derives from literary closure, but he has been shown the path to that Unity no more than is the postulant.

Similarly Yeats appears as Ireland's spokesman and this too is a victory. But the refusal of Ireland throughout *Autobiographies* to be led gives the heroic victory its futile aspect and its element of disappointment. Yeats's "stylistic arrangements of experience" remain dualistic: through the Mask he transcends biography in mythic pattern but, because always tinged with ironic despair, the myth in its turn is suffused with biographic limitations. *Autobiographies* charts the patterning of the self between the two tensions; except for rare moments, they have not engendered and become one.

SEVEN: *ON THE BOILER:* The Fanatic Heart

In *Autobiographies,* Yeats's choice of a Mask of heroic defeat rather than of heroic victory is the result of his feeling himself out of phase with his age; indeed his heroism arises out of that feeling. So too is much of the lack of Unity in *Autobiographies* due to lack of Unity of the autobiographer and his age. A man who finds his intellectual and artistic antecedents in the most aristocratic of all feudal courts needs to tread softly in the twentieth century and in a country rebelling to free itself of sovereign rule and to establish representative government. That necessary care had determined the impersonal tone of much of *Autobiographies.* It had in part dictated the transformation of "First Draft" into *The Trembling of the Veil* by the imposition of the "Lunar parable" on anecdotes and characterizations and by the overall structure of waxing and waning. It had also acted as one principle of selection of those passages from his *Journal* that Yeats published as *Estrangement* and *The Death of Synge:* he toned down or omitted some of the franker political passages such as that at the end of Entry 65 of the *Journal* against the "active state of democratic envy and jealousy" which he saw as preventing the Irish play-goers from accepting "the pre-eminence of one or two writers" and as making them dread "all liberated things" (Mem, 168-69).[1] Writing in 1938 to George Barnes of the BBC, Yeats *was* frank about his need for mythic structure and a Mask in lieu of direct statement: "surely a man so intelligent as you, " he flatters Barnes before refusing him, "understands that if I were to write whatever I would 'most like to say to the country as a whole' or to my own family as a whole, it would be altogether unprintable."[2]

Not long before writing that letter, in a last autobiographical gesture, Yeats had found a Mask through which to come close to writing what he would most like to say to his country and his age. Adopting the persona of a figure remembered from childhood, a mad ship's carpenter, he metaphorically announces that, although he is "very good at his trade"—carpentry/poetry—, he has no intention of sticking to it; instead he is about "to read the Scriptures and denounce his neighbours" (OB, 9). But both law-giving and denunciation demand an attention not granted the figure from Yeats's childhood, for his use of the Mask of the mad old carpenter carries with it an archetypal wisdom. Denouncing that destruction of what had seemed promised which had also shaped the "tragedy" of *Autobiographies,* Yeats justifies both the Mask and the oracular tone of *On the Boiler:*

> Young men know nothing of this sort,
> Observant old men know it well;
> And when they know what old books tell
> And that no better can be had,
> Know why an old man should be mad. (OB, 9)

120

"Preliminaries" takes up the themes which in *Estrangement* had turned *Autobiographies* from personal to national considerations even more markedly than had the antithetical myth of *The Trembling of the Veil.* Yeats once again decries contemporary leaders' desires to be popular and the "ignorance" which is the result of governments' "Forcing reading and writing on those who wanted neither" and which has resulted in Ireland's being given "to the incompetent" (OB, 11). The argument is that which, in *Estrangement,* had led Yeats to set Ireland's rising middle class against the ideal of an Urbino, but in *On the Boiler* the symbolic Urbino is displaced in favour of an antithesis based on the actual composition of the Irish Senate: Yeats praises the nominated Senator, "always speaking with undisturbed self-possession," and "sets up against him some typical elected man, emotional as a youthful chimpanzee, hot and vague, always disturbed, always hating something or other" (OB, 12).

What distinguishes "Preliminaries" and much of the rest of *On the Boiler* from *Estrangement* are its tone and its rhetoric. In *Estrangement* the tone was angry, strident, while the rhetoric, denunciatory as it was, was also expository, rationalizing. Here the tone is more measured and denunciation is combined with a more overtly vatic rhetoric, culminating in an imperative to Ireland. That imperative is finally directly stated as, the Mask of the mad carpenter and all Masks set aside, Yeats speaks out of personal experience: "I was six years in the Irish Senate; I am not ignorant of politics elsewhere . . . . I say to those that shall rule here: If ever Ireland again seems molten wax, reverse the process of revolution." The image of Ireland as "molten wax" ready to receive a political imprint is that of the nation in "Ireland after Parnell," rendered by upheaval momentarily receptive to political direction before succumbing to the misdirection of hatred. Yeats's command to Ireland goes on to denounce all government, whether democratic or dictatorial, in favour of "the politics of the intellect":

Do not try to pour Ireland into any political system. Think first how many able men with public minds the country has, how many it can hope to have in the near future, and mould your system upon those men. It does not matter how you get them, but get them. Republics, Kingdoms, Soviets, Corporate States, Parliaments, are trash, as Hugo said of something else "not worth one blade of grass that God gives for the nest of the linnet." These men, whether six or six thousand, are the core of Ireland, are Ireland itself. (OB, 13)

Section IV of "Preliminaries" takes the reader back to Yeats's touchstone for what he hoped to achieve in Ireland, the plays of the Abbey Theatre which "are taking the place of political speakers, political organisations, in holding together the twenty scattered millions conscious of their Irish blood" simply because their choice is sometimes dictated by such an aristocracy of the intellect— "'Not what you want but what we want.'" But it is in this alone that the Abbey has

121

succeeded for, if it has "produced some of the best plays of modern times," it has also produced "a far greater number of the worst" (OB, 13-14) and has followed no other direction Yeats would have wished. As so often in *Autobiographies,* so here denunciation and prophetic utterance subside into an autobiographical moment expressive of defeat: "I have wondered if I did right in giving so much of my life to the expression of other men's genius," Yeats asks and goes on to console himself with a personal victory dependent on a cultural tradition which is the antithesis of his age: "I have aimed at tragic ecstasy and here and there in my own work and in the work of my friends I have seen it greatly played. What does it matter that it belongs to a dead art and to a time when a man spoke out of an experience and a culture that were not of his time alone, but held his time, as it were, at arms length, that he might be a spectator of the ages." His consolation lies in images of great intensity: "These thing will, it may be, haunt me on my deathbed; what matter if the people prefer another art, I have had my fill" (OB, 14). As in *Autobiographies,* personal victory and heroic defeat are each other's doubles.

Personal memories also provide the transition to a consideration of the nature of the revolution—should Ireland ever again be "molten wax"—needed to mould the nation. Yeats opens "To-morrow's Revolution" with quarrels that are but "superficial" conflict, quarrels with his father, with "dominant opinion," quarrels which led him to invent "a patter," to permit himself "an easy man's insincerity, and for honesty's sake a little malice." "I think I have succeeded," he concludes archly of the patter, "and that none of my friends know that I am a fanatic." The "fanatic heart" asserts the Yeatsian mythology of a more profound conflict, a "slow-moving" reversal of gyres "where opposites die each other's life, live each other's death," a conflict that lets Horne find his Mask in Botticelli, Ricketts his in Delacroix, that lets Synge find among the "forgotten people" of the Aran Islands "a mirror for his bitterness," and lets Yeats write "plays in Shakespearean blank verse about Irish kings for whom nobody cared a farthing" (OB, 15). These conflicting gyres in which cycles increase and diminish and come round again, whether in architecture and art, in literature, or in the rituals of war ("Asiatic conquerors before battle invoked their ancestors, and a few years ago a Japanese admiral thanked his for guiding the torpedoes" [OB, 15]) are metaphor, myth, expressing "things too deep for my intellect and my knowledge" (OB, 25), neither patter nor plain-speaking.

"But now I must . . . put away my patter," Yeats declares his intention, and, an observant old man, "speak to the young men before the ox treads on my tongue" (OB, 15). The patterer has revealed himself Preacher, had he finds his Scripture in the seventeenth century *The Anatomy of Melancholy.* That text is no symbolic evocation, like

Yeats's frequent allusions to Urbino or Coole Park, of an inherited tradition for the artist; it is a practical call for eugenics:

"'It is the greatest part of our felicity to be well born, and it were happy for human kind, if only such parents as are sound of body and mind should be suffered to marry. An husbandman will sow none but the best and choicest seed upon his land; he will not rear a bull or an horse except he be right shapen in all parts, or permit him to cover a mare, except he be well assured of his breed; we make a choice of the best rams for our sheep, rear the neatest kine, and keep the best dogs, *quanto id diligentius in procreandis liberis observandum!* and how careful then should we be in begetting our children!' " (OB, 15—16)

Although he abandons both "patter" and metaphor and myth in favour of a more direct statement of what he "would 'most like to say to the country as a whole,' " Yeats does not abandon rhetorical strategy. The greater part of "To-Morrow's Revolution" rests on an appeal to external authorities—Burton, the psychologists reporting on intelligence testing—, an appeal made more overt by Yeats's atypical care in documenting the sources of his information. The strategy is a clever one; no lover of science himself, Yeats is willing to use its information to suggest ways of controlling its effects. Moreover, given that references to eugenics were not apt to sit lightly with many of his readers, Yeats's indirect discourse provides him with a Mask of reason with which to present a doctrine little likely to be popular. The appeal to Burton is an appeal to the authority of the established literary canon; the appeal to the evidence of intelligence testing is an appeal to the authority of science: both appeals are for the maintenance of a traditional class system to the end of fostering the highest cultivation of the arts among a gifted, wealthy and educated few. Yeats's selection of data points to an increase in "mother-wit" as one moves up the class structure from paupers to the sufficiently well-off. He speculates from this about the threat of the increasing families of those of the lower ranks who, protected from infant mortality by science and encouraged to procreate by governments offering baby bonuses, mar all with "ill-breeding."

Moving forward from behind the impersonality of his data, Yeats interprets his "text" from Burton as a program for "revolution." As he had in *The Bounty of Sweden,* he names Stockholm as the contemporary model of a cultured city-state: there the largest families are those of the intelligentsia. For the rest of Europe, he predicts that science and economic re-organization will "remove the last check upon the multiplication of the uneducatable masses." If Culture is to be preserved, if Europe is not, "like those older civilisations that saw the triumph of their gangrel stocks," to "accept decay," "it will become duty of the educated classes to seize and control one or more . . . necessities. The drilled and docile masses may submit, but a prolonged civil war seems more likely" (OB, 19). Yeats frankly asserts that this is a plain-speaking of the personal conviction behind his mythology when he recalls Robartes' words, "'Love war because of its horror, that belief may be changed, civilisation renewed'" (OB, 20).[3] Like Robartes' visions, both early and late, Yeats's is not only terrifying but apocalyptic, ending "with the victory of the skilful, riding their machines as did the feudal knights their armoured horses" (OB, 19). As the simile makes plain, the argument is for a political program to effect the return of feudal values.

As in *Autobiographies* where the defeat of Yeats's hopes for Ireland gives way to personal breakdown or in "Preliminaries" where his remarks about the mis-education of the Irish quieten into an assessment of the personal value of his work at the Abbey, so the political manifesto of "To-Morrow's Revolution" cedes to the "Private Thoughts" behind Yeats's acceptance of the data he cites and his appeal to authority shows itself as resting on personal conviction. "I am philosophical, not scientific," he explains, "which means that observed facts do not mean much until I can make them part of my experience" (OB, 21-22). The statement makes autobiography the basis of theory and myth; the form of "Private Thoughts" demonstrates the expanding significance of "observed facts" in the context of individual experience. Recollections of ancestors (reminiscent of the passage in *Autobiographies* in which Yeats turns over miniatures of his dead relatives and places his own thoughts in their historical context) imaginatively become his own experience so that his single mind becomes analogous to "all human destiny" (OB, 22). As the individual mind expands outward to incorporate its civilization in Yeats's myth, so too history can be contracted to "my own particular amusements and interests . . . for Heraclitus was in the right": in history, in love, in horse-racing, in all things whatsoever, "Opposites are everywhere face to face, dying each other's life, living each other's death" (OB, 22).

These "Private Thoughts" seem a précis of *A Vision;* Yeats himself saw them as a statement of those convictions about the individual mind on which he had founded the historical generalizations of his "philosophy": "(The *Vision* is my 'public philosophy'). My 'private philosophy' is the material dealing with the individual mind which came to me with that on which the mainly historical *Vision* is based" (L, 916). Thus the historical sketch of the waxing and waning of our civilization, presented theoretically in *A Vision,* posited as the source of tragedy in *Autobiographies,* is given in *On the Boiler* in anecdotes about individual persons and places. The culture reaches its apex in Castiglione's record of conversations at Urbino and its remnants live on in a "City Father of a defeated Spanish town [who] said that he could not understand it because their commander was not less well born than his opponent" or in Bishop Berkeley who refused to design a facade because "too many country gentlemen were already at the task" (OB, 23). Yeats took his class-consciousness seriously, yet is wit in these examples. Playfulness disappears as he goes on to examples of deterioration: "coarse, arrogant Bentley" refutes the scholarship of gentlemen; upstarts gain power; "culture, unity of being, no longer sufficed, and the specialists were already there" (OB, 23); it is time for Swift's satire.[4]

Like Yeats's program for revolution, his "Private Thoughts" predict an apocalypse. He sees the civilization ending, the individual submerged in the multitude: "the old classes, with their power of co-ordinating events, evaporate, the mere multitude is everywhere with its empty photographic eyes" (OB, 25). Against that multitude, Yeats re-asserts the individual mind in both theoretical and autobiographical terms: objectivists hide "from the mass of the people that the grave diggers have no place to bury us but in the human mind"; he himself, grown old, can no longer live among masterpieces and try "to make the like" but is convinced that genius is "'mad as the mist and snow'" (OB, 26). He seems to withhold judgment of the multitude—"Civilisation slept in the masses, wisdom in science. Is it criminal to sleep? I do not know; I do not say it" (OB, 26)—but his restraint is rhetorical, not actual, for like Robartes' all his convictions do point to an energetic acceptance of some new dispensation: approaching "the phoenix nest . . . we who have hated the age are joyous and happy"(OB, 25).

Revolution, a "tragic crisis" to be embraced with joyous energy, is "assume[d]" in *On the Boiler*. Hence "Ireland After The Revolution" opens with an exhilarated spoof of a manifesto for educational reform:

. . . the Irish Government will teach the great majority of its school-children nothing but ploughing, harrowing, sowing, curry-combing, bicycle-cleaning, drill-driving, parcel-making, bale-pushing, tin-can-soldering, door-knob polishing, threshold-whitening, coat-cleaning, trouser-patching, and playing upon the Squiffer, all things that serve human dignity, unless indeed it decide that these things are better taught at home, in which case it can leave the poor children at peace. (OB, 27—28)

The spoof is pointed in its feudalism: universal literacy and, therefore, the mis-education of the Irish is to be ended. A more seriously phrased proposal for educational reform follows; it suggests a curriculum so traditional as to exclude even Latin as "a language of the Greco-Roman decadence, all imitation and manner and other feminine tricks" (OB, 28). The government and military institutions of the nation are to be equally traditional, equally individualistic, equally "masculine." Yeats desires military families, "efficient and self-reliant, . . . [that] could throw back from our shores the disciplined uneducated masses of the commercial nations" (OB, 29—30), a military institution that would command loyalty because it embodied "human violence." Shifting back into the imperative, he directs the Irish to "Desire some just war, that big house and hovel, college and public house, civil servant—his Gaelic certificate in his pocket—and international bridge-playing woman, may know that they belong to one nation" (OB, 30). All is to be the creative impulse of an intellectual elite that the Irish masses might be "moulded and cast" (OB, 30) into Unity, that Irish minds' "ancient, cold, explosive, detonating impartiality" might displace in their own nation the "alien appeal to mass instinct" of the English mind, a mind transformed by journalism and ill-conceived education into "a bed-hot harlot" (OB, 31).

Yeats's rhetoric in these passages is powerful and frequently abusive, a mixture of political manifesto, philosophy and demagogeury which demands the rights of a traditional order through the restoration of "the responsibilities of the family" (OB, 29). Even George V's accession to the Prime Minister's wish that the King's Russian relatives not be brought to England is seen by Yeats as the betrayal of family for the sake of popularity in a democracy. Both Yeats's doctrine and his rhetoric in *On the Boiler* counteract the trends of his age to such an extent that, his position stated in the book's three central sections, some rhetorically strategic summation and withdrawal seems tactically appropriate. "Crazy Jane on the Mountain" summarizes the conflict of the previous chapters. The popular George V is considered[5] —"A King had some beautiful cousins/But where are they gone?/Battered to death in a cellar/And he stuck to his throne"—and opposed to the Irish tradition:

> Last night I lay on the mountain
> (Said Crazy Jane)
> There in a two horsed carriage
> That on two wheels ran
> Great bladdered Emer sat,
> Her violent man
> Cuchulain, sat at her side,
> Thereupon,
> Propped upon my two knees,
> I kissed a stone;
> I lay stretched out in the dirt
> And I cried tears down. (OB, 31)

The responsive emotion evoked by the Irish vision mythologizes what has been political rhetoric in the previous chapters as well as bringing to the fore again the mad persona through which Yeats had initially eased the reader into his thoughts. He manipulates that mad persona's ambivalence: it disarms us even while it demands that its observations are to be taken seriously; it heightens the literal political rhetoric between its appearances even while it casts that rhetoric in a literary frame. Initially a means of putting forward what Yeats believes, the persona finally enables him to withdraw once again from literal to symbolic statement.

Yeats's opening rhyme suggests that "Observant old men" have a right to be listened to simply because of their experience. In "Other Matters," the old man on the boiler finally rests on his autobiographical and familial experience, on his own work at the Abbey and at Cuala to create Unity of Culture in Ireland. Admitting himself "a biassed man"

126

(OB, 32), he reiterates many of his points through personal reference. Reading for the Abbey has taught him that tradition is being shaken at one extreme by "a form of jocularity" which "has begun to replace or degrade characterisation," at the other extreme by plays which substitute opinion for action (OB, 33). A third example leads Yeats to the formulation of an aesthetic: "The arts are all the bridal chambers of joy. No tragedy is legitimate unless it leads some great character to his final joy" (OB, 35). The aims of Higgins, Yeats and Dorothy Wellesley in their new editions of the Cuala Press Broadsides state the theme another way: "where the poem is Irish of Irish national tradition, no churl must be present. We, like all good poets, turn our backs on the heterogeneous, seek out our own kindred" (OB, 36). So too Jack B. Yeats's *The Charmed Life:* "He does not care that few will read it, still fewer recognize its genius; it is his book, his 'Faust,' his pursuit of all that through its unpredictable, unarrangeable reality least resembles knowledge" (OB, 36). The Cuala embroideries will also serve "to keep the name of the designer and the Yeats name in memory" (OB, 37). The structure of "Other Matters" is suggestive rather than rhetorically suasive but the cumulative effect of its examples establishes the Yeats family as an artistic family, trustee of Ireland's inherited tradition, on the model of those Renaissance or Oriental families whose obligation it was to ensure the continuation of an inherited artistic tradition.

First his political and now his aesthetic position enunciated, Yeats once again withdraws into his role as poet: "In my savage youth I was accustomed to say that no man should be permitted to open his mouth in Parliament until he had sung or written his Utopia, for lacking that we could not know where he was taking us, and I still think that artists of all kinds should once again praise or represent great or happy people" (OB, 37). *On the Boiler* is a Senator's and a Poet's Utopia. It completed, politician and poet are opposed one final time: "somebody talked of a man with a monkey and some sort of stringed instrument, and it has pleased me to imagine him a great politician" (OB, 37–38). "Some knew what ailed the world/But never said a thing," the imagined politician confesses while Yeats's bandwagon rhythms, pronounced caesurae and vulgar images in his last stanza satirize him as a tinker:

> With boys and girls about him,
> With any sort of clothes,
> With a hat out of fashion
> With old patched shoes,
> With a ragged bandit cloak,
> With an eye like a hawk,
> With a stiff straight back,
> With a strutting turkey walk,
> With a bag full of pennies,
> With a monkey on a chain,
> With a great cock's feather,
> With an old foul tune.

Yet, transformed, that imagined politician also rhymes:

> So I have picked a better trade
> And night and morning sing:
> *Tall dames go walking in grass green Avalon.* (OB, 38)

That he can so sing of a traditional order marks him as a "great politician" in Yeatsian terms. His song epitomizes the Utopian order for which Yeats argues in *On the Boiler* and once again lifts the tract above political rhetoric, transforms it into a final autobiographical and mythological gesture towards Unity of Being in Yeats's own life as poet, nationalist and sometime political figure, towards hoped-for Unity of Culture in Ireland.

But in Yeatsian mythology all things have their double: the interface of Utopia is reality, of Unity of Culture is chaos and destruction. Yeats assumes one last persona in *On the Boiler,* a persona the more terrifying for its being less self-consciously rhetorical and ironic than that of the ship's carpenter or the politician. "A silly old man" (OB, 39), a pedlar, he too is versed in political thought. But where the mad ship's carpenter gave us Yeats's program of "revolution" by which a better Ireland might be built, the old man of *Purgatory* gives us the other side of the penny in his prognostications for his nation.

In many ways the personae are parallel. The Old Man in *Purgatory* draws a lesson from gaunt tree and burned house just as Yeats-cum-ship's carpenter had done from Dublin's eighteenth-century Mansion House, all but destroyed by "Gin Palace" embellishments (OB, 10), and from Burton's *The Anatomy of Melancholy;* the Mansion House of "Preliminaries" provides what Donald Torchiana has termed the "framework" of *Purgatory*[6] and makes the play symmetrically complete the tract's political rhetoric. Similarly, Yeats metaphorizes Ireland as the ruined house, whether Mansion House or country house. The house, whether the nation's or the family's, is founded upon the maintenance of tradition:

> Great people lived and died in this house;
> Magistrates, colonels, members of Parliament,
> Captains and Governors, and long ago
> Men that had fought at Aughrim and the Boyne.
> Some that had gone on government work
> To London or to India came home to die,
> Or came from London every spring
> To look at the May-blossom in the park.
> They had loved the trees that he cut down
> To pay what he had lost at cards
> Or spent on horses, drink and women;
> Had loved the house, had loved all
> The intricate passages of the house . . . . (OB, 41)

Both houses owe their ruin to "gangrel stock." The Lord Mayor will not restore House or Ireland to her former dignity because, like George V, "Stuck to his throne," "he thinks . . . that his duty is to make himself popular among the common people" (OB, 10); the old man on the boiler moves from this "ignorance" to the lesson on eugenics he draws from Burton. The mother of the Old Man of *Purgatory*, having married a groom who "killed the house" (OB, 41) has "passed pollution on" (OB, 45) so that, two generations later, the Boy of the play is no learned gentleman who loves the house and the tradition it stands for but an uneducated bastard upon whose slow wits the ideas of theft or murder come as possibilities for self-betterment.

The penalty for this destruction is greater even than the bloodshed *On the Boiler* prophesied and *Purgatory* enacts. In the play Yeats not only makes a statement about Ireland but is more direct than he has been before about the nature of his belief in an after-life. In a passage which states as law what he had only hypothesized in *The Celtic Twilight*, he has the Old Man explain the vision, which is to come, of his mother's remorse: souls must

> Re-live
> Their transgressions, and that not once
> But many times; they know at last
> The consequence of those transgressions
> Whether upon others or upon themselves;
> Upon others, others may bring help,
> For when the consequence is at an end
> The dream must end; upon themselves
> There is no help but in themselves
> And in the mercy of God. (OB, 40)

The other side of the Utopian "revolution" outlined in *On the Boiler* is Yeats's growing conviction of the impossibility of saving Ireland. At the literal level, the play condemns the individual (like the Japanese ghost Yeats had cited many years earlier) to continuous dreaming back so long as it believes in its own deeds: "Twice a murderer and all for nothing," the old man exclaims after having tried to end his mother's purgatory, "And she must animate that dead night/Not once but many times!" (OB, 46). The "remorse of the dead" will ensure the "misery of the living" (OB, 46). At the symbolic level, the action asserts the impossibility of Unity of Culture to Ireland "after Parnell,"[7] after her moment for revolution has passed and she has fallen. If there is completion in the individual life (the man kills his son and so finishes "all that consequence" [OB, 45]), there is none in the supernatural life or in the national life: the woman "dreams back" still; the house of Ireland remains a charred shell, "Its threshold gone to patch a pig-sty" (OB, 39); the tree, Yeatsian symbol of Ireland and of Unity of Being since his earliest prose, the tree which recalls Lady Gregory's planting of trees that, reaching maturity only after fifty years, would be bearers of tradition, the once fecund tree of "Green leaves, ripe leaves, leaves thick as butter," that tree stands at the play's end as at its beginning, barren and "riven" (OB, 39).

Nor can one even claim the ecstasy of tragedy for this end. "No tragedy is legitimate," Yeats has told us before giving us *Purgatory*, "unless it leads some great character to his final joy." Many characteristics of the tragic hero can be claimed for the Old Man: that he takes action to right what is wrong even though that action may be futile, that he is bound upon a wheel of fire, that he achieves some recognition of the nature of himself and the world. But I doubt we can claim "joy" for him. He remains too bound to the misery of the world for that, too unable to transcend himself and the endless round of purgatorial experience he has come to understand. In the Old Man's failure to achieve the "tragic joy" Yeats granted his earlier heroes, *Purgatory* is Yeats's most pessimistic play. Ireland herself has provided him with his Body of Fate. Its failure to achieve Unity of Culture has done for Yeats what Florence's banishment of Dante had done for that poet: it has enabled him to see the Vision of Evil which instructs him in necessary pessimism; it has given him that loss, greater than any personal loss, necessary to lead him, through transforming vision, to Unity of Being. As in *Autobiographies,* so too in *On the Boiler* the reader encounters Yeats's individual Unity of Being as a *fait accompli,* as a governing vision presented through assertion and, more powerfully, through his controlling metaphors. But in *Autobiographies* Yeats retreats from his plaint against Ireland and her failure to achieve Unity of Culture and rests on his personal achievement; allowing savage rhetoric full sway for a time, he mutes it again in the images of personal rebirth that end *The Trembling of the Veil,* the images of literary rebirth that end *Dramatis Personae,* the dignified acceptance of the recognition owed himself and his efforts in behalf of his country of *The Bounty of Sweden.* In *On the Boiler* and particularly in *Purgatory,* he presents his nation's failure to match his Unity of Being with a corresponding Unity of Culture with unmediated directness and bitterness. That directness, that bitterness, show him confronting his "Body of Fate." Facing "the greatest obstacle" he "can confront without despair" and transforming it in the lasting beauty of art, he retrieves for himself what he denies the Old Man of *Purgatory;* in this last autobiographical gesture he uses myth to gain for himself a tragic joy that transcends the particular obstacle. For in terms of the total construct of *On the Boiler* it is Yeats to whom we respond, not any one of his personae. Leaving us with an uncompromising and unsoftened view of Ireland's failure to attain Unity of Culture in a drama which yet displays worlds beyond this, Yeats boldly takes to himself the heroic mind implied by the mythic structure of *Autobiographies.*   *June, 1979.*

APPENDIX: *AUTOBIOGRAPHIES* AND PHILOSOPHY: Their Publication

An examination of manuscript versions of *Autobiographies* points out the indebtedness of all Yeats scholars to Curtis Bradford's careful description of a large part of the Yeats papers. Readers are referred to his *Yeats at Work* (Carbondale, Edwardsville: Southern Illinois University Press, 1965), pp. 337—77, for an extensive discussion of versions of *Autobiographies*. Denis Donoghue has published in *Memoirs* "First Draft" (the continuation of *Reveries over Childhood and Youth* which Yeats said he intended for his "own eye alone" but which covers much of the same ground as *The Trembling of the Veil*) and the *Journal* from which Yeats drew *Estrangement* and *The Death of Synge;* he has also collated passages from the *Journal* and *Estrangement* and *The Death of Synge* in *Memoirs,* pp. 303—04 (Appendix G). The primary source for the publication history of *Autobiographies* is, of course, Allan Wade, *A Bibliography of the Writings of W.B. Yeats* (3rd ed., rev. and edited by Russell K. Alspach; London: Rupert Hart-Davis, 1968). Joseph Ronsley, *Yeats's Autobiography: Life as Symbolic Pattern* (Cambridge, Mass.: Harvard University Press, 1968), includes a chapter on the work's "Publishing History" which brings together the material in Wade, in Bradford and in several of Yeats's letters.

While I have verified what follows by my own examination of the manuscripts of *Autobiographies,* it will be readily apparent that only occasionally and in relatively minor matters do I supplement Bradford's detailed description. The description is briefly recapitulated here along with references to the publication of Yeats's mature philosophical writings for two reasons: that the reader tracing Yeats's use of autobiography through the preceding discussion might have ready to hand information about the texts' composition and publication pointing to Yeats's self-conscious use of the genre, and that he might have obtruded on his attention more forcefully than is generally the case that autobiographical and philosophical writing were, for Yeats, intimately interrelated modes for some twenty years.

Many of Yeats's early essays obviously qualify as "philosophical." But he began to move tentatively towards the *systematic* presentation of his occult beliefs only with "Swedenborg, Mediums, and the Desolate Places," written in 1914. In 1914 too, he had written his first autobiography, announced by The Cuala Press as *Memory Harbour: A Revery on my Childhood and Youth* and published by that press in 1916 (although publication date in the text is 1915), in an edition of 425 numbered copies, as *Reveries over Childhood and Youth.* The edition was accompanied by separately bound *Plates to Accompany Reveries over Childhood and Youth* (three plates: Jack B. Yeats, *Memory Harbour,* colour, with W.B. Yeats's explanatory note on the facing page; *Mrs. Yeats,* from a drawing by John Butler Yeats made in 1867; *John Butler Yeats,* from a watercolour drawing by himself). Both the English and the American MacMillan editions of the text appeared the same year. As Bradford has noted, Yeats deleted from the typescript of the book passages about his family which might have offended and the description of his first orgasm which occurs again in "First Draft." 1914, then, marks the beginning of a long period during which Yeats wrote both autobiography and, in the words of "Swedenborg, Mediums, and the Desolate Places," essays "discovering a philosophy" (Ex, 31), along with his poetry.

In 1915–16, Yeats wrote the "First Draft" of a further autobiography. Letters and his notation on the manuscript's envelope indicate that he regarded this manuscript as far too private to publish. Although it has not figured largely in my own discussion because I have been more concerned with Yeats's *public*—i.e., published—versions of his self, it bears comparison with *Autobiographies;* it contains many of the reminiscences but not the structuring myth of *The Trembling of the Veil.*

During 1917, Yeats worked on *Per Amica Silentia Lunae* (published in 1918). This first philosophical fruit of George Yeats's attempts to amuse her new husband with automatic writing contains many of the basic ideas of *A Vision,* although it lacks the terminology, the characterology, the historical perspective and much of the complexity of thought of the larger work. During 1917 too he began taking notes for *A Vision* and writing the first of many drafts of the work which he intended to be a major systematization of his personal convictions, his knowledge of the occult, and the material he received via Mrs. Yeats from "communicators." (As Northrop Frye has felicitously remarked, we may as well accept Yeats's explanation of the source of this material since we have no better explanation to offer; moreover, hundreds of pages of automatic writing pertaining to *A Vision* exist among the Yeats papers to testify to his explanation.) He drafted and redrafted the text more or less continously between 1917 and 1925 when the first edition of *A Vision* was published by T. Werner Laurie.

During this period of intensive work on his philosophy, Yeats also did his most sustained autobiographical writing. Returning to the events covered in "First Draft," although perhaps not to the text itself—the tone, style and controlling metaphors of the two texts differ markedly—, he wrote *Four Years.* Bradford notes those passages which parallel in content passages from "First Draft" and Yeats's re-ordering of events between "First Draft" and *Four Years* and tentatively dates the composition of this autobiography, no doubt correctly, as the winter of 1920–21. Portions of the text were published in installments between June and August, 1921 in *The Dial* and *The London Mercury;* the Cuala Press published it entire in 1921. There are extant two complete manuscript versions of the text, one exceptionally tidy and one even fuller of cancellations and emendations than Yeats's manuscripts usually are; in addition there are a number of manuscript and typescript fragments pertaining to Florence Farr, Maud Gonne, Mme. Blavatsky and MacGregor Mathers (Mrs. Mathers would object strongly to the description of her husband) that Yeats seems to have written when revising *Four Years* for inclusion in *The Trembling of the Veil* (Bradford gives details of these fragments). Yeats seems still to have been making minor additions and revisions in proof since short passages appear in the Cuala Press edition which are not in either manuscript. The stylistic revisions between the two complete manuscripts are innumerable; they show Yeats very carefully and very deliberately putting forward a literary and philosophical construct of his life and his self. More interesting is the amount of emendation and re-writing it took to work certain passages of his life into the pattern of *Autobiographies,* most notably his love for Maud Gonne. Yeats tried the Gonne passage several times in the hope of getting it right; Bradford notes that the most completely developed of these efforts closely parallels "First Draft" in several places and may have been written with reference to the earlier manuscript. Much of the passage is an extension of the praise of Maud Gonne as a "commendation of Spring" which eventually found its way into *Four Years.* What is more unexpected in the manuscript passage which is omitted from the published version is Yeats's allusion to a "prophecy" which prefigures the one hundred twenty year cycles of the historical description in *A Vision.* He speaks of the day on which he met Maud Gonne:

> her that
> Was it that day or a little later that I told [4 ~~indecipherable words~~] I had found a prophesy by Abbot Trithermires [?] dividing the ~~world~~ his history into periods of a hundred and twenty years a piece, and that in 1800 began ~~a hun~~ a period consecrated to Mercury or intelligence & in 1920 a hundred years of brute force, a prophesy . . . I have not since been able to trace and may have dreamed, but which gave us both [~~word~~] ~~pleasure~~ considerable pleasure.[1]

Yeats was undoubtedly sincere about the manner in which is "communicators" gave him the material for *A Vision,* but they had a good deal to draw on.

He seems to have continued writing his autobiography without cease for "Ireland after Parnell" and some of "Hodos Chameliontos" and "The Tragic Generation" were published serially as "More Memories" in *The Dial* and *The London Mercury* between May and October, 1922. (The section on Verlaine was transposed with some revision from a sketch in *The Savoy,* April, 1896, titled "Verlaine in 1894.") That same year, all of *The Trembling of the Veil,* including *Four Years*—revised and the ending altered to make the transition to "Ireland after Parnell" —, was published in a limited edition by T. Werner Laurie. The remainder of *The Trembling of the Veil* seems, as Bradford hypothesizes, to have been written as a single unit; the major manuscript shows no chapter divisions. The manuscript is exceedingly difficult to sort out; there is one continuous and obviously major draft and also many "Stray Pages" which Bradford thinks constitute an earlier, probably chronological, draft. Yeats's drafts reveal him re-ordering his events so as to gain cohesiveness for his text and to lead into "Hodos Chameliontos" (incorrectly spelled "Hodos Chamelionis" in the first edition; Yeats corrected his Latin as he clarified his philosophy). He took particular pains over the drafts and extensive revisions of his account of The Young Ireland Movement and of the failure of his own plans for Ireland, of his description of the Ely Place theosophists (this passage is as often rewritten as that about Maud Gonne) and of his description of Taylor and Dowden. Some of this care was doubtlessly dictated by tact: Dowden had been one of his father's best friends and it would have seemed rather strong to publicly characterize Taylor as "notorious for a temper that carried him to the edge of insanity"[2] or as "the tyrant of a society that turned everything to argument."[3] Some of his deletions—descriptions of Mary Battle's visions or of a seance, for example—were probably made for the sake of concision and to place emphasis on what would seem authoritative and systemic in his lunar myth while minimizing what would seem merely superstitious or folk-loric. The "failure" of his plans for literary nationalism and his life at Ely Place needed particular care in the telling since they are crucial in Yeats's account of the ways in which he sought his Mask. Revelatory in this context is a passage Yeats deleted from Section III between the principal manuscript of "Ireland after Parnell" and the published version: "Looking backward after all these years I think I was doing work of great importance, though it was not such a waste of vitality as I have sometimes thought it. Young men in Paris or in London had for a generation or so been fighting the same fight."[4] *Autobiographies* ascribes political activity to Yeats's anti-self and finally moves to a view of Ireland as failing to achieve Unity of Culture: this passage is not consonant with the larger pattern of the work and perhaps that is why it is dropped.

The composition of the remainder of *The Trembling of the Veil* gave Yeats considerably less trouble. The principal manuscript of "Hodos Chameliontos" is relatively clean and there are few "Stray Pages" redrafting its passages. Revisions of the principal manuscript for "The Tragic Generation" and "The Stirring of the Bones" are nothing like so extensive or numerous as those for "Ireland after Parnell" although a number of drafts do exist of the section on Wilde and Yeats added material about William Sharp between the principal manuscript and publication.

Yeats published a short note titled "A Biographical Fragment" in *The*

Dial and in *The Criterion* in July, 1923; it concerned "The Vision of the Archer" and was added to *Autobiographies* along with "The Vision" in 1926. In 1923, he also received the Nobel Prize. The text of his lecture, "The Irish Dramatic Movement" was published in Stockholm that year and would be appended to The Cuala Press edition of *The Bounty of Sweden.* He finished writing that autobiography (the manuscript of which shows unusual ease of composition) in January, 1924; the Cuala Press published it in July, 1925.

1925 also saw the publication of the first edition of *A Vision.* Dissatisfied with it, Yeats began revising it immediately, doing most of the work by 1934–35. During those nine years he collected his autobiographical writings and published two further volumes. *Autobiographies: Reveries over Childhood and Youth and The Trembling of the Veil* appeared, with further revisions of the initial published versions, with MacMillan in 1926. Some of the description of Dowden, Taylor and O'Leary Yeats deleted from this edition of *Reveries over Childhood and Youth* because he had covered it again in *The Trembling of the Veil.* A long passage about his youthful literary and occult ideals for Ireland is also cut, I suspect because it contradicted the view of Ireland which fitted Yeats's doctrine of the Mask. It also showed the young Yeats as more naive than does the final version of *Autobiographies:*

I had planned a drama like that of Greece, and romances that were . . . to bring into the town the memories and visions of the country and to spread everywhere the history and legends of mediaeval Ireland and to fill Ireland once more with sacred places. I even planned out, and in some detail . . . , another Samothrace, a new Eleusis. I believed, so great was my faith, or so deceptive the precedent of Young Ireland, that I should find men of genius everywhere. I . . . believed I had devined [sic] the soul of the people and had set my shoes upon a road that would be crowded presently.[5]

The major revisions to the content of the remainder of *The Trembling of the Veil* serve to strengthen Yeats's controlling "Lunar metaphor." Section VI was added to "Hodos Chameliontos" in this edition. So too were the powerful image for Unity of Being of Hérodiade's dancing alone in her spotlight-moon and the lines from Mallarmé's poem which Yeats quotes. Finally, "The Vision of the Archer" and the notes to it Yeats had published as "A Biographical Fragment" introduced that section of "The Stirring of the Bones" in which Yeats describes himself and Lady Gregory as beginning their collection of folk-belief; added to the visions already recorded there, it considerably intensifies the strength of Yeats's "one myth" as a structuring device in *Autobiographies.*

In 1926 Yeats also published *Estrangement,* first in *The London Mercury* and *The Dial* and then at Cuala Press. He followed this in 1928 with *The Death of Synge,* again in *The London Mercury* and *The Dial* and at Cuala. Bradford notes that four extracts which are part of

Estrangement had appeared in 1911 in *The Manchester Playgoer;* Lady Gregory had quoted from a journal entry included in *The Death of Synge* in 1913 in *The English Review.* Both books are selections of entries from a journal Yeats kept between 1908 and 1914 (published in *Memoirs*). There is no clue extant as to when Yeats made the selections but, since he usually published prose as soon as it was ready for the printer and since Cuala Press often looked to him for copy, it seems not unreasonable to assume that he made the selections for *Estrangement* in 1925–26, and those for *The Death of Synge* perhaps later, in 1927– 28. Although the selection of entries is much more stringently limited for the second book, in both cases Yeats seems to have used concision and their relevance for issues he wished to raise publicly as his criteria. Nearly all astrological references are dropped, as are the more personal comments, daily events of merely passing interest as opposed to those with something to say about Ireland or the arts, and the harshest of his indictments of the Irish. Yeats adds no new material although he does make numerous stylistic revisions.

Working the while on *A Vision,* Yeats returned to autobiography late in 1933 and in 1934 when he wrote *Dramatis Personae* (published entire by Cuala Press in 1935 and in part in *The London Mercury* and *The New Republic* in 1936). Yeats's letters testify to the care he took in planning his presentation of Moore. The manuscript version itself of *Dramatis Personae* shows little revision, but the typescript is considerably revised. Bradford suggests that this is because Yeats had by this time developed the practice of dictating to a typist from the manuscript and then heavily and very efficiently revising the typescript. Those revisions in *Dramatis Personae* show Yeats honing his style the better to impale Moore, making passage after passage more concise, more rhetorically pointed (see Bradford for a very convincing comparison of the original manuscript version and the revised typescript).

In 1936 MacMillan brought out the previously uncollected autobiographies, arranged in the order in which they now appear in the standard edition, in *Dramatis Personae 1896–1902. Estrangement. The Death of Synge. The Bounty of Sweden.* The text follows that of earlier editions except for the omission of the Preface and Notes to *The Bounty of Sweden.* In 1937 the second, extensively rewritten version of *A Vision* was published and, in 1938, MacMillan brought out *The Autobiography of William Butler Yeats,* all the autobiographies collected in a single volume which altered the previous texts only by the deletion of "The Irish Dramatic Movement." That lecture would be restored in the 1955 standard edition of *Autobiographies.*

NOTES

ONE: PERSONAL UTTERANCE AND THE LUNAR PARABLE:
Early Prose and *A Vision*

1 For a description of Yeats's dissatisfaction with *The King of the Great Clock Tower*, his decision to rewrite it completely in verse, and his writing of *A Full Moon in March*, see Curtis B. Bradford, *Yeats at Work* (Carbondale, Edwardsville: Southern Illinois University Press, 1965), pp. 268—69, and Liam Miller, *The Noble Drama of W.B.Yeats* (Dublin: The Dolmen Press; North America: Humanities Press Inc., 1977), pp. 293—97, 299—301.

2 *The Savoy* (January, 1896), 135—38; *The Secret Rose* (London: Lawrence & Bullen, 1897), 1—10. See P.L. Marcus, "Yeats and the Image of the Singing Head," *Eire*, IX, 4 (1974), 86—93 for the Irish sources of this story and its sources in Yeats's relationship with Olivia Shakespear. Marcus also cites an unpublished revision, titled "A Very Pretty Little Story," in which the alterations of the plot from the original version anticipate *The King of the Great Clock Tower* and *A Full Moon in March.*

3 VI, misprints "exultation" for "exaltation."

4 See James Lovic Allen, "Belief versus Faith in the Credo of Yeats," *Journal of Modern Literature*, 4, 3 (Feb., 1975), 692—716, for evidence of Yeats's literal belief in the system of *A Vision.*

5 Joseph Ronsley, *Yeats's Autobiography: Life as Symbolic Pattern* (Cambridge: Harvard University Press, 1968) analyzes *Autobiographies* as beginning "as if it were the beginning of the world" and closing with "Yeats's vision of unity of culture as the ultimate stage in the world's spiritual evolution, as if the apocalypse had at least drawn nearer" (p. 134). Ronsley relies on *Per Amica Silentia Lunae* rather than on *A Vision* to explain Yeats's philosophy.

6 Ibid., p. 33.

7 A, 102 records that Yeats read the poem at The Young Ireland Society. The passage follows immediately after the recollections of O'Leary and Taylor at the Society. O'Leary returned from exile in 1884; Yeats wrote his first "Irish" and "autobiographical" poem, *The Wanderings of Oisin,* under the influence of O'Leary and Katherine Tynan in 1886. See Richard Ellmann, *Yeats: The Man and the Masks* (1948; rpt. N.Y.: E.P. Dutton & Co. Inc., n.d.), p. 51, on the autobiographical nature of this poem.

8 See also, A, 102.

9 M.C. Flannery, *Yeats and Magic: the earlier works* (Gerrards Cross: Colin Smythe, 1977), p. 43, finds the antinomy of *A Vision*, "Solar vision (objectivity) versus Lunar vision (subjectivity)," already formulated in an 1889 diary.

10 That this formulation remained important to Yeats is indicated by his reprinting it as "The Moods" in *Ideas of Good and Evil* (EI, 195).

11 Ecclesiasticus, 42:24: "All things go in pairs, one the opposite of the other;/he has made nothing incomplete." Frayne and Johnson footnote this passage with a

reference to Henry Wace's 1888 edition of *The Apocrypha* which "reads: 'All things are double one against another'" (UP, II, 195).

12 A, 102: "my father would hear of nothing but drama"; YP, 30: "I got a conviction which my father did not share."

13 Joseph Hone, *W.B. Yeats: 1865–1939* (2nd ed.; London: MacMillan, 1962), p. 58. Quoted also by Norman Jeffares, *W.B. Yeats: Man and Poet* (N. Y.: Barnes & Noble, Inc., 1966), p. 63, and Richard J. Finneran, "Introduction," JS&D, 9.

14 cf. A, 35, of his English school companions: "our mental images were different."

15 See Ellmann, *Yeats: The Man and the Masks*, p. 78.

16 Ellmann, *Yeats: The Man and the Masks*, p. 78; Finneran, JS&D, 10; Hone, *W.B. Yeats*, p. 58; Jeffares, *W.B. Yeats: Man and Poet*, p. 63.

17 See Finneran, JS&D, 27–31; Richard J. Finneran, *The Prose Fiction of W.B. Yeats: The Search for 'Those Simple Forms'* (Dublin: The Dolmen Press, 1973), p. 11; Ellmann, *Yeats: The Man and the Masks*, pp. 78–79; Phillip L. Marcus, *Yeats and the Beginning of the Irish Renaissance* (Ithaca, London: Cornell University Press, 1970), pp. 37–39.

18 See Finneran, *The Prose Fiction of W.B. Yeats*, p.11, and his introduction to JS&D, pp. 27–32, for Sherman (self) and Howard (anti-self).

19 Ibid.

20 See the closing description of her love for Sherman, "a reverberation of the feeling of the mother for the child at the breast" (JS&D, 111).

21 See Robert O'Driscoll, *Symbolism and some Implications of the Symbolic Approach: W.B. Yeats during the Eighteen-Nineties* (Dublin: The Dolmen Press, 1975), pp. 20-21 for an analysis of this passage and pp. 21-24 for a discussion of the reasons Yeats turned to folk belief.

22 See Richard J. Finneran, "Yeats's Revisions in *The Celtic Twilight*, 1912–1925," *Tulane Studies in English*, 20 (1972), 97–105, for these and other late revisions.

23 *Fairy and Folk Tales of the Irish Peasantry*, 1888; *Representative Irish Tales*, 1889.

24 See Richard Ellmann, *The Identity of Yeats* (rev. ed.; London: Faber and Faber, 1964), pp. 56–61 for Yeats's use of the term "mood."

25 See Allan Wade, *A Bibliography of the Writings of W.B. Yeats* (3rd ed., revised and edited by Russell K. Alspach; London: Rupert Hart-Davis, 1968), pp. 54–56, and Bradford, *Yeats at Work*, p. 316.

26 Bradford, *Yeats at Work*, p. 314.

27 Ibid.

28 Ibid., pp. 317—26; Wade, *Bibliography,* pp. 40—41; Marcus, *Yeats and the Beginning of the Irish Renaissance,* pp.51—54.

29 For considerations of the spiritual values symbolized by Aodh, see Augustine Martin, "'The Secret Rose' and Yeats's Dialogue with History," *Ariel,* 3, 3 (July, 1972), pp. 93—94, and O'Driscoll, *Symbolism and some Implications of the Symbolic Approach,* pp. 25—27.

30 For consideration of the spiritual in "Out of the Rose," see also Martin, "'The Secret Rose,'" pp. 96—97, and O'Driscoll, *Symbolism and some Implications of the Symbolic Approach,* pp. 30—31.

31 See Finneran, *The Prose Fiction of W.B. Yeats,* pp. 18—19; O'Driscoll, *Symbolism and some Implications of the Symbolic Approach,* pp. 29—30; and Thomas R. Whitaker, *Swan and Shadow: Yeats's Dialogue with History* (Chapel Hill: The University of North Carolina Press, 1964), p. 37: "It is the moment of the lark's song in Blake's *Milton*—that of Christ's descent into the wheel and Milton's redemption of his shadow." See also, Marcus, *Yeats and the Beginning of the Irish Renaissance,* p. 47, for alternative interpretations of the thrush's song in terms of Yeats's treatment of the Church.

32 See also O'Driscoll, *Symbolism and some Implications of the Symbolic Approach,* p. 27.

33 See O'Driscoll, *Symbolism and some Implications of the Symbolic Approach,* p. 31: "The wisdom of the king is in recognizing that supernatural wisdom and natural law are incompatible."

34 See L, 280; W.B. Yeats, *Early Poems and Stories* (London: MacMillan, 1925), p. 528; Finneran, *The Prose Fiction of W.B. Yeats,* p. 34; Marcus, *Yeats and the Beginning of the Irish Renaissance,* p. 56.

35 For other discussions of these three stories see Whitaker, *Swan and Shadow,* pp. 39—49; O'Driscoll, *Symbolism and some Implications of the Symbolic Approach,* pp. 37—48; Finneran, *The Prose Fiction of W.B. Yeats,* pp. 19—22. Much of Robert O'Driscoll's discussion is also presented in his "Critical Introduction" to *"The Tables of the Law:* A Critical Text," *Yeats and the 1890s,* eds. Robert O'Driscoll and Lorna Reynolds, *Yeats Studies,* I (1971), 87—98.

36 O'Driscoll, *Symbolism and some Implications of the Symbolic Approach,* p. 37.

37 Ibid., p. 48.

38 Ibid., p. 38, for the narrator's refusal to see that "it is only through the constant activity of art, not in merely surrounding oneself with works of art, that ecstasy can be experienced and a changing heart transmuted for a moment into a changeless work of art."

39 See Michael Fixler, "The Affinities between J.-K. Huysmans and the 'Rosicrucian' Stories of W. B. Yeats," *PMLA,* LXXIV (Sept., 1959), 466—67. Whitaker, *Swan and Shadow,* p. 39, suggests that the narrator "imagines himself another Pater." For a discussion of the narrator as modelled on Marius the Epicurean, see also F.C. McGrath, "Heroic Aestheticism: Yeats, Pater, and the Marriage of Ireland and England," *Irish University Review,* 8, 2 (Autumn, 1978), p. 184.

40 See O'Driscoll, *Symbolism and some Implications of the Symbolic Approach*, pp. 38–39, for an analysis of the narrator's failure to recognize the contradictions in his position, "poised uncomfortably between the material and spiritual, the definite and indefinite worlds."

41 Whitaker, *Swan and Shadow*, p. 305.

42 This passage originally read "souls trembling between the excitement of the spirit and the excitement of the flesh" (TL, 105). Yeats revised the phrase to the reading I have given in the text in 1908 when he republished the story for the fourth time. The revision is obviously to make the syntax point to the nature of the revelation.

43 The "trembling of the veil" is quoted from Stéphane Mallarmé, "Crise de vers":

La littérature ici subit une exquise crise, fondamentale.

. . . on assiste, comme finale d'un siècle, pas ainsi que ce fut dans le dernier, à des bouleversements; mais, hors de la place publique à inquiétude du voile dans le temple avec des plis significatifs et un peu sa déchirure *(Oeuvres complètes,* eds., Henri Mondor and G. Jean-Aubry [Paris: Gallimard, 1945], p. 360).
This passage of the essay first appeared in *The National Observer,* under the title "Vers et Musique en France," on March 26, 1892 (Mallarmé, *Oeuvres,* p. 1574). See Ellmann, *Yeats: The Man and the Masks,* pp. 86–91, for Mallarmé's involvement with French Rosicrucianism and for his and Yeats's contributions to *The National Observer.*

44 H.P. Blavatsky, *Isis Unveiled: A Master-Key to the Mysteries of Ancient and Modern Science and Theology* (New York: J.W. Bouton and London: Bernard Quaritch, 1886), II, 640.

45 H.P. Blavatsky, *The Secret Doctrine: The Synthesis of Science, Religion, and Philosophy* (London: The Theosophical Publishing Society, 1893), II, 294.

46 The phrases come from the ritual entitled "De L'Aigle et du Pélican ou Souverain Prince Rose-Croix" reproduced in Pierre Mariel, *Rituels des Sociétés Secrètes* (Paris: La Colombe, 1961), p. 123. The ritual of the 18th Degree, p. 104, contains much the same formula. MacGregor Mathers knew the leaders of Le Grand Ordre Kabbalistique du Rose Croix and Yeats met two principal French Rosicrucians, Sâr Joséphin Péladan and Stanislaus de Guaïta, in Paris in 1894; see Fixler, "The Affinities between J.-K. Huysmans and the 'Rosicrucian' Stories of W.B. Yeats," p. 464.

47 ts., "Paths and Portals. Part I. Concerning the Portal and Path of π. Issued by V.H. Fra. Sub Spe. Th. A.M. as Flying Roll to the Adepti," Microfilms of Yeats papers, National Library of Ireland, Center for Contemporary Arts and Letters, SUNY, Reel 6.

48 ms. (not in Yeats's hand), "$4^0 = 7^0$ Philosophus," Yeats papers, Reel 6.

49 ts., "$7^0 = 4^0$ Ritual," Yeats papers, Reel 6.

50 ts., "Ceremony of 5=6" (covering page contains Yeats's signature and the designation 5=6), Yeats papers, Reel 6.

51 ts., "Consecration Ceremony of Vault of Adepti," Yeats papers, Reel 6.

52 Quoted by Ellmann, *Yeats: The Man and the Masks*, p. 188.

53 cf. the horses in the Japanese painting, "'trembling into stillness,'" of *Autobiographies* (A, 186).

54 For discussions of the story as advocating the overthrow of Christianity and of its parallels with the historical antitheses of *A Vision* and the later poetry, see Whitaker, *Swan and Shadow*, pp. 41—43, and O'Driscoll, *Symbolism and some Implications of the Symbolic Approach*, p. 41.

55 Whitaker, *Swan and Shadow*, pp. 47—48, identifies the harlot as Sophia, of the Book of Enoch, married by Simon Magus, and used by Yeats for her cabbalistic value as Holy Shekinah, the fallen female divine principle.

56 See Fixler, "The Affinities between J.-K. Huysmans and the 'Rosicrucian' Stories of W. B. Yeats," pp. 467—68; Ellmann, *Yeats: The Man and the Masks*, pp. 89—90; and Virginia Moore, *The Unicorn: William Butler Yeats' Search for Reality* (N.Y.: MacMillan, 1954), pp. 191—92.

57 William H. O'Donnell, "Yeats as Adept and Artist: *The Speckled Bird, The Secret Rose* and *The Wind among the Reeds,*" in *Yeats and The Occult*, ed., George Mills Harper, Yeats Studies Series (Toronto: MacMillan of Canada, 1975), p. 56, suggests that Yeats's belief extended to the possibility of a mortal's becoming one of the "supernal creatures."

58 MacGregor Mathers has been suggested as a model for Robartes by Moore, *The Unicorn*, p. 191; Michael J. Sidnell, "Mr. Yeats, Michael Robartes and Their Circle," in *Yeats and The Occult*, pp. 231—32; Laurence W. Fennelly, "W.B. Yeats and S.L. MacGregor Mathers," in *Yeats and The Occult*, p. 305; and William H. O'Donnell, ed., *The Speckled Bird*, xxxi. Warwick Gould, "'Lionel Johnson Comes the First to Mind': Sources for Owen Aherne," in *Yeats and The Occult*, pp. 256—84, suggests Lionel Johnson and John O'Leary as "live" models for Owen Aherne, Captain John Aherne and Dr. Maurice Aherne as historical models. Fixler, "The Affinities between J.-K Huysmans and the 'Rosicrucian' Stories of W.B. Yeats," p. 465, first suggests Lionel Johnson as a source for Aherne.

59 Ellmann, *Yeats: The Man and the Masks*, p. 83, points out Yeats's "almost constant use of autobiographical material" in the 1890s. However, he sees Aherne and Robartes as the only personae of Yeats in the stories, assuming that Aherne is the narrator in "Rosa Alchemica" and "The Adoration of the Magi." Finneran, *The Prose Fiction of W.B. Yeats* and O'Driscoll, *Symbolism and some Implications of the Symbolic Approach*, have assumed the same narrator for all three stories.

60 See the reference to Robartes' "letters and table talk" in the Preface to *Michael Robartes and the Dancer* (Dundrum: The Cuala Press, 1920); Ellmann, *Yeats: The Man and the Masks*, pp. 234—35; Walter Kelly Hood, "Michael Robartes: Two Occult Manuscripts," in *Yeats and The Occult*, pp. 204—24. One of the mss. Hood reproduces, "Michael Robartes Foretells," is also printed as Appendix B of Hazard Adams, *Blake and Yeats: The Contrary Vision* (Ithaca: Cornell University Press, 1955), pp. 301—05.

61 See Ellmann, Hood and Adams, Ibid., for published portions of this dialogue, or, more often, monologue by Robartes.

141

62 e.g., Joseph Ronsley, "Yeats as an Autobiographical Poet," in *Myth and Reality in Irish Literature*, ed., J. Ronsley (Waterloo: Wilfred Laurier University Press, 1977), p. 140, interprets Robartes' presence as "an ideogram which effectively obscures, though it does not eliminate, the presence of the actual poet."

63 For different views of the irrationality of the world of *Stories of Michael Robartes* and an analysis of the John Bond-Mary Bell sequences and the import of the cuckoos, see Adams, *Blake and Yeats*, pp. 196—98; Hazard Adams, "Some Yeatsian Versions of Comedy," in *In Excited Reverie: A Centenary Tribute to William Butler Yeats 1865—1939*, eds., A. Norman Jeffares and K.G.W. Cross (London: MacMillan, 1965), pp. 165—67; and Sidnell, "Mr. Yeats, Michael Robartes and Their Circle," pp. 252—54.

64 For an analysis of the persona of Robartes in the sequence of dialogue poems at the end of *The Wild Swans at Coole* and in *Michael Robartes and the Dancer*, see Sidnell, "Mr. Yeats, Michael Robartes and Their Circle," pp. 224—54. He presents the dancer as image "of the apotheosis of the human soul" (p. 239).

65 O'Donnell, ed., *The Speckled Bird*, p. xxiii; Finneran, *The Prose Fiction of W.B. Yeats*, pp. 23, 36—37.

66 Finneran, *The Prose Fiction of W.B. Yeats*, pp. 24—27, finds that each of the four sections of *The Speckled Bird* recalls a genre of prose fiction Yeats had used previously: Section I is "legendary" *(The Celtic Twilight)*, Sections II and IV "esoteric and occult" ("Rosa Alchemica"), and Section III "realistic" *(John Sherman)*.

67 Modelled on Mathers (see note 58, and O'Donnell's notes, *The Speckled Bird*, pp. 21, 57, 58, 62—65), perhaps named after Sir Eric Robert Dalrymple Maclagan, 1879—1951 (Finneran, *The Prose Fiction of W. B. Yeats*, p. 36).

68 See particularly O'Donnell's notes to *The Speckled Bird;* Finneran, *The Prose Fiction of W.B. Yeats*, pp. 36—37; and David G. Wright, "The Elusive Self: Yeats's Autobiographical Prose," *The Canadian Journal of Irish Studies*, IV, 2 (Dec., 1978), p. 41.

69 Identified by Martin, "'The Secret Rose' and Yeats's Dialogue with History," p. 91, as an unacknowledged paraphrase of the life of the street singer, Zozimus, from Gulielmus Dubbinesis Humoriensis, *Zozimus* (Dublin: M'Glashan and Gill, 1871).

70 Martin, "'The Secret Rose' and Yeats's Dialogue with History," p. 95, and O'Driscoll, *Symbolism and some Implications of the Symbolic Approach*, p. 28, identify Yeats's source as Kuno Meyer's translation (1892) of the eleventh-century *Aisling Meic Conglinne*. In the original the gleeman is victorious over the monks.

71 See Martin, "'The Secret Rose' and Yeats's Dialogue with History," pp. 95, 102, for a discussion of Cumhal and Hanrahan as Romantic artists.

72 This story was replaced in the 1905 *Stories of Red Hanrahan* by "Red Hanrahan," (first published in 1903). See Wade, *Bibliography*, pp. 40-42, 74; Marcus, *Yeats and the Beginning of the Irish Renaissance*, pp. 51—54; Bradford,

Yeats at Work, pp. 318–20; Richard J. Finneran, " 'Old lecher with a love on every wind': A Study of Yeats' STORIES OF RED HANRAHAN,'" *Texas Studies in Literature and Language,* XIV, 2 (Summer, 1972), p. 349; Michael J. Sidnell, "Versions of the Stories of Red Hanrahan," *Yeats Studies,* 1 (1971), pp. 119–22, 166–67; and Cara Ackerman, "Yeats' Revisions of the Hanrahan Stories, 1897 and 1904," *Texas Studies in Literature and Language,* XVII, 2 (Summer, 1975), pp. 505–512, for this portion of the publication history and revisions of the Hanrahan stories.

73 See Whitaker, *Swan and Shadow,* p. 195; Marcus, *Yeats and the Beginning of the Irish Renaissance,* p. 55; Grace J. Calder, *George Petrie and 'The Ancient Music of Ireland'* (Dublin: The Dolmen Press, 1968), pp. 43–45; Martin, "'The Secret Rose' and Yeats's Dialogue with History," p. 99; Finneran, "'Old lecher with a love on every wind,'" p. 350, for this identification. Martin, pp. 98–100, suggests that Hanrahan also owes a good deal to Carleton; Finneran, p. 351, names William Dall O'Heffernan as another contributor to Hanrahan's character.

74 O'Driscoll, *Symbolism and some Implications of the Symbolic Approach,* pp. 32–36, sees Hanrahan's error in the separation of the physical and spiritual worlds which dictates his refusal of Cleena; he goes on to trace Hanrahan's growing awareness of his mortality in terms of images and incidents of deterioration and decay in the stories.

75 These identifications have been made by Moore, *The Unicorn,* pp. 58–61; Kathleen Raine, *Yeats, The Tarot and The Golden Dawn* (Dublin: The Dolmen Press, 1972), pp. 20, 28; Finneran, *The Prose Fiction of W.B. Yeats,* p. 28, and "'Old lecher with a love on every wind,'" p. 352; and Ackerman, "Yeats' Revisions of the Hanrahan Stories," pp. 512–24. Yeats draws an analogy between the treasures and the Grail legend in EI, 185.

76 Ackerman, Ibid.

77 Calder, *George Petrie and 'The Ancient Music of Ireland,'* p. 45, links the two songs.

78 Ellmann, *The Identity of Yeats,* pp. 31–32, speaking of *The Secret Rose* version of "Red Hanrahan's Song about Ireland" noted that Yeats begins each stanza with one of the three "inferior elements" ("the winds of Knocknarea," "the waves of Cummen Strand," "dark and dull and earthy the stream of Drumahair" [RH, 148–49]) and associates Cathleen ni Houlihan with fire.

79 Finneran, "'Old lecher with a love on every wind,'" interprets these stories in terms of "sin, suffering, repentance, and redemption" (p. 354) and the encounter with Diarmuid and Dervorgilla as "patriotic conversion" (p. 355).

80 This account replaces the first versions of the story in which Owen O'Sullivan the Red/Red Hanrahan is knocked unconscious by the collaboration of the three elements (yew/earth, eagle/air, pike/water) which had not yet retaliated for his cursing of them.

81 Ackerman, "Yeats' Revisions of the Hanrahan Stories," pp. 515–16, makes an identification of Winny and Echtge, and, therefore, Winny and Ireland.

82 See Finneran, "'Old lecher with a love on every wind,'" pp. 357–58, and Ackerman, "Yeats' Revisions of the Hanrahan Stories," p. 517, for such parallels.

83 See George Mills Harper, *Yeats's Golden Dawn* (London: MacMillan, 1974), pp. 14–98, for the history of these quarrels.

84 O'Donnell, Critical Introduction to *The Speckled Bird*, p. xxv. See also Harper, *Yeats's Golden Dawn*, p. 164, for Yeats's collaborators in the planning of rituals for The Celtic Mysteries.

85 David S. Thatcher, *Nietzsche in England 1890–1914* (Toronto: University of Toronto Press, 1970), p. 141, discusses the Nietzschean allusion in this statement.

86 Ronsley, Introduction to "Yeats's Lecture Notes for 'Friends of My Youth,'" notes that the lecture "is perhaps the earliest version of much of the material in *The Trembling of the Veil*" and suggests the notes may be "even a first rough draft, for much of 'Four Years' and 'The Tragic Generation'" (FMY, 61). He also quotes from this lecture in his *Yeats's Autobiography*, pp. 2, 89.

87 Quoted by O'Driscoll, in his Introduction to "Yeats on Personality" (p. 4) and made central to his argument.

88 This phrase is dropped from subsequent drafts and appears in the lecture, as recorded by the stenographer and corrected by Yeats, modified thus: "Again I am going —*that I may* escape from rhetoric—to be biographical . . ."(YP,29).

89 Ellmann, *Yeats: The Man and the Masks*, pp. 70–74.

90 Yeats tentatively dates this dinner in *Autobiographies* as "1887 or 1888?" (p. 134), after the publication of his *The Wanderings of Oisin* (January, 1889) and before that of Wilde's "The Decay of Lying" (January, 1889); he clearly is little help in dating the meeting. Ellmann, *Yeats: The Man and the Masks*, p. 74, sets early 1889 as the date of Yeats's meeting with Wilde. cf. Yeats papers, Reel 22: "In I think 1887—a couple of years after I first arrived in London. . . ."

91 Oscar Wilde, *The Works of Oscar Wilde*, ed., G. F. Maine (London, Glasgow: Collins, 1948), p. 914.

92 Yeats's annotated copy of the Thomas Common edition is now in the possession of Northwestern University Library. This passage is quoted by Thatcher, *Nietzsche in England*, p. 151, and by P. Bridgwater, "The Strong Enchanter: W. B. Yeats and Nietzsche," in *affinities: Essays in German and English Literature*, ed., R. W. Last (London: Oswald Wolff Limited, 1971), p. 72. For Nietzsche's influence on Yeats see Ellmann, *The Identity of Yeats*, pp. 91–98; Denis Donoghue, *William Butler Yeats* (New York: Viking, 1971), pp. 52–61; F. A. C. Wilson, *Yeats's Iconography* (London: Victor Gollancz, 1960), pp. 177–86; Erich Heller, "Yeats and Nietzsche: Reflections on a Poet's Marginal Notes," *Encounter*, xxxiii, 6 (Dec., 1969), 64–72; Thatcher, pp. 139–73; and Bridgwater, 68–87.

93 *The Philosophy of Neitzsche* (New York: The Modern Library, n.d.), p. 956. Common's *Nietzsche* includes only two passages from *The Birth of Tragedy* but F.A.C. Wilson, *W.B. Yeats and Tradition* (London: Victor Gollancz, 1958), p. 58, and *Yeats's Iconography*, p. 177, indicates that Yeats read *The Birth of Tragedy* in 1903 and that it was his "favourite reading in Nietzsche."

94 This is Yeats's own recollection (L, 592). Ellmann, following the account of Ernest Boyd, *Ireland's Literary Renaissance* (London: Grant Richards, 1923), pp. 213–14, places Yeats's first acquaintance with *Esoteric Buddhism* in the spring of 1885 *(Yeats: The Man and the Masks,* p. 61).

95 "A Second Letter to the Adepti of R.R. et A. C. on the Present Crisis," reproduced in George Mills Harper, ed., *Yeats's Golden Dawn*, p. 245.

96 W.B. Yeats, *The Writing of "The Player Queen,"* Manuscripts of W.B. Yeats transcribed, edited and with a commentary by Curtis Baker Bradford (DeKalb: Northern Illinois University Press, 1977), p. 21.

97 Ibid.

98 Bradford, Ibid., p. 40, dates Draft 5 as completed by Spring, 1908 on the basis of a tentative table of contents for Bullen's *Collected Edition* published later in 1908 which Yeats has written at the end of the draft.

99 Ibid., p. 39 (Bradford's summary of Draft 3).

100 Bradford, Ibid., p. 33, dates the composition of Draft 16 as 1910 and suggests, p. 43, that Yeats had worked out some of Draft 16 before completing Draft 6 with the song.

101 Ibid., p. 46.

102 cf. St. John Ervine on meeting Yeats late in 1910: "He was then interested in the more esoteric forms of drama, and was eager to put masks on the actors' faces. He wished to eliminate the personality of the player from the play, and had borrowed some foolish notions from Mr. Gordon Craig about lighting and scenery and dehumanized actors. He had a model of the Abbey Theatre in his rooms and was fond of experimenting with it. There was some inconsistency in his talk about acting: at one moment he was anxious for anonymous, masked players, 'freed' from personality, and at the next moment, he was demanding that players should act with their entire bodies, not merely with their voices and faces" (IR, I, 106).

103 Ellmann, *Yeats: The Man and the Masks,* pp. 195–97, and Moore, *The Unicorn,* pp. 235–37.

104 Allen, "Belief versus Faith in the Credo of Yeats," pp. 702–03.

105 Ellmann, *Yeats: The Man and the Masks,* p. 197, quotes this passage.

106 Allen, "Belief versus Faith in the Credo of Yeats," p. 709, quotes this passage.

107 Ibid., and Bradford, *Yeats at Work,* p. 307.

108 See particularly Roy Pascal, *Design and Truth in Autobiography* (Cambridge, Mass.: Harvard University Press, 1960); Jean Starobinski, *La relation critique* (Paris:

Gallimard, 1970), pp. 83–87; James Olney, *Metaphors of Self: The Meaning of Autobiography* (Princeton: Princeton University Press, 1972); Jeffrey Mehlman, *A Structural Study of Autobiography: Proust, Leiris, Sartre, Lévi-Strauss* (Ithaca: Cornell University Press, 1974); Philippe Lejeune, *Le pacte autobiographique* (Paris: Editions de Seuil, 1975).

109 Blake had also formulated a set of antitheses to contrast mental and physical reality and has posited the union of such antitheses in a single form. See Northrop Frye, *Fables of Identity: Studies in Poetic Mythology* (New York: Harcourt Brace & World, Inc., 1963), p. 232.

110 The comparison occurs several times in Dante's *Convivio* (*Opere minori*, ed., Alberto del Monte [2nd ed.; Milan: Rizzoli, 1966]). In that which Yeats uses most frequently, a comparison he would have had also from Pietro Bembo's oration in *Il Libro del cortegiano*, beauty of soul manifests itself in bodily perfection: "E quando elli [il corpo] è bene ordinato e disposto, allora è bello per tutto e per le parti; ché l'ordine debito de le nostre membre rende uno piacere non so di che armonia mirabile . . ." (p. 503). On other occasions Dante compares beauty to the well-proportioned body in general terms (p. 254) or the beauty of philosophy (its morality or wisdom) to the beauty of the harmoniously proportioned body (p. 397).

111 *Poetry and Ireland: Essays by W.B.Yeats and Lionel Johnson* (Dundrum: Cuala Press, 1908).

112 Hargrave Jennings, *The Rosicrucians: Their Rites and Mysteries* (3rd rev. ed.; London: John C. Nimmo, 1887), II, 65. See Arthur Edward Waite, *The Brotherhood of The Rosy Cross, Being Records of The House of the Holy Spirit in its Inward and Outward History* (London: William Rider & Son Limited, 1924), p. 87, for variants of the Adonis tradition.

113 Waite, *The Brotherhood of The Rosy Cross*, p. 90.

114 "Beyond its edge" because the enclosing sphere is also a Yeatsian symbol of Unity of Being.

115 Frye, *Fables of Identity*, p. 233, compares the "cones" of Blake, Dante, and Yeats.

116 Hugh Kenner, *The Pound Era* (Berkeley, Los Angeles: University of California Press, 1971), pp. 146, 239. The development of Vorticism was Wyndham Lewis's, the name Pound's (p. 238).

117 Ezra Pound, "I Gather the Limbs of Osiris, IX. On Technique," *The New Age*, X, 13 (Jan. 25, 1912), 298.

118 See Harbans Rai Bachchan, *W.B. Yeats and Occultism* (Delhi: Motilal Banarsidass, 1965), Appendix VI, for the contrasted significance of the upright and inverted triangle in the systems of different writers and traditions.

119 Blavatsky, *The Secret Doctrine*, I, 44.

120 Ibid., p. 132.

121 cf. Madame Blavatsky's remark (A, 175): "'there is another globe stuck on to this at the North Pole, so that the earth has really a shape something like a dumbbell.'" cf. also her description of the first stages in the development of a germ cell: "Its nucleus grows, changes and forms a double cone or spindle, thus X *within* the cell" (*The Secret Doctrine*, II, 123).

122 Reproduced in R.G. Torrens, *The Golden Dawn: The Inner Teachings* (N.Y.: Samuel Weiser, 1973), p. 182. The passage is substantially the same as that reproduced by Israel Regardie, *The Golden Dawn: An Account of the Teachings, Rites and Ceremonies of The Order of the Golden Dawn* (4th rev. ed.; Saint Paul, Minnesota: Llewellyn Publications, 1971), IV, 251.

123 cf. Jenning's demonstration of the power of triangles in towers, *The Rosicrucians*, II, 4. Two of his illustrations show stairs or paths winding, gyre-like, around the outside of the tower.

124 Waite, *The Brotherhood of The Rosy Cross*, p. 99.

125 cf. *Per Amica Silentia Lunae:* "it may be 'sexual love,' which is 'founded upon spiritual hate,' is an image of the warfare of man and Daimon; and I even wonder if there may not be some secret communion, some whispering in the dark between Daimon and sweetheart . . . . I remember an old Irish story of three young men who went seeking for help in battle into the house of the gods at Slieve-na-mon. 'You must first be married,' some god told them, 'because a man's good or evil luck comes to him through a woman'" (M, 336–37). Again, Yeats would have had the symbolism from theosophy. Harold Bloom, *Kabbalah and Criticism* (N.Y.: The Seabury Press, 1975), pp. 29–32, traces the male-female imagery of the *Sefirot*, parenthetically noting that "Kabbalah is nothing if not sexist" and concluding that the direction from which the Cabbalist encounters the *Sefirot* makes it "necessarily a sexual mysticism or erotic theosophy."
     The sexual analogy is fundamental to Blavatsky's discussion of lunar symbolism. She quotes Gerald Massey: "'In the lunar phenomena the moon was one, as *the* moon, which was two-fold in sex, and three-fold in character, as mother, child and adult male. Thus the child of the moon became the consort of his own mother!'" (*The Secret Doctrine*, I, 422). Massey finds in these lunar myths "'the very foundations of the Christian Trinity in Unity'" (Ibid.) and Blavatsky, by way of an allegory in the *Zohar*, uses them to explain the nature of Jehovah, citing the *Demon est deus inversus* contrary Yeats adopted as his personal motto: "She-He (Yah-hovah) is the supernal Hé, and Eve. This Yah-hovah then, or Jehovah, is identical with our Chaos—Father, Mother, Son—on the material plane, and in the purely physical World; Deus and Demon, at one and the same time; the Sun and Moon, Good and Evil, God and Demon" (Ibid., p. 423).

126 cf. the description of the white heron in *Calvary:*
     Although half famished he'll not dare
     Dip or do anything but stare
     Upon the glittering image of a heron,
     That now is lost and now is there. (VPl, 780–81)
"Moon-crazed," it symbolizes antithetical Unity of Being, absorption in the self.

127 Ellmann, *Yeats: The Man and the Masks*, pp. 236–38, suggests that Yeats's decision to place himself in Phase 17 was an arbitrary one to gratify his ego but that, having done so, he then tried to make his life consonant with the image. Moore, *The Unicorn*, pp. 269–70, sees Yeats as placing himself midway between Maud

Gonne (Phase 16) and his wife (Phase 18) without much regard for the logic of the positioning. Gerald Levin, "The Yeats of the Autobiographies: A Man of Phase 17," *Texas Studies in Literature and Language*, 6 (1964–65), 398–405, demonstrates the parallels between Yeats's description of himself in *Autobiographies* and his description of the man of Phase 17 in *A Vision*. Levin also shows Yeats tracing his life in terms of his progression through the different phases, an idea that corresponds to the astrological concept (which he does not cite) of the progressed horoscope. Stuart Hirschberg, "Why Yeats Saw Himself as a '*Diamonic* Man' of Phase 17: A Complementary View," *English Language Notes*, XI (1973–74), 202–05, notes the factual basis for Yeats's self-assignment; the 218.62 degrees which separate the sun and the moon in Yeats's natal horoscope are equivalent to the 218.62 degree angle between the sun and the moon at Phase 17 of the Lunar cycle (12.86 degrees per phase [360 ÷ by 28] x 17). Marilyn Busteed, Richard Tiffany and Dorothy Wergin, *Phases of the Moon: A Guide to Evolving Human Nature* (Berkeley: Shambhala, 1974), develops the correspondences between traditional astrology and Yeats's system.

128 Yeats seems to be referring to the following passage: "Ahi, piaciuto fosse al dispensatore de l'universo che la cagion de la mia scusa mai non fosse stata! ché né altro contra me avria fallato, né io sofferto avria pena ingiustamente, pena, dico d'essilio e di povertate. Poi che fu piacere de li cittadini de la bellissima e famosissima figlia di Roma, Fiorenza, de gittarmi fuori del suo dolce seno . . . per le parti quasi tutte a le quali questa lingua si stende, peregrino, quasi mendicando, sono andato . . . " (Dante, *Convivio*, p. 247). Yeats's construction of "exile and poverty" into "solitude, lost through poverty" is probably due to a faulty memory. He may have known of the passages he quotes only at secondhand.

129 Blavatsky, *The Secret Doctrine*, I, 131. Bloom, *Kabbalah and Criticism*, stresses the interplay between literal belief and metaphor in Cabbalistic writings: "The *Sefirot* then are ten complex images for God in His process of creation, with an interplay between literal and figurative meaning going on within each *Sefirah*" (p. 27).

130 Bradford, *Yeats at Work*, p. 346.

131 See William M. Murphy, *Prodigal Father: The Life of John Butler Yeats (1839–1922)* (Ithaca, London: Cornell University Press, 1978), p. 436.

132 e.g.: "Yesterday I finished my memoirs; I have brought them down to our return to London in 1886 or 1887. After that there would be too many living people to consider and they would have besides to be written in a different way" (L, 589); "You need not fear that I am not amiable" (L, 589); "I am rather nervous about what you think. I am afraid you will very much dislike my chapter on Dowden, it is the only chapter which is a little harsh, not, I think, really so, but as compared to the rest, which is very amiable . . . " (L, 602). See Murphy, *Prodigal Father*, pp. 446–48 for John Butler Yeats's reactions to *Reveries over Childhood and Youth:* "it was 'as bad to be a poet's father as the intimate friend of George Moore.'"

133 She appears in "First Draft" as "Diana Vernon." The pseudonym, unusual in this draft, was surely to protect her from the knowledge of her son-in-law Ezra Pound who acted as secretary to Yeats in 1915–16 when "First Draft" was written.

134 See the reference at the beginning of Section XVI of "First Draft" to "these plans, in which there was much patriotism and more desire for a fair woman . . ." (Mem, 59).

135 He responded indirectly several times. Ronsley, *Yeats's Autobiography*, p. 36, writes of *Reveries over Childhood and Youth:* "In chronicling his family history he rebuts George Moore, who had accused him of being ashamed of his middle-class background." Ian Fletcher, "Rhythm and Pattern in 'Autobiographies,'" in *An Honoured Guest: New Essays on W.B. Yeats,* eds., Denis Donoghue and J. R. Mulryne (New York: St. Martin's Press, 1966), pp. 175–76, sees *Autobiographies* as challenging "Moore's version of history." The poem "A Coat" is considered a response to Moore as is the "Closing Rhyme" of *Responsibilities* with its reference to "passing dogs." Yeats often remarked that the two beggars of *The Cat and the Moon* were based on Edward Martyn and George Moore. See Murphy, *Prodigal Father*, pp. 418–19, for Yeats's anger at Moore's portrait of him.

136 See Philippe Lejeune, *Le Pacte autobiographique*, p. 23: "Un auteur, c'est n'est pas une personne. C'est une personne qui écrit et qui publie." Lejeune goes on to point out that the sign by which the reader perceives the literary autobiographers's reality "est la production antérieure *d'autres textes* (non autobiographiques), indispensable à ce que nous appellerons 'l'espace autobiographique.'"

137 Jean Starobinski, *La relation critique* (Paris: Gallimard, 1970), p. 85.

138 Paul Valéry, *Oeuvres*, ed., Jean Hytier (Paris: Gallimard, 1957), I, 565.

139 Ibid., 566.

140 Ibid., 760.

TWO: *REVERIES OVER CHILDHOOD AND YOUTH*

1 Henry James, *A Small Boy and Others* (New York: Scribner's, 1913), p. 285; *Notes of a Son and Brother* (New York: Scribner's, 1914), pp. 87, 360, 384.

2 Ronsley, *Yeats's Autobiography*, p. 34, notes that "Yeats begins *Reveries Over Childhood and Youth* as if he were writing about the beginning of the world. He enumerates sense impressions and random glimpses of his surroundings to produce an image of childhood, and in this way unfolds an Edenic view of his own beginnings." Marjorie Perloff, "'The Tradition of Myself': The Autobiographical Mode of Yeats," *Journal of Modern Literature*, 4, 3 (Feb., 1975), p. 542, draws attention to Yeats's exactitude about places in *Reveries over Childhood and Youth* and to his establishing "Sligo as a world of Edenic innocence."

3 The design on the spine carries this coyness to the point of preciousness. Only the hand of the upper portion and the figure appear. The divine hand plucks a flower, while the figure seems to peek around a door only slightly ajar.

4 Porphyry, "Concerning the Cave of the Nymphs," trans., Thomas Taylor, in *Thomas Taylor the Platonist: Selected Writings*, eds., Kathleen Raine and George Mills Harper (Princeton: Princeton University Press, 1969), p. 304.

5 Reproduced in R.G. Torrens, *The Secret Rituals of the Golden Dawn* (New York: Samuel Weiser, Inc., 1972), p. 171. The passage also appears in a copy of "$4^\circ = 7^\circ$ Philosophus" (not in Yeats's hand), Yeats papers, Reel 6.

6 cf. his father's selection of passages to read aloud ("All must be an idealization of speech, and at some moment of passionate action or somnambulistic reverie" [A, 65]) and Yeats's attribution, in a letter to Arthur Power dated June 20, 1935, of what he has done to the influence of his "father's studio" (ms. 5918, National Library of Ireland). For assessments of the nature and extent of John Butler Yeats's influence on his son, see Ellmann, *Yeats: The Man and the Masks*, pp. 13—20; A. Norman Jeffares, "John Butler Yeats," in *In Excited Reverie*, pp. 39—47; Ronsley, *Yeats's Autobiography*, pp. 38—44; William M. Murphy, "Father and Son: The Early Education of William Butler Yeats," *Review of English Literature*, VIII, 4 (Oct., 1967), 75—96, and his *Prodigal Father*, particularly pp. 230, 378—79, and 415. Wright, "The Elusive Self," p. 48, suggests that the structure of *Reveries* is provided by "the increasing then declining influence of Yeats's father"; Fletcher, "Rhythm and Pattern in 'Autobiographies,'" pp. 170—72, traces the father's influence on the style of *Reveries* and on Yeats's concept of "personality" as it controls characterization.

7 James Olney, "W.B. Yeats's Daimonic Memory," *The Sewanee Review*, LXXXV, 4 (Fall, 1977), pp. 590—91.

8 Wayne Shumaker, *English Autobiography: Its Emergence, Materials and Form* (Berkeley, Los Angeles: University of California Press, 1954), p. 86, first employed this term to describe autobiographies which "adopt as their subject some aspect of psychic development, some process of intellectual or affective becoming."

9 Yeats uses the same simile in a text written for a 1938 radio broadcast (his ill health prevented its being given): "I have sometimes wondered if I did not write poetry to find a cure for my own ailment, as constipated cats do when they eat valerian" (UP, II, 507). Frayne and Johnson draw attention to his expression of "a similar idea in 'The Circus Animals' Desertion'" (UP, II, 507).

10 Ronsley, *Yeats's Autobiography*, pp. 20—21, compares Yeats's reveries to Joyce's method in *A Portrait of the Artist as a Young Man* and to Synge's style in his fragments of autobiography.

11 Robert Corbet Yeats, 1870—1873.

12 At the one point in *Reveries* at which he did use a technical term, "pathic," Yeats was careful to identify it as a term the boy to whom it was applied "would not have understood" (A, 26). Its inclusion is an instance in which Yeats's desire for discretion did not modify his text for John Quinn, in a letter dated July 16, 1915, acknowledging receipt of the ms. of *Reveries*, takes exception to the word's inclusion, suggesting that the passage was inappropriate to Yeats's memoirs (Yeats papers, Reel 16); Yeats did not alter or delete it.

13 Adams, "Some Yeatsian Versions of Comedy," pp. 152—70, sees the child's perception of the irrationality of the adult world as central to *Reveries over Childhood and Youth*. Perloff, "'The Tradition of Myself,'" pp. 556—58, discusses several incidents of *Reveries* as indicative of the child's discernment of "a gap between appearance and reality" and of "comic futility."

14 Stephen A. Shapiro, "The Dark Continent of Literature: Autobiography," *Comparative Literature Studies*, 5 (1968), p. 441, draws attention to Yeats as "a master of the character" in *Autobiographies*.

15 Yeats tended to romanticize the Pollexfen family who seem to have been melancholic and unnaturally unaffectionate. See William M. Murphy, *The Yeats Family and the Pollexfens of Sligo* (Dublin: The Dolmen Press, 1971), pp. 9–25 for a sketch of the Pollexfen family, pp. 20–22, 25, for William Pollexfen in particular.

16 Ibid., pp. 16–17, for the history of this statement. John Butler Yeats seems to have initially used the image of "'giving a voice to the sea cliffs'" in reference to the inarticulateness of the Pollexfens.

17 See the essay "Poetry and Tradition": the artist "is known from other men by making all he handles like himself, and yet by the unlikeness to himself of all that comes before him in a pure contemplation" (EI, 255). This essay had first appeared in 1908.

18 *Plates to Accompany Reveries over Childhood and Youth* (Dublin: Cuala Press, 1915). See also George Mills Harper, *"Go Back to Where You Belong": Yeats's Return from Exile* (Dublin: The Dolmen Press, 1973), pp. 9–12, 15–19, 24, for Yeats's use of Sligo in shaping for himself a mythology of exile.

19 See Ronsley, *Yeats's Autobiography*, pp. 40, 41, 43–45; Ellmann, *Yeats: The Man and the Masks*, pp. 21–22; and Murphy, "Father and Son," pp. 75–77, for Yeats's youthful rebellion against his father's ideas.

20 See Ellmann, *Yeats: The Man and the Masks*, pp. 45–47, and Ronsley, *Yeats's Autobiography*, pp. 47–48, for estimates of the influence of O'Leary's nationalism on Yeats.

21 ms. 13,576, National Library of Ireland; quoted by Thomas Parkinson, *W.B. Yeats: The Later Poetry* (Berkeley, Los Angeles: University of California Press, 1964), p. 93.

THREE: *THE TREMBLING OF THE VEIL*

1 The "sacred book" seems to be another reference to Mallarmé's "Crise de vers" (see One: note 43): "Je me figure par un indéracinable sans doute préjugé d'écrivain, que rien ne demeurera sans être proféré; que nous en sommes là précisément à rechercher . . . un art d'achever la transposition, au Livre, de la symphonie . . ." (p. 367). Yeats probably knew this essay through Arthur Symons: "nor shall I ever know how much my practice and my theory owe to the passages that he read me from Catullus and from Verlaine and Mallarmé" (A, 319–20).

2 Thatcher, *Nietzsche in England*, p. 149.

3 Walter Pater, *Marius the Epicurean: His Sensations and Ideas* (Library ed., 1910; rpt. Oxford: Basil Blackwell and New York: Johnson Reprint Corporation, 1967), II, 91.

4 William Butler Yeats, *Four Years* (Dundrum: The Cuala Press, 1921), p. 79. cf. his description of the "communicators" of *A Vision* as figures in a dream shared by himself and Mrs. Yeats and occasionally taking forms external to them.

5 cf., for example, the description of Aherne in the opening of *The Tables of the Law* (103): a "nature, which is half monk, half soldier of fortune, and must needs turn action into dreaming, and dreaming into action."

6 ". . . I have a ring with a hawk and a butterfly upon it, to symbolize the straight road of logic, and so of mechanism, and the crooked road of intuition: 'For wisdom is a butterfuly and not a gloomy bird of prey'" (VPo, 827).

7 cf. Yeats's 1892 introduction to William Allingham's poetry: "In greater poets everything has relation to the national life or to profound feeling; nothing is an isolated artistic moment; there is a unity everywhere, everything fulfils a purpose that is not its own; the hailstone is a journeyman of God, and the grass blade carries the universe upon its point" (UP, I, 260).

8 *Prometheus Unbound,* for Yeats, had associations not only with Shelley's poem but also with theosophical doctrine. Mme. Blavatsky explains the hero as bringing *spiritual* gifts to man *(The Secret Doctrine,* II, 99). His stolen fire symbolized a "divine spark" but, because mankind was unable to approach the spiritual quality of Prometheus, that fire created "the eternal vulture of ever unsatisfied desire, of regret and despair," instead of bringing the wisdom that can now be realized only when Prometheus is released by Herakles *(The Secret Doctrine,* II, 431, 546ff).

9 cf. "the Gift of Harun Al-Rashid," (VPo, 463): "violent great hearts can lose/Their bitterness and find the honeycomb."

10 1886, in a review, "The Poetry of Sir Samuel Ferguson," which Frayne identifies as Yeats's "second known published prose piece" (UP, I, 87): "The mind of the Celt loves to linger on images of persistance [sic]; implacable hate, implacable love . . ." (UP, I, 104).

11 "But I know that a nation cannot be powerful, cannot be ready for necessary battle, unless it has hatred as well as love in its heart. A nation is like a great tree and it must lift up its boughs towards the cold moon of noble hate no less than to the sun of love, if its leaves are to be thick enough to shelter the birds of heaven. Nor can its fruit be worthy to be eaten by men unless it have a harsh as well as a sweet savour" (UP, II, 323).

12 Porphyry, in his treatise on the symbolism of the cave at the head of the Ithacan harbour to which Odysseus returns, is at pains to explicate the significance of stone amphorae filled with honey. The waters of the cave, he tells us, represent the waters through which the souls of the dead are reborn onto the earth. cf. "News for the Delphic Oracle" (VPo, 612).

13 Porphyry, "Concerning the Cave of the Nymphs," p. 307.

14 Pater, *Marius the Epicurean,* I, 83.

15 Wilson, *Yeats and Tradition,* pp. 211–13, 216–17, 222, discusses at length Yeats's use of Porphyry in "The Delphic Oracle upon Plotinus," "News for the Delphic Oracle" and "The Stare's Nest at my Window."

16 My attention was drawn to Patmore's essay by Wilson, *Yeats and Tradition,* pp. 66–67, who, discussing the association of St. John with Dionysus, identifies the essay.

17 Coventry Patmore, "The Precursor," *Religio Poetae etc.* (London: George Bell and Sons, 1893), p. 12.

18 Ibid., p. 11.

19 Ibid., p. 10.

20 Porphyry, "Concerning the Cave of the Nymphs," p. 308. cf. Edmund Spenser, whom Yeats imitated in his youth (A, 66), "March," *The Shepheardes Calendar:* "Of honey and of gall in love there is store;/The honey is much, but the gall is more."

21 *Secret Symbols of the Rosicrucians* (Abdiel Lodge, 1967), p. 1. This text is "An exact reproduction of the original [1785 Altona ms.] but with the German text and terms literally translated." Portions of the Altona ms. were translated and published in Boston in 1888; a facsimile edition of the German ms. appeared in 1919. ʹI cannot prove Yeats's familiarity with this particular ms., but the honeycomb symbol is a common one in Rosicrucianism.

22 Daniel O'Hara, "The Irony of Tradition and W.B. Yeats's *Autobiography:* An Essay in Dialectical Hermeneutics," *Boundary 2,* V, 3 (Spring, 1977), pp. 692–93, notes that Yeats lifts his portrait of Russell out of its chronological position in the narrative in order to make a transition to "Hodos Chameliontos" and to establish Russell as "a figure of imaginative difference" from himself.

23 cf. "Crazy Jane Reproved" (VPo, 509). O'Hara, "The Irony of Tradition in W.B. Yeats's *Autobiography,*" p. 693, remarks upon the "'shell-like'" involution of the rhetorical question and suggests that it "projects its own craftsman-like Deity for the artist in Yeats to emulate."

24 cf. UP, II, 127 (1898): "Our Irish romantic movement . . . should always, even when it makes new legends about traditional people and things, be haunted by places. It should make Ireland, as Ireland and all other lands were in ancient times, a holy land to her own people."

25 See Ronsley, *Yeats's Autobiography,* pp. 76–82, for an interpretation of this passage in terms of *Per Amica Silentia Lunae* and Ellmann's explanation of Yeats's interpretation of the *anima mundi.* The symbol of rebirth and the pessimism at the core of the passage become clearer in the context, presented in the previous chapter chapter of the present study, of *A Vision.*

26 Yeats seems to have admired *Axel* chiefly for this quality of pessimism: "The lovers resolve to die . . . and so complete the four-fold reunciation—of the cloister, of the active life of the world, of the labouring life of the intellect, of the passionate life of love. The infinite is alone worth attaining, and the infinite is the possession of the dead . . . . Seldom has utmost pessimism found a more magnificent expression" (UP, I, 324).

27 Yeats had first written, more prosaically and accurately, of The Rhymers in *Letters to the New Island,* pp. 142–48.

28 Fletcher, "Rhythm and Pattern in 'Autobiographies,'" p. 182.

29 The central thesis of Olney, "W.B. Yeats's Daimonic Memory."

30 Fletcher, "Rhythm and Pattern in 'Autobiographies,'" p. 182.

31 Ibid., p. 173.

32 Ibid., pp. 183–84, for discussion of the episodes involving Todhunter's *Sicilian Idyll* and his *Comedy of Sighs*, p. 185, for Yeats's response to *Ubu Roi*.

33 Yeats particularly remembers the marionette quality of the actors. An earlier version of *Ubu Roi*, titled *Les Polonais*, was given privately December, 1888–January, 1889 using the marionettes of the Théâtre des Phynances.

34 See Mallarmé, *Oeuvres complètes*, pp. 47–48, and Arthur Symons, *Poems* (New York: John Lane Company, 1907), I, 205–06, for the passage Yeats quotes. It was first published in 1893.

35 J.-K. Huysmans, *A Rebours* (Paris: Bibliothèque-Charpentier, 1912) pp. 70–79. Yeats does not refer specifically to these paintings but does allude to Moreau's *Jason* immediately following his remarks about "Hérodiade."

36 Ibid., p. 260.

37 cf. "The Tribes of Danu," (1897) (UP, II, 69).

38 Bradford, *The Writing of "The Player Queen,"* p. 31.

39 *The King of the Great Clock Tower, A Full Moon in March* and *The Death of Cuchulain.* Wilson, *W.B. Yeats and Tradition*, interprets the dance in the first two of these plays in terms of the ritual slaying of the god in the Minerva-Dionysus myth (pp. 90–92) and that of the third as an embodiment of Platonic doctrine (p. 174). Yeats obviously fuses his sources to weld a symbology both highly personal and traditional.

40 See Arthur Symons, "The Dance," in *Poems* (New York: Dodd, Mead and Company, 1924), II, 41:

> For the immortal moment of a passionate dance,
> Surely our two souls rushed together and were one,
> Once, in the beat of our winged feet in unison,
> When, in the brief and flaming ardour of your glance,
> The world withered away, vanishing into smoke;
> The world narrowed about us, and we heard the beat
> As of the rushing winds encompassing our feet;
> In the blind heart of the winds, eternal silence woke
> And, cast adrift on our unchainable ecstasy,
> Once, and once only, heart to heart and soul to soul,
> For an immortal moment we endured the whole
> Rapture of intolerable immortality.

41 A version of the sequence of visions appears in *Memoirs*, pp. 100–04. Yeats published the incident as "A Biographical Fragment" in *The Criterion*, I, 4 (July, 1923), 315–21, and *The Dial*, LXXV (July, 1923), 13–19. He included it for the first time in *The Trembling of the Veil* in the 1926 edition of *Autobiographies*.

42 William F. Halloran, "W.B. Yeats and William Sharp: The Archer Vision," *English Language Notes*, VI, 4 (June, 1969), pp. 273–80, traces the events between

Yeats's writing to Sharp about the archer vision (shortly after Aug. 9, 1896) and Sharp's writing of "The Archer" (about Sept. 23, 1896) and draws the conclusion that the thought transference "almost certainly took place through the mails."

43 cf. "Discoveries": "Instinct creates the recurring and the beautiful, all the winding of the serpent; but reason, the most ugly man, as Blake called it, is a drawer of the straight line, the maker of the arbitrary and the impermanent . . . . Sanctity has its straight line also, darting from the centre, and with these arrows the many-coloured serpent, theme of all our poetry, is maimed and hunted. He that finds the white arrow shall have wisdom older than the serpent. . ." (EI, 288).

44 R.F. Rattray, Principal of University College in Leicester in the 1920s, writes that Yeats was unaware of the analogies between his vision and Greek legend until the occasion of a dinner party in Leicester (1922 or early 1923?) at which Vacher Burch (later lecturer at Liverpool Cathedral) pointed them out to him when Yeats spoke of his archer vision (IR, I, 157). In his introduction to the publication of the vision as "A Biographical Fragment" in *The Criterion* (July, 1923), Yeats claimed, "When lecturing in England the other day," to have "met a man learned in Cretan and other East Mediterranean antiquities" who encouraged him to publish the addition to *The Trembling of the Veil* and provided the explanatory notes for it (315). Yeats calls Burch simply "my learned man" in *The Criterion*, fearing to name him, he says, lest he "compromise his scholarship by joining it to such an outlawed doctrine as that of the Race Memory" (320). By the time he published the 1926 edition of *Autobiographies*, including this new beginning to Section VI of "The Stirring of the Bones," he evidently could no longer remember Burch's name or find his letter (A, 576—77).

45 This later interpretation of Yeats's corresponds with his interpretation of this same dream in *Per Amica Silentia Lunae:* "we who are poets and artists, not being permitted to shoot beyond the tangible, must . . . live but for the moment when vision comes to our weariness like terrible lightning, in the humility of the brutes. . . . We seek reality with the slow toil of our weakness and are smitten from the boundless and the unforeseen. Only when we are saint or sage, and renounce experience itself, can we in imagery of the Christian Cabbala, leave the sudden lightning and the path of the serpent and become the bowman who aims his arrow at the centre of the sun" (M, 340).

46 Regardie, *The Golden Dawn*, I, 191.

47 See particularly, O'Hara, "The Irony of Tradition and W.B. Yeats's *Auto-biography*," pp. 690—92 ("Yeats lives through his crisis of identity by re-living and re-shaping the crises of his friends, each of whom, like Russell, becomes in the process representative of another of Yeats's imaginative potentialities"), and Olney, "W.B. Yeats's Daimonic Memory," pp. 590—95 ("he replaces individual men and women with types and then, going the last logical step, replaces those types with archetypes").

48 Yeats papers, Reel 6.

49 Yeats had recounted this story earlier in "Swedenborg, Mediums, and the Desolate Places." cf. also the lines of the Fool in *The Hour Glass*: "When it is spring with us, the trees are withering there, when it is summer with us, the snow is falling there, and have I not myself heard the lambs that are there all bleating on a cold November day . . . ?" (VPl, 585).

50 Yeats had added the two experiences to *The Celtic Twilight* ("A Voice") in 1902. He also records the "Emmanuel" vision in *Memoirs*, 126, in *The Speckled Bird*, 30, at the end of *Per Amica Silentia Lunae*, discussing his need to seek an Image of the self, and in *A Vision* (VII, 233), to explain that "A living man sees the Celestial Body through the Mask."

FOUR: *DRAMATIS PERSONAE*

1cf.: "My first fifty pages . . . begin where my old autobiography ends. It is curious how one's life falls into definite sections—in 1897 a new scene was set, new actors appeared" (L, 820).

2 Critics have been quick to point out Yeats's attempt to satirize Moore by Moore's own method. See particularly, Fletcher, "Rhythm and Pattern in 'Autobiographies,'" p. 186, and Meredith Cary, "Yeats and Moore—An Autobiographical Conflict," *Eire—Ireland*, IV, 3 (Autumn, 1969), 94–109, who suggests that Yeats attempts and fails to master Moore's technique.

3 See particularly, Cary, "Yeats and Moore," pp. 94–101, and Ronsley, *Yeats's Autobiography*, pp. 107–109, for summaries of Moore's portrait of Yeats, and Cary, pp. 101–04, for Yeats's specific responses.

4 George Moore, *Ave*, Vol. I of *'Hail and Farewell!'* (New ed., 1914; rpt. London: William Heinemann Ltd., 1927), p. 46.

5 Ibid., p. 62.

6 Ibid., p. 56.

7 George Moore, *Vale*, Vol. III of *'Hail and Farewell!'* (1914; rpt. London: William Heinemann Ltd., 1926), pp. 256–60.

8 Moore, *Ave*, pp. 110–11.

9 "I have suppressed the last two paragraphs . . . and have made up the deficiency, very ingeniously I think, from your letter. Your letter is most complete and I had little more to do than to arrange it for the narrative. I am most grateful to you for your assistance, but I will suggest that you do not take any one into your confidence regarding this little collaboration. To do so would merely give occasion for some vain merriment and would prevent the beauty of the present creation from being seen. *I am willing to take the credit for work which I have not done without assistance so that the few who are capable of seeing may see its beauty.* I long to show you the new text: for I think I have made very dexterous use of the material" (Moore to Yeats, L—WBY, 45, my italics).

10 e.g., in his assessment of their quarrel over *Where There is Nothing*: "on my side distrust remained, on his disgust. I look back with some remorse . . . . Had I abandoned my plot and made him write the novel, he might have put beside *Muslin* and *The Lake* a third masterpiece, but I was young, vain, self-righteous, and bent on proving myself a man of action" (A, 454).

11 "George Moore's *Hail and Farewell* . . . is not at all malicious. Of course there isn't the smallest recognition of the difference between public and private life . . . . It

156

is curiously honest, very inaccurate and I think, for anyone not in the book itself, rather dull. Of course he has lots of unfavourable things to say about everybody but they are balanced by favourable things too and he treats himself in the same way. . . . There are things which would seem undignified and spiteful if taken by themselves, but the total impression is more than usually sincere. He certainly does not see either you or I as we are seen by a sympathetic friend. It is a slightly humourous, slightly satirical but favourable impression. A stranger's impression" (L, 564, to Lady Gregory).

12 Moore, *Vale*, p. 172.

13 Ibid., p. 174.

14 A draft of a letter from Yeats to Moore about the concessions each must make to the other is in The National Library of Ireland, ms. 8777. A portion of the letter appears in L, 347—48.

15 Fletcher, "Rhythm and Pattern in 'Autobiographies,'" p. 188, notes of this passage that Moore's "lack of physical definition is brilliantly suggested by the use of near-synonyms, each purporting to catch at the oddity, the absence of style . . . ."

16 cf. Yeats's *Tribute to Thomas Davis* [delivered Nov. 20, 1914] (Cork: Cork University Press; Oxford: B.H. Blackwell, 1947), pp. 17—18: "Davis could shew forth the service of Ireland as heroic service worth a good man's energy, because he had in his words and in his actions a moral quality akin to that quality of style which can alone make permanent a picture and a book."

17 See Ronsley, *Yeats's Autobiography*, pp. 110—21, for Yeats's thematic use of antinomies as outlined in *Per Amica Silentia Lunae* in characterizing the "bifurcation" of Lady Gregory's and Edward Martyn's minds, and in the oppositions of Coole Park and Tulira, Moore and Martyn, Moore and Lady Gregory. O'Hara, "The Irony of Tradition and W.B. Yeats's *Autobiography*," interprets the antithesis of *Dramatis Personae* as well of all of *Autobiographies* as "between tradition and modernity, between a genealogical paradigm of imaginative descent and, apparently, no model at all" (p. 682).

18 Moore, *Vale*, p. 176.

19 Ibid., p. 187.

FIVE: *ESTRANGEMENT* AND *THE DEATH OF SYNGE*

1 The *Journal* begins in December 1908 and the distribution of entries is as follows: 1908, 3 entries; 1909, 202 entries; 1910, 25 entries; 1911, 3 entries; 1912, 7 entries; 1913, 4 entries; 1914, 2 entries; 1915, 1 entry; 1917, 2 entries; 1918—19, 3 entries (all drafts of poems); 1930, 2 entries. The entries included in *Autobiographies* date from January 14, 1909 to October, 1914. Denis Donoghue has reprinted the *Journal* in *Memoirs*.

2 Alain Girard, *Le Journal intime* (Paris: Presses Universitaires de France, 1963), pp. 4, 131, outlines the *intimistes'* characteristics.

3 cf. the 1907 essay, "Poetry and Tradition": "Power passed to small shopkeepers, to clerks, to that very class who had seemed to John O'Leary so ready to bend to the power of others, to men who had risen above the traditions of the countryman, without learning those of cultivated life or even educating themselves, and who

because of their poverty, their ignorance, their superstitious piety, are much subject to all kinds of fear. Immediate victory, immediate utility, became everything . . ." (EI, 260).

4 For the influence of Castiglione and the idea of courtly societies like that of Urbino on Yeats's concept of the artist as aristocrat and on *A Vision*, see Corinna Salvadori, *Yeats and Castiglione: Poet and Courtier* (Dublin: Allen Figgis, 1965); F.A.C. Wilson, *Yeats and Tradition*, p. 200, and *Yeats's Iconography*, pp. 92–95, 101, 211–12, 325, also traces Castiglione's influence on Yeats.

5 "Ma quello che senza lacrime raccontar non si devria é che la signora Duchessa essa ancor é morta; e se l'animo mio si turba per la perdita de tanti amici e signori mei, che m'hanno lasciato in questa vita come in una solitudine piena d'affanni, ragion é che molto più acerbemente senta il dolore della morte della signora Duchessa che di tutti gli altri, perché essa molto più che tutti gli altri valeva io ad essa molto più che a tutti gli era tenuto" (Baldesar Castiglione, *Il Libro del cortegiano* con una scelta delle *Opere minori*, ed., Bruno Maier [Torino: Unione Tipografico–Editrice Torinese, 1964], p. 71).

6 Wyndham Lewis, *The Art of Being Ruled* (London: Chatto and Windus, 1926), p. 431.

7 Ibid., p. 432.

8 Ibid.

9 See the comments about Lewis in his letters: "we are in *fundamental* agreement" (L, 733); "He . . . is on my side of things philosophically" (L, 739); "I have read *Time and Western Man* with gratitude . . . . It has given, what I could not, a coherent voice to my hatred" (L-SM, 122). In a diary begun Sept. 23, 1928 (ms. 13, 580, The National Library of Ireland) which contains notes for the revision of *A Vision*, he particularly praised *The Art of Being Ruled* and *Childermass* for their attack on what was artificial in contemporary culture, on what belonged to the mechanism of Phase 26 of his lunar model.

10 cf. the lines in "Solomon and the Witch" explaining a moment which at first seems to be one of Unity of Being:

> 'Maybe the bride-bed brings despair,
> For each an imagined image brings
> And finds a real image there;
> Yet the world ends when these two things,
> Though several, are a single light,
> When oil and wick are burned in one;
> Therefore a blessed moon last night
> Gave Sheba to her Solomon.' (VPo, 388)

11 cf. *On the Boiler*, 22: "When a man loves a girl it should be because her face and character offer what he lacks, the more profound his nature the more should he realise his lack and the greater be the difference. It is as though he wanted to take his own death into his arms and beget a stronger life upon that death."

12 cf. "On those that hated 'The Playboy of the Western World', 1907" (VPo, 294).

13 Michel de Montaigne, *Les Essais de Michel de Montaigne*, ed., Pierre Villey (Paris: Presses Universitaires de France, 1965), p. 665.

14 The reference is to a translation entitled "Venetian Costume" by D. Neville Lees of portions of Cesare Vecellio's *Degli Abiti antichi e moderni di diverse parti del mondo* (Venice, 1590) which appeared with illustrative engravings in *The Mask*, I, 12 (Feb., 1909), 226–31.

15 For evaluations of the extent of Synge's influence on Yeats's aesthetic and on his style, see Robert O'Driscoll, "Yeats's Conception of Synge" and Suheil Badi Bushrui, "Synge and Yeats," in Bushrui, ed., *Sunshine and The Moon's Delight: A Centenary Tribute to John Millington Synge 1871–1909* (New York: Barnes & Noble, Publishers, 1972).

16 Denis Donoghue, in *Memoirs*, 206, identifies the source for the first of these allusions as Byron's *The Bride of Abydos*, II, ii, 26–27, and the second as Homer's "Hymn to Apollo."

17 cf. Yeats's 1910 lecture on "The Theatre" (delivered in London to raise money for the Abbey) in which he contrasted performances of Grassi's Sicilian troupe and Galsworthy's *Justice*. Grassi's troupe played in the co̤ ṟedia dell'arte tradition. "All depended upon the joyous spontaneity of their art"; the theme of all their plays was human nature, human life. *Justice* Yeats took as representative of a studied art, only partly engaging its actors, an art about external characterization, circumstance, and things (YP, 17–19).

18 He repeats this comparison in more measured tones in his address to the Royal Academy of Sweden: "He [Synge] was to do for Ireland, though more by his influence on other dramatists than by his direct influence, what Robert Burns did for Scotland. When Scotland thought herself gloomy and religious, Providence restored her imaginative spontaneity by raising up Robert Burns to commend drink and the Devil" (A, 567). As early as 1886, Yeats had distinguished between poets like Shelley, Wordsworth and Coleridge (poets who "investigate what is obscure in emotion, and appeal to what is abnormal in man," poets who form groups and leave "schools" behind them) and national poets (poets who "sing of the universal emotions") like Homer and Hugo, Burns and Scott (UP, I, 105).

19 The thought became "When Helen Lived," fusing once again Helen, Maud Gonne and the poetic Muse.

SIX: *THE BOUNTY OF SWEDEN*

1 Ronsley, *Yeats's Autobiography*, p. 128, has discussed the statement in similar terms: "he [Yeats] suggests as in the other books following *Dramatis Personae*, that these disconnected passages are to be read without expectation of an overall coherence. Moreover, the statement again serves to disarm his critics, here in regard to what would certainly, and rightly, be considered an overly idealistic view of Swedish culture. Without entirely rejecting Yeats's assertion that his book is an impressionistic record," Ronsley goes on to trace the "narrative continuity" of *The Bounty of Sweden*.

2 "He watched Margaret Henderson, moved to wondering pleasure by her face, delicate as a shell" (SB, 20).

3 Ronsley, *Yeats's Autobiography*, pp. 129–33.

4 William Butler Yeats, *The Bounty of Sweden: A Meditation, and a Lecture Delivered before The Royal Swedish Academy and Certain Notes* (Dublin: The

Cuala P
from th

5 Ronsley, *Yeats's Autobiography*, p. 129, notes that Yeats was "prepared to find this achievement in Scandinavia long before any visit to Sweden had ever been projected."

6 This paraphrase of the hero paradigm is obviously indebted to Joseph Campbell, *The Hero with a Thousand Faces* (1949; rpt. Cleveland, New York: Meridian Books, 1956).

7 O'Hara, "The Irony of Tradition and W.B. Yeats's *Autobiography*," pp. 698—703, treats Yeats's use of a "tradition of irony" and concludes that he uses it to become "authentically imaginative." My own argument obviously takes a different turn.

SEVEN: *ON THE BOILER:* The Fanatic Heart

1 Bradford, *Yeats at Work*, p. 343, notes that in revising the *Journal* "Yeats appears to have tried systematically to soften the statement of his growing conservatism and generally antidemocratic bias."

2 Copy of a letter from W.B. Yeats to George R. Barnes; ms. 5918, The National Library of Ireland.

3 See Fahmy Farag, "Needless Horror or Terrible Beauty: Yeats's Ideas of Hatred, War and Violence," in *The Opposing Virtues* (Dublin: The Dolmen Press, 1978), pp. 7—19, for the consistency of Yeats's early occultism and his later political beliefs.

4 Donald T. Torchiana, *W.B. Yeats and Georgian Ireland* (Evanston: Northwestern University Press, 1966), 348—49, discusses the influence of the eighteenth century on *On the Boiler*.

5 Torchiana, *Ibid.*, 353—54 links the King of this section with George V in the previous section.

6 *Ibid.*, p. 347.

7 Torchiana, *Ibid.*, pp. 359—60, assuming the events of the play to take place in 1938, points out that the Old Man's sight of the live tree fifty years earlier would have occurred just before the rejection of Parnell in 1889, that the Old Man would have been sixteen and would have murdered his father at the time of Parnell's death in 1891, and that the Boy would have been born in August, 1922, when the Free State was formed. In the pages which follow, Torchiana reads the play as a symbolic rendering of Irish history since the eighteenth century.

APPENDIX: *AUTOBIOGRAPHIES* AND PHILOSOPHY: Their Publication

1 Yeats papers, Reel 24.

2 Quoted by Bradford, *Yeats at Work*, p. 358.

3 Yeats papers, Reel 21; quoted by Bradford, *Yeats at Work*, p. 366.

4 Yeats papers, Reel 21; quoted by Bradford, *Yeats at Work*, p. 365.

5 W.B. Yeats, *Reveries over Childhood and Youth* (London: MacMillan, 1916), pp. 121—22.